INCLUSION REVOLUTION

THE ESSENTIAL GUIDE TO DISMANTLING
RACIAL INEQUITY IN THE WORKPLACE

DAISY AUGER-DOMÍNGUEZ

SEAL PRESS

New York

Seal Press
Hachette Book Group
1290 Avenue of the Americas, New York, NY 10104
www.sealpress.com
@sealpress

Printed in the United States of America

First Edition: March 2022

Published by Seal Press, an imprint of Perseus Books, LLC, a subsidiary of Hachette Book Group, Inc. The Seal Press name and logo is a trademark of the Hachette Book Group.

The Hachette Speakers Bureau provides a wide range of authors for speaking events. To find out more, go to www.hachettespeakersbureau.com or call (866) 376-6591.

The publisher is not responsible for websites (or their content) that are not owned by the publisher.

Print book interior design by Jeff Williams.

Library of Congress Cataloging-in-Publication Data

Names: Auger-Domínguez, Daisy, author.
Title: Inclusion revolution: the essential guide to dismantling racial inequity
   in the workplace / Daisy Auger-Domínguez.
Description: First edition. | New York: Seal Press, [2022] |
   Includes bibliographical references.
Identifiers: LCCN 2021045105 | ISBN 9781541620124 (hardcover) |
   ISBN 9781541620148 (ebook)
Subjects: LCSH: Racism in the workplace. | Diversity in the workplace. |
   Personnel management. | Corporate culture.
Classification: LCC HF5549.5.R23 A94 2022 | DDC 658.30089—dc23
LC record available at https://lccn.loc.gov/2021045105

ISBNs: 9781541620124 (hardcover), 9781541620148 (ebook)

LSC-C

Printing 1, 2021

In memory of my late grandfather,
Ramón Arcadio Fernández Domínguez—

Te digo adiós para toda la vida, aunque toda la
vida siga pensando en ti.

To Christopher and Emma, siempre.

CONTENTS

Introduction   I

1. Your Inclusion Ambitions   15
2. Build Better Teams...Period.   37
3. Overhaul Your Recruitment   59
4. Make Better Hiring Decisions   83
5. Nurture a People-First Culture   III
6. Set Psychological Safety in Motion   I4I
7. Tune In to the Whispers and Screams (and Everything in Between)   I7I
8. No Talent Left Behind   205
9. Build Support Scaffolding   239
10. Get to the Heart of Accountability   265
11. Persist   295

Further Resources for the Inclusion Revolution   317
Acknowledgments   319
Notes   323
Bibliography   331

INTRODUCTION

S ITTING AT A sleek white conference table, surrounded by some of the most credentialed HR executives in the world, a humming laptop in front of me and a free chai latte in my hand, I felt like I'd finally arrived. I was just hired into a newly created global diversity recruitment role at Google—a role that was elevated to an executive level to recruit me specifically—with an ambitious charge to "hire the most diverse talent." Here I was, a Dominican and Puerto Rican woman in leadership, recruited by arguably the world's most powerful company to create the very change I had dreamed of as a young girl growing up in Santo Domingo. This was my moment.

My new team's mission was to build a workforce that better represented the world and Google's users, specifically by increasing the hiring rates of female, Black, and Latinx employees. We enthusiastically set out to redesign how to find, cultivate, and convert a robust and steady stream of candidates. We took a deep dive into the experience of female, Black, and Latinx software engineers and came up with a set of recommendations to be presented to company decision-makers. These recommendations included solutions for reducing bias in job descriptions and the interview process and expanding our talent markets beyond traditional target schools and companies largely lacking in racial and ethnic representation.

Minutes before I unveiled my biggest, boldest diversity hiring strategy yet, I paused to think about all the experiences, experiments, wins, and losses that led me to this moment. This had been my life's work for nearly two decades. I was ready for this. But what happened next shattered my natural optimism. The big bets we presented—like expanding our offices in communities rich in Black and Latinx talent—were perceived as impractical and unimaginative. This was 2016, yet these top executives weren't ready to take bold action.

I presented to a room of mostly white men and women. The team leader, who was of Indian descent, and my own manager, a white man, dominated the conversation, clearly signaling to the rest of the team whose opinion mattered. What followed felt like hours of intellectual debate over the source of our inability to hire more Black and Latinx software engineers, while the leaders dismissed the changes I had proposed as not scalable or tractable enough. Finally, I nearly lost my mind when I was asked, "What's the root cause?" for what seemed like the millionth time. I blurted out, "RACISM! The root cause is racism. Our recruitment process was designed with a racist lens, and we need to reexamine and rebuild every stage of the hiring journey with an anti-racist lens in order to achieve different outcomes."

The room went *qui-eeeet*. The discomfort was palpable. It was the truth that no one wanted to hear. But it was the truth. Up until that moment, I didn't dare to speak my whole truth because I was afraid of being misjudged or penalized, like many underrepresented and marginalized employees feel every day, regardless of their place in the pecking order. I shared the truth that causes even well-intended people to become defensive and dismissive. And the room did just that.

Many brilliant Google employees before me had designed a highly efficient recruitment process to hire the world's brightest minds. Many also had advocated for changes to enhance the company's overall people systems and culture. While the company had doubled in size and had seen increases in hiring and representation for women globally and for Black and Latinx employees in the United States, turnover rates for underrepresented employees of color remained just as high, if not higher. It was clear that the culture at Google also needed to change if we wanted to retain this talent we were working so hard to bring through our doors. However, tolerance for behavioral and operational change was low, even in an organization that brazenly set out to "change the world."

There was also work to do on the personal level, but white leaders were not listening to their BIPOC (Black, Indigenous, and people of color) colleagues. Suppose you're a Black entry-level employee asking leadership to hire a more diverse workforce, help employees of color advance through the ranks, and facilitate conversations about racial inequality. Well, in that case, there's little chance leadership will listen, much less take action. That is, before now.

There's been a sea change globally: a candid and courageous conversation about systemic racism, a reexamination of the role that race plays at work, and a call to dismantle racial injustice. We are in the midst of a global reckoning on racism, and corporations are on high alert, from the executives, shareholders, and boards of directors to employees. CEOs are hyperaware that their companies—and their public personas—are one social media cycle away from reputational (and share price) oblivion.

Let's face it, in 2020 everything changed—and there is no going back. We can't unsee what we've witnessed during this period of compound crises: a once-in-a-century pandemic, economic fallout, and public scrutiny to racialized violence. Black and brown people are saying, "We've had enough. We want real change. And we're keeping score."

There is a need for national changes to our criminal justice system and society, and one place we can all start is taking a close look at our workplaces. Inequity in the workplace is a problem you can solve. I want *you* to be that leader who shines a light on others, not the one who dims it.

Everyone has a relationship to work. It is how we get paid and are able to put food in our children's bellies. Work is where we spend the majority of our days outside of the time spent with our families and loved ones. Over the years, I've worked for managers and leaders who emboldened my sense of what's possible. They went beyond saying, "I want you to be successful" to "I am going to ensure that you are successful." They said: "I see you. I value you. You matter. You make a difference." You can never hear "I believe in you" too often. But I've also had managers and peers who have set up roadblocks for my success and questioned my value on a daily basis. Even as I pushed to bring more seats to the table, I have had to fight to keep my own while watching white colleagues face far fewer hurdles.

The business case for diversity in the workplace is overwhelming: companies with diverse boards of directors, C-levels, and employee bases consistently outperform those without. Yet, workforce statistics show a persistent lack of progress for non-white workers in the corporate workforce, from entry-level to executive. And while much attention is focused on corporate boards, progress is slow, with the spotlight primarily on placing women—mostly white—on S&P 500 boards. The Rooney Rule—a commitment, first used by the National Football League and now broadly embraced by other businesses, to interview at least a certain number of underrepresented candidates for certain positions—is more of a symbolic gesture. Just like with diversity training and conversation series, attempts at a quick fix are often a wasted effort. Unless you're discussing the why and are ready to act on those often-hard-to-swallow answers, these well-intentioned solutions fail to deliver meaningful progress.

The urgency is clear, but the road map is not.

The diversity problem many are trying to solve is at its core about addressing racial and gender dynamics, harm in the workplace, and power imbalances. This problem affects what products, services, and content companies create, who they are designed to serve, and who benefits. It prompts the questions: What can be done to dismantle centuries of discrimination and anti-Blackness globally? How can fairer workplaces be achieved? Many organizations are now at the starting point: deeper awareness and recognition of the long-standing and systemic racial inequities they perpetuate. This moment is prompting reflections about how they need to change to achieve a fairer and healthier future for all, with many taking action to become the companies where we all want to work. This should be the time for institutions to finally tip toward fairness, belonging, and an end to systemic racism and other "isms." But will they? Will leaders and managers apply the courage and rigor it takes to shift the culture, processes, and practices that perpetuate inequity across their teams and workplaces?

In 2020, nearly every major company made corporate pledges and public commitments on expanding racial equality. They accelerated timelines for "change," appointed chief diversity officers, delivered anti-racism and belonging training, and launched listening series, educational forums, guides, and resources. They hired racially diverse talent, created supplier diversity programs, and made philanthropic contributions.

These are all good actions—and they are *reactive*. Hiring sprees and ad hoc, piecemeal solutions won't change organizational behavior, systems, and cultures that are misaligned with equity, inclusion, and belonging. Everyone is asking for receipts, not "diversity theater." People don't want to associate themselves with brands that under-deliver on their promises.

We have work to do. Pursuing diverse representation in the workplace alone won't ensure that all employees feel included, valued, and physically and psychologically safe. Instead of filling the void with short-lived promises, we need to approach this work with empathy and resolve, and we need to examine the root causes of racial inequity across the employee life cycle (recruiting, onboarding, developing, retaining, and offboarding). We need to define inclusive values and behavioral expectations, rethink the way things have always been done, and allow for more transparency about how we track our goals. In other words, we need a fundamental shift in organizational thinking, culture, norms, processes, and practices.

An entrenched culture like the one I experienced at Google, and that exists at many other organizations, can be masked by a company's strong financial performance or brand. A company can appear from the outside to be forward-thinking and progressive, while its internal culture quietly erodes the morale, well-being, and professional advancement of BIPOC employees, as well as the effectiveness of its diversity, equity, and inclusion programs.

In scenarios such as this one, organizations often experience one or more of these pitfalls:

1. Having diversity, equity, and inclusion decisions made by an ill-informed leadership team while highly competent BIPOC talent cycle in and out of the organization.

2. Continuing to misdiagnose diversity problems and failing to recognize them as leadership problems.

3. Focusing on quick wins (e.g., speaker series, Rooney Rule practices), a misguided strategy that leads to solving for the wrong things.

These pitfalls are challenging in any organizational context, but especially when you consider that the roadblocks to inclusive and equitable workplaces are hiding in plain sight: insidiously exclusive cultures marked by bias, prejudice, bullying, discrimination, and harassment, plus incompetent leaders and misaligned human resource programs. Instead of addressing the root causes, organizations continue to blame the lack of representational diversity on a "supply issue." They ignore subjective hiring ("Hey, this kid played lacrosse at Dartmouth and he interned at Goldman, he knows how to compete"), performance, pay processes, and toxic behavioral norms. Most of all, they are unwilling to hold leaders and managers accountable for their behavior and actions.

How do we reduce the structural inequities that limit access and potential, and what would it take to change? These have been central questions throughout my career. Inspired by historian Ibram X. Kendi's work and that of pioneering scholars Walter Stafford, Kimberlé Crenshaw, Frantz Fanon, and Anita Hill, I believe that eliminating racism requires challenging it before *and* after it appears. White supremacy and white privilege influence not only who gets hired, included, and promoted in an organization, but what we think of as normal or desirable, whether we are white or not. Instead of working toward populating organizations with more racial representation—the common aim of diversity, equity, and inclusion practices—we should address and dismantle the root causes of how racism systematically advantages white people and disadvantages BIPOC.

We have all witnessed racism at work. Early on in my career, I watched talented women and BIPOC employees be sidelined, marginalized, and silenced. These experiences led me to spend the past two decades designing and executing diversity, equity, and inclusion strategies across large, global companies and, in more recent years, at start-ups and nonprofit institutions. I worked at known and revered companies like Google, Disney, and Viacom—companies at which we got some things right and some things wrong. This has been my journey, but I can guess that many of you reading this right now have experienced something similar in your own lives and careers.

My commitment to creating workplaces that work for everyone comes from a personal place. I know firsthand how companies and organizations are strengthened when they make their cultures more inclusive and equitable, and I know why that shift is hard.

The greatest gifts my family gave to me, at the expense of their own comfort, were the educational tools to access and navigate a wide range of professional experiences and environments, including spaces not designed for people like me. I have been sought after and hired at some of the most admired companies because I've learned how to navigate predominantly white spaces. But that doesn't mean that I have always felt welcomed and valued. The real shame is that it has been up to me—and others like me—to neutralize passive and sometimes outright racism and construct our own personal safety nets. Now it's time for everyone to step in.

What Is Change?

Throughout my career, I've contributed my voice, experience, and bits of my soul to solve complex issues of workplace culture, identity, access, opportunity, and power from the inside. Many of my fellow diversity, equity, and inclusion leaders and practitioners have also been at this for a long time, and they're exhausted, frustrated, and burned-out. Yet I am more hopeful than ever. Why?

You.

I'm writing this book for you: The white or BIPOC manager. The leader who recognizes that diversity, equity, and inclusion are necessary for your teams. The aspiring manager who wants to dismantle old systems in your workplace from the inside out and build bridges and connections. The manager sandwiched between the C-suite and your entry-level workers, who feels that you don't have the power and influence to effect the level of change you want to see in your organization. I have been there. And I am here to tell you that you *do* have the power.

You who are often given directions instead of time, guidance, and budget. You who feel unable to move forward because you lack answers to your questions about purpose and opaque processes. You who want to ensure that everyone who works with you feels better after an interaction with you, not diminished and depleted. You who want to clear the pathway for success for everyone on your team.

So, what's in it for you? Think of this book as a how-to manual for building a more inclusive company or organization. I'll offer tangible advice to dismantle exclusive practices throughout the employee life cycle and show you how to do this work, step-by-step. But ultimately you have to put in the work if you believe that this is important to you, your team, and your organization. If you've picked it up because you're either anxious or dismayed with the lack of progress, this book shares stories to ground and inspire you. If you want to support this work indirectly or take it on yourself, this book offers tools and resources to help you do that. And if you've picked up this book even though you doubt this work is worthwhile or valuable—I hope you give me the chance to prove otherwise.

We all interact in workplaces and have a million opportunities to influence change. Throughout this book, I present bold policies, better practices, and real ideas that anyone can implement to chip away at the problematic biases, norms, behaviors, processes, and systems across our organizations. I ask targeted and perhaps uncomfortable questions for you to consider. And I share my own stories of how I've been on both sides of the equation and how I've learned from my mistakes.

While you may not have the power to replace your company's leadership, there are important steps that all managers and aspiring managers, both white and BIPOC, can take today toward the goal of building more diverse, equitable, and inclusive workplaces that are successful both commercially and culturally. You'll need to focus on those interventions most pertinent to your culture and business, and state clearly what you're trying to achieve. This is a book of action for those who are willing to find the courage to realize equity in their organizations and confront pervasive whiteness at work. And it's a book for those who are struggling with moving past the trending hashtags, political landmines, and pervasive blind spots. All of this is here so that you can hire, engage, retain, and grow diverse talent and sharpen your equity and inclusion lens.

Change means creating a fervent sense of belonging for everyone, no matter their background, ethnicity, gender, sexual identity, religious beliefs, physical ability, or any other identity. Everyone is welcome to this Inclusion Revolution, and the invitation explicitly states to show up as you. The experience of women of color in the workplace—women like me—is like walking a tightrope every day. I have to make daily decisions that take a toll on my physical and mental well-being—which parts of myself to bring forward and which parts to blend. Which parts will threaten or offend the least? How much space can I take? How many mistakes can I afford? Will I constantly have "un pie aquí y un pie allá" (one foot in and one foot out), always exceeding the most unreasonably high standards while watching mediocrity succeed upwardly? Or will I be able to breathe and be me?

I've found many leaders eager for actionable frameworks and advice to create more inclusive cultures. But again and again I find one thing plaguing their attempts: *fear*. They are so terrified about messing up and saying the wrong thing to all their stakeholders: employees, board members, funders, clients, customers, or the wider world via social media. They are so afraid of losing their job, professional footing, and ability to provide for their families that they're paralyzed into inaction.

There is a very special energy in organizations where fear doesn't exist. Where people feel seen, heard, and valued. Where people feel that they can engage, perform, and contribute without judgment and retaliation. It keeps workplaces from feeling dark and heavy. It keeps the mistrust out of the air. It keeps employees from leaving the organization or, worse, sustaining repeated trauma to survive financially. It breeds the highest levels of creativity, innovation, and collaboration. That is the workplace I want for you!

Over the years, I have tested and developed different models for dismantling inequities across many organizations and industries. I have seen what works and what doesn't. I've learned that best practices and research are starting points. There are no silver bullets or shortcuts, but you must start somewhere. Here's my formula: **reflect**, **visualize**, **act**, and **persist**. As you tackle any challenge or consider new opportunities for your organization, **reflect** on what you and others are experiencing at this moment, **visualize** what is possible for you and your organization, **act** on what you've heard and learned, and **persist** when obstacles appear, because they will.

This book begins with an internal lens (**reflect**) to help you get clear on your truth and the truths of your coworkers—the variations in your points of view, feelings, and identities; your motivations; and how this impacts the organizational climate.

The bulk of the book walks you through steps two and three (**visualize** and **act**) as we address big topics like hiring, onboarding, and transforming culture. This will start you on your path to use your knowledge of the organization's climate and systemic and structural barriers. The invitation here is to approach this work from a place of ideas, values, and pure pragmatism—fixing one part of a broken system at a time. Create your own best-practice learning lab through constant testing and iteration, and define the role you want to play. This is where you invite engagement and collaboration.

The final chapters are when we rumble with the uncomfortable (**persist**) and hold ourselves and others accountable. Discomfort is an inevitable result of confronting the places where we've fallen short. It should be uncomfortable to hear about the times when the company has let employees down or when you have fallen short as a manager or colleague. Lean on courage and fortitude to stay the course, respond proactively, track progress, and celebrate your wins. Make small tweaks over time. You need to see what sticks.

I believe this model can be cultivated in every company and organization. Use it as your guide on your own journey.

If this sounds intimidating, don't worry. Small, consistent, deliberate, and sustainable actions made over time deliver the greatest impact. I'll show you how to come at it with a compassionate, realistic, and accessible approach. Your goal is not to change your entire organization overnight; it's to make a plan that reflects your values and aspirations. It's to increase the capacity of others to do good.

Embrace the Revolution

Real revolutions are the ones no one sees coming. But we have all seen this coming. It is no surprise that those most harmed by racial hierarchies are crying out to be heard and demanding fairness. White supremacy and systemic racism have been built into our institutions and legislated into every aspect of our society. The media further legitimizes overrepresented and idealized representations of white Americans while marginalizing and minimizing BIPOC experiences. We are a nation with a fraught history of slavery and racial segregation that has long emboldened people to think in racist ways. But if we understood the root cause of our thinking, I believe we would begin to question and change these racist patterns. To create fair and inclusive workplaces, we need to understand the hidden power structures and toxic cultures that block full inclusion and racial equity, and commit to changes in hiring, pay, and performance management. It is no longer an option for any of us to remain passive.

I want to inspire new levels of ownership and to strengthen our collective capacity to drive change, recognize the pitfalls, and keep going. This is about how we as a people can learn to work together. That has always been the revolution: how we drive change, together. This is not about culture by default but rather culture by deep intention and action. What does it look like? Work that feels generative, effortless (despite the hard work you do), productive, and joyful.

What works, what has proven to work for generations before us, is millions of people acting in millions of different ways and across millions of moments, not just completing one discrete task at a time. To dismantle inequity in the workplace, we must translate good intentions into impactful and sustained actions. We must generate better decisions, better strategy, better conversations and debate, better risk and performance management, better investments, and better career *and* business outcomes.

The model for impacting real change in the workplace that I'm presenting is a revolutionary approach that is within our reach. It does not require us to tear down the existing structure and create something from scratch. It is meant to increase our capacity to make this moment a movement. The steps of this model are incremental enough that everyone can do them, including *you*.

Inclusion Revolution is not a blueprint for check-the-box diversity training; it's not a prescription for being politically correct in the workplace. This is a book of action for those who are willing to confront the pervasive inequities at work. Let's raise the bar by fighting back against the lack of purposeful attention and effort coupled with the fatigue and inertia that comes from years of trying to get diversity, equity, and inclusion right. Let's turn goodwill and intent into real results. And let's build change that lasts, because through the best teams—and the broadest client, customer, investor, and audience reach—companies can build a stronger future.

Welcome to the Inclusion Revolution!

1

YOUR INCLUSION AMBITIONS

T HERE'S A FAMOUS story about President John F. Kennedy visiting the NASA space center in 1962. Kennedy noticed a man carrying a broom, and when the president introduced himself, he asked the man what his job was. The employee, a janitor, responded, "Well, Mr. President, I'm helping to put a man on the moon." Achieving that sense of shared purpose is a foundation for true and lasting inclusion and belonging in the workplace.

Right now, diversity, equity, and inclusion is our moon landing, and to make this mission successful we need everyone, from interns to executives, to contribute to creating a culture of belonging. Imagine that you can make work easier for all kinds of people in your organization, to allow them to use their skills and thoughtfulness for innovation and problem-solving. Imagine that you can create a sense of psychological safety where everyone feels confident and comfortable to take risks, make mistakes, contribute opinions, and be candid about what they are up against. Managers have this power. *You* have this power. It starts with making a visible commitment to inclusion and belonging across your teams, because work cultures are not all created equal.

Some people experience the workplace as it should be: challenging—it is work after all—and rewarding, if you're lucky. For others, that same workplace is overlaid with microaggressions, gender violence, systemic racism, outright discrimination, and the nagging feeling that you're going crazy as you try to get through each day. Underrepresented employees across many workplaces feel like their background, ideas, and experiences are routinely being discounted. These feelings of exclusion are among the primary reasons for the revolving door of talent for employees of color. Over and over, outstanding people are hired for their magic—and then that magic is sucked dry when they are ostracized for not "fitting in" within the broader culture. When that happens, they either underperform, quit, or get pushed out. Those are the circumstances for so many, and that's what I want to change. If you're reading this book, you do too.

This book is full of concrete, accessible, and research-based tools that can be applied immediately. But before you roll up your sleeves and try to leapfrog the process, commit to first understanding who you are and what have been the barriers to racial equity in your organization. This first chapter is an essential moment of truth that will encourage you to act with intention.

We first need to clear the air and be honest with ourselves, and our colleagues, about why corporate America is so white. White people have had decades of advantages in professional workplaces, mostly through the nation's systemic segregation of neighborhoods, schools, and social and professional networks, to the point where it seems normal that most white people only move through all-white spaces, have all-white friend circles, and have all-white colleagues. This chapter is about being willing to interrogate why and to understand how ill-prepared everyone is—white and BIPOC managers alike—to discuss the true root causes in a constructive way.

"What's one thing you like about being white?" That's the question writer, scholar, and TV host Dr. Marc Lamont Hill asked his guest, a conservative activist, in a discussion on race theory. The guest didn't respond, deflecting the question, but if every white person took a moment to stop and consider their own answer, they might begin to understand why it's so essential to confront racial inequity in our workplaces.

I'm hopeful because I believe more and more managers are beginning to understand that they will have trouble achieving anything unless they first create a welcoming environment where their team members feel encouraged to be themselves and speak up, feel a sense of connection to their work and their peers, and feel that they receive equitable treatment and have a fair chance to succeed. When you understand this and why it's necessary to create a culture of belonging—why these actions will work, what challenges they are helping solve, and how they will benefit everyone—you will become a stronger champion, a better ally, and an admirable leader.

Get on the Balcony

Goals are necessary and milestones are measurable, but the real transformation comes when you align them with the spirit of *why* it's important to hire, retain, and engage a diverse workforce; *what* biases and dated practices have kept you from making progress; and *what* steps you can take to mitigate bias and microaggressions. That's when the work of creating a fair, equitable, and inclusive organization becomes clear.

Ron Heifetz and Marty Linsky coined the leadership skill "getting off the dance floor and going to the balcony" in their book *Leadership on the Line*. They describe the dance floor as being in the middle of the action, bogged down in the details, and getting on the balcony as the practice of taking a step back and taking everything in. That is, asking, "What's really going on here?" The operational pressures of diversity, equity, and inclusion work—such as needing to show nearly immediate results in workforce representation—often mean that those tasked with achieving a company's diversity, equity, and inclusion aspirations go for quick-fix approaches that do not address the root cause of racial disparities in their organizations. They are pushed and pulled by events, people, and opaque and conflicting agendas. This often leads to misdiagnosed problems and well-known yet inadequate stand-alone solutions—like diverse candidate slates, employee resource groups, culturally immersive programs, and unconscious bias training—that perpetually keep them on the dance floor, rather than taking the time to step back and pause for reflection.

When you're feeling lost or stuck, bring it back to the why: define it, then refine and redefine the opportunities. Get clear on how diversity, equity, and inclusion will contribute to your mission and performance, and what you will do to make your insights a reality for your business. Be willing to surface hidden flaws that, if left unattended, could fester into unmanageable problems.

Getting on the balcony takes discipline, courage, and a willingness to stay the course. Allow yourself the time to think, reflect, and observe the patterns of behaviors, norms, actions, and inactions to understand what might get in the way of dismantling inequity in your workplace. The best leaders, managers, and individual contributors learn how to move gracefully between the balcony and the dance floor. Try this exercise to help you do just that.

Define what you're trying to solve for and why:

- What motivates me to build a diverse workforce and inclusive culture?

- What makes me nervous or confused?

- What gets in our way as an organization, as a team?

- What am I missing or have I been unwilling to see?

- What is possible that we have not thought of yet?

- What's working and what can we share with or borrow from others?

- How do we bring others along?

Then get back on the dance floor to define interventions based on what you've gathered. Try building an opportunity statement:

- Creating a more diverse, equitable, and inclusive workplace at _____ is critical because _____.

- As a/an (individual contributor, team leader, senior executive) at _____, I will _____ and _____ and _____ in the next six to twelve months.

You can move back and forth, dynamically and collaboratively. When employees clamor for public statements, ask them to challenge their assumptions about how and where work gets done and about the behavioral norms and expectations across teams. When executives are eager to jump into action, encourage them to pause, listen to what their team members need, build solutions based on the insights they gather, and show evidence of care even when they don't know what to say.

"The work has to start with an internal focus before it turns to an external focus," says Freada Kapor Klein, founding partner at Kapor Capital, a venture capitalist, social policy researcher, and philanthropist who has advocated for diversity and inclusion in tech since the 1980s.

Center what you want to achieve. Well-curated performances won't do. You must answer that core question: Why do I want to do this? Followed by: Where do I want to enter this work? If your answer is "I want to avoid imploding from this scandal" or "I'm being told it's important," you will not make the right choices or investments. Achieving a more diverse, equitable, and inclusive workplace is not a box to check off. A common answer is that it's the right thing to do, but achieving an inclusive workplace is not just about ethics and morality.

If you're not yet sure of your why, know this: when we improve belonging and inclusion at work, success follows. Belonging improves retention. Workplace belonging can lead to a 56 percent reduction in turnover risk. That's because people who feel they belong perform better, become more willing to challenge themselves, and are more confident and resilient. The positive stats keep on coming: workplaces with inclusive cultures are six times more likely to innovate and weather market change, and workplace engagement (an additional indicator of belonging) is closely correlated with increased productivity, profit, and innovation, as well as decreased employee turnover. *Harvard Business Review* attempted to quantify this impact, stating that increased job performance, reduced turnover, and fewer sick days for a ten-thousand-person company would result in annual savings of more than $52 million.

That's $52 million in savings just when someone feels comfortable and safe in their place of work. The message is loud and clear: diversity and inclusion will bring profits and innovation. But it's still not breaking through.

Doing good and doing well are not mutually exclusive. You should frame the value proposition of nurturing a diverse, inclusive, and equitable workplace as both the right and the smart thing to do. You should aim to be the company that everyone else wants to emulate—the one receiving awards for the best place to work because your employees are able to share ideas openly, explore disagreements, and talk through tensions as a team, not because you had the most press attention. Making people feel included and connected and fostering an embrace of belonging is not just a nice thing to do; it's necessary to heal the harm that exists across workplaces. Leaders who wish to build innovative and agile teams must embrace this role. To prime yourself for this work, it's essential to understand your power as a manager or coworker to eliminate disparities and inequities. You can show up for your teams in ways that are meaningful to them and build genuine connections based on empathy and trust. Figure out their unique challenges and reduce the barriers to their success. This drives empathy, understanding, and in the end, innovation, experimentation, and agility.

You will need to reflect. Think about your vision. Be clear about your intentions. What are you trying to do, and what do you hope to gain? Get grounded in your motivation so that you can better define your role in the Inclusion Revolution and recruit others to your cause. You must think, then act. Being at the forefront of this revolution will make you a better, more in-demand leader.

Your Mindset Matters

This work is hard, complex, and triggering. It fundamentally requires you to acknowledge your personal blind spots and your organization's cultural and systemic sore spots. You will need to confront deep-seated beliefs and unconscious habits—including guilt and shame, common obstacles to change. You will need to explore your identity and privilege in relation to others and ask for feedback that may be hard to hear. You will need to build new muscles, including the capacity to interpret new information, to sit in ambiguity, conflict, and discomfort, and to determine what's possible when you witness workplace inequities. You will need to act on the knowledge you gain and embrace and admit your fears about what change means for you. You will need to come face-to-face with the missed opportunities where you were complicit by looking away or letting something slide. I know that may feel like a lot, but when you open your mind and heart to the possibility of making a difference in someone's life, these efforts will feel worthwhile.

"In any given moment, we have two options: step forward into growth or step backward into safety," said psychologist Abraham Maslow, the architect of Maslow's hierarchy of needs. Safety looks like short-term policies and public campaigns; growth looks like taking the time to find the most inclusive solution, not the fastest one. Instead of clinging to what we can or can't control, or fearing that we will be slapped down for trying to be helpful, we can meet this overwhelmingly complex diversity, equity, and inclusion work with curiosity, openness, resilience, and agility. I want to invite you to think more expansively and imaginatively about your role, conscious or unconscious, as a leader or aspiring manager in creating feelings of exclusion or inclusion.

We all have the capacity to lead and collaborate fairly and with compassion. Whether you're a diversity, equity, and inclusion professional or a leader, ally, or accomplice trying to cultivate better workplace culture, here's how you can get in the right mindset:

1. **Embrace courage**. Know you're going to make mistakes along the way. Don't let the fear of putting your foot in your mouth keep you silent. Learn from your gaffes or things you might not have done right in the past and make a promise to yourself to do better next time.

2. **Tame your defensiveness**. It's a natural by-product of feeling uncomfortable and questioning your privilege or your habits. Sit with those emotions, ask yourself what you are trying to protect and why, and watch for any tendencies to make excuses, deny facts, or blame others.

3. **Be transparent**. If you don't know an answer, or if you are genuine about your desire to do better, say so. Transparency and vulnerability build trust, which is an essential tool in this work. Be frank about what you do not know, what you wonder about, what blind spots you are working on.

4. **Own your power**. Know that you can make a difference. It will take time to radically transform your organization, but it's worth it. While it's crucial that your CEO and senior executives are driving change from the top, a survey from the Boston Consulting Group found that 80 percent of a company's workforce is mid-level managers who influence most day-to-day decisions and culture building. Whether you're a manager or aspiring to be one, you can be a leader for change.

5. **Think like a beginner**. A beginner's mindset stems from a concept in Zen Buddhism called shoshin. Wikipedia defines it as "having an attitude of openness, eagerness, and lack of preconceptions when studying a subject, even when studying at an advanced level, just as a beginner in that subject would." It's crucial to have an open mind that enables you to be willing to experiment, seek feedback, and admit your fears and mistakes.

An important first step is to put your mind in an inquisitive, reflective state. Be ready to ask *why*. Go deeper and question norms, assumptions, policies, and procedures. Question everything—even what I write here! Observe yourself and look for blind spots. Challenge my assumptions and yours at every step. A truly remarkable number of things you do every day, regardless of their complexity, operate outside of your awareness: how you respond to the people around you, how you select the news you watch, the way you conduct yourself in a meeting, the candidates you select for jobs, and even where and what you eat. You do these things automatically. You do them by habit. This is implicit bias; your brain creates biased shortcuts to help you make decisions quickly.

Hold Up a Mirror to Bias

The task of inclusion, let alone a full Inclusion Revolution, is a challenging endeavor because of the well-researched existence of an us-versus-them bias. Take this quote from Mary E. Casey and Shannon Murphy Robinson in their book *Neuroscience of Inclusion*: "When we meet someone and the brain doesn't like their differences—the way they think, the color of their skin, what they believe, how they dress, or any other characteristics the brain perceives as outside its comfort zone—this is no small event. When the brain registers differences as discomfort, it sends an 'away' impulse and even regards these differences as potential threats."

University of California, Berkeley, professor John A. Powell's work on belonging asks, "How do we build bridges?" In short, how do we move away from an us-versus-them mindset and toward a "we" mindset. He says that belonging requires us to hear others' stories with compassion, and he believes that we can achieve that through "bridging"—the practice of turning outward to connect with others. This contrasts with what we currently see in the workplace: we turn inward, connecting only to what we know and who we know, diminishing our ability to listen and collaborate.

This lifetime of social programming and biased mental shortcuts can prevent people from reaching their full potential and cause harmful setbacks. You can get over the invisible barriers caused by implicit bias by pausing, reflecting, and taking different actions. It requires a deep examination of history, motives, and intentions. Preconceived notions, biased interpretations, and social conditioning can foster unjust practices.

The first step: rewrite the old rules. Stop saying (and thinking) that's how it's always been done, or that's what has been passed down as the right way to do something. Question a practice or policy's legacy. Does it still make sense to do things that way?

For example, when you're writing a job description or asking for referrals for a new role, ask yourself, "Why am I doing it this way?

What am I missing? Whose voice or experience am I discounting? Who could I be creating access for?" We don't have to continue with oppressive practices that allow inequities to persist. We can transform our organizations for good, and in the process show up differently in our workplaces, with our families, in our communities.

This requires a willingness to interrogate the ways your behavior or organizational habits may reinforce advantages for white coworkers and marginalize BIPOC coworkers. It means being mindful that anti-Blackness is a material factor that harms and holds back your Black coworkers. It is up to you—the white or BIPOC manager—to develop the skills to help you discern between when you experience an emotional reaction because someone has violated a legitimate boundary of yours, versus because you expect coworkers to comply, appease, and defer, and you're not getting it.

It's rare for a manager, even BIPOC managers, to have received racially sensitive management training that will help them understand how to do this. Instead, most managers come up in a working world that was built for an assumed white, male workforce, and very few organizations have challenged those norms. Women and BIPOC have been shown that the only way to succeed professionally is to act like a successful white man, even though that playbook does not recognize the realities of racism and sexism.

Every employee deserves a workplace culture and manager that brings out their best professional performance. And no employee can bring their best self and talents to the table if they feel that they have to armor up and overcome their manager's low expectations from the start. But just because you're a person of color doesn't mean you know what it's like to create an inclusive, welcoming workplace. You've likely learned to put up with a lot to survive all-white spaces, and there is a danger that you could be normalizing bad behaviors (ever hear someone say, "He didn't mean it that way"?).

At the core of this book is the thesis that racial exclusion, discrimination, and harassment across all industries is a systematic problem, that a misuse of power is at the root of inequity, and that in order to achieve inclusion in the workplace, we need to dismantle the practices, behaviors, and systems that exclude. We live in a white supremacist culture that privileges white norms, values, and behaviors. When I say that we need to adopt an equity mindset, that means treating people equally and with respect and committing to fair outcomes, regardless of race, gender, sexual identity, religion, or age, among other differences.

Create a Road Map for Change

For far too long, managers have believed that creating a fair, inclusive, and equitable working environment is somehow separate from their core job as a leader. That's what chief diversity officers are for, right? As if a manager's only job is achieving operational goals.

Employees have become more vocal and persistent in challenging leadership on controversial issues—including immigration, harassment, arbitration clauses, and pay equity—yet we are all stuck in the gray space between awareness and effective action. There are reasons: a fear of saying the wrong thing, confusion as to what to prioritize first or where and how much to invest, or frustration about the lack of impact of previous efforts. We need to get out of this space.

We all interact in workplaces and have a million opportunities to influence change. You can create change in your organization through small and constant actions that over time affect hearts, minds, and systems. Activist and author Angela Davis says we need to "make the radical imaginable" and empower ordinary people to put pressure on the existing state of affairs to create conditions for change. She calls these strategies "reform tactics," though you may think of them as operational practices, such as designing new hiring policies, launching new management training programs, and setting targets for achieving representational diversity. I think of this as affecting the conditions for change, one effort, conversation, or key performance indicator at a time.

Waiting for change to happen means abdicating your responsibility to lead and missing your chance to create conditions for your entire team to succeed. You must act. There is no other choice if you believe that building inclusive, equitable, and diverse workplaces is the priority of the decade. Reading anti-racist books doesn't magically turn you into an anti-racist activist, just as reading about inclusive practices doesn't make you an inclusive leader. These are not topics to be tucked away and brought out for periods of curious examination or social pressure. In fact, acting on the lessons, ideas, and awakening that comes from reading a book takes you on the path to course correct years of systematic bias and racism in the workplace.

A thoughtful, committed call to action is what's needed. It can feel necessary to act quickly and react defensively to what's being said around you. But more often, a thoughtful response and an action plan to make things right is far more necessary when, for example, harassment or toxicity is reported. The key ingredients to success are introspection, thoughtful responses, and committing to meaningfully and materially changing what needs to change. What works best is not always what comes first, but what has the most lasting impact.

"This work needs to be done in the true spirit of reparations if we're going to do anything differently," says Freada Kapor Klein. An exploration of reparations—typically discussed as a way to redress the injustices of slavery, Jim Crow, and anti-Black institutional racism—can also apply more broadly to the workplace by acknowledging that institutional and structural inequities exist and that they limit Black people's professional opportunities in particular. "It is as though we have run up a credit-card bill, and having pledged to charge no more, remain befuddled that the balance does not disappear," said Ta-Nehisi Coates in his article "The Case for Reparations." "The effects of that balance, interest accruing daily, are all around us."

On a practical level, what do reparations look like in the workplace? In relation to work, it is not about placing guilt on white people or excusing BIPOC employees not performing their job duties, but about acknowledging that four hundred years of slavery and subsequent racial segregation in our schools, neighborhoods, and workplaces have stunted economic and social outcomes for Black communities. So what's a business leader to do?

Shift your mindset to focus on achieving fair outcomes for all your people. What do they need to feel a sense of belonging and connection to you and your organization? Start with these questions:

1. **What do your customers want?**

    The audiences you build for, sell to, and speak to around the world are richly diverse, so you can't serve them well if your company doesn't reflect their voices, culture, perspectives, and needs. If a high percentage of your customers are Black, doesn't it make sense to have Black leaders be the ones approving marketing plans? Black leaders who understand the demographic and what they value from a personal and professional lens. Companies who are profitable understand this and create room for diverse ideas to be welcomed and challenged, for creative tensions to exist, and for excellence, innovation, and inspiration to thrive.

    In 2014, Apple made a strategic acquisition to engage Black consumers, 71 percent of whom own smartphones. Apple purchased Dr. Dre's Beats Electronics for $3 billion to add a product line favored by a Black audience and featured celebrities like Kendrick Lamar in advertising. Apple recognized the purchasing power of their consumers.

    Every company has a customer, and the most successful companies know to put that customer—no matter who they are, what they believe, where they are from, or what they identify with—first. Diversity of thought, experience, and background is good for business, but it's also better for the customers who *are* your business.

2. **Who are you leaving out?**

The smallest changes can have the biggest impact on the most people. For an LGBTQ event at Twilio, a cloud software company, an organizer taped a sheet of paper on a bathroom door that declared it "all gender" for the day. They never took it down. A candidate who interviewed at Twilio reportedly joined the company because of that sign; it was a literal signal of inclusion, and the candidate felt comfortable coming out as transgender. In response to that feedback, Twilio added gender-neutral bathrooms across the office.

Some diversity advocates use the calendar as a way to make inclusion sustainable in the form of Black, Hispanic, and Asian heritage months, Pride month, women's history month, and so on. This must be done tastefully and sensitively— having Taco Tuesday during Hispanic heritage month is one big eye roll. Do something more impactful. Several organizations, such as Barclays UK, have held global Wikipedia edit-a-thons, where teams get together to literally change the narrative of history. Less than 20 percent of Wikipedia biographies are about women, and an estimated 90 percent of Wikipedia editors are men, so these companies set out to fix this by writing and uploading articles about women. Art+Feminism, a national campaign to improve coverage of cis and transgender women and the arts, did the same and teamed up with UC Berkeley's Race+Justice edit-a-thon to fire up their laptops and add or edit articles.

3. **What do your managers need to know?**

Everyone in corporate America has gone through some type of diversity training. The truth is, it's not working. There is scant research-based evidence to demonstrate the effectiveness of generic training and cookie-cutter diversity, equity, and inclusion practices. Instead, you need to tailor solutions to the individual needs of the people in your workplace. And you need to provide reinforcing mechanisms—such as continuous tips and tricks and resources for managers—to help teams internalize what they've learned within their day-to-day operations, along with clear accountability expectations.

You have to get down to the basics of how people manage, lead, operate, and hire in an inclusive way. You need to build a shared understanding of what you're trying to solve and who should do it. Be careful with what you expect to get out of training and research and the impact it will have. Training can introduce very complex topics, new vocabulary, and an expectation for immediate expertise, as if a one-day exploration of racism at work is all it takes to turn managers into gold-star inclusive leaders.

Instead, leadership and management development should prioritize giving managers the tools to spot where change can happen: Where are the biggest gaps in your company culture? What direct or indirect experiences at work cause racial trauma? What specifically do you want people to do, think, or feel differently after the training? Start by determining your focus, where your most significant opportunities are, and where you want to make an impact.

I have attended my fair share of diversity workshops as a participant. My fellow colleagues of color and I would often joke, "Hey, you're also here to learn about how to work with yourself?" But we learned about our own blind spots too. When delivered with care and in alignment with ongoing organizational commitments to diversity, equity, and inclusion, these trainings can help build better managers of all backgrounds.

One of the key blind spots many white managers have is that they believe all women and BIPOC are coming into meetings and group discussions at the same baseline. Use these trainings as an opportunity to point out that women and BIPOC are conditioned over a lifetime to defer to white men and to never take up space. While many white men assume that colleagues are not interrupting or talking at length because they have nothing to say, the reality is that many women and BIPOC staff are reluctant to speak, even when they have abundant ideas. A useful leadership hack is setting up a new norm where women and BIPOC are asked to speak first and are brought in by explicit invitation from a leader, rather than expecting them to interrupt and dominate the conversation. People are immediately credentialed when someone in power speaks about them. Mention them in a meeting; invite them to join a planning session. Note, though, that this doesn't work for everyone. Ask your BIPOC colleagues whether they're willing to engage.

Many BIPOC have had to conform to white norms in order to rise, so BIPOC managers may also need to find ways to create paths for people to succeed as themselves. For example, ideally, in the future BIPOC won't have to code-switch, the act of adjusting one's style of speech, behaviors, appearance, and expressions in order to seem "professional." It can be damaging if junior BIPOC staff meet senior BIPOC staff who pressure them into respectability politics and encourage code-switching in order to fit in.

The Belonging Effect

Belonging—a word I'm sure you've heard a lot—is key to creating environments where everyone feels they can thrive. Belonging is not just getting in the door and being invited to a meeting; belonging is the feeling that you're respected, valued, and essential. Our words and actions must signal to others that we really do care enough to notice—to see them for who they really are. To belong is not just to be a team member but to be able to participate in creating the workplace that you belong to. It's also consistently and universally tied to a person's workplace commitment, motivation, and pride, according to Culture Amp, a culture-driven people analytics platform. Asking the question, "Will this help someone feel like they belong?" is a good starting place throughout the work we will do together.

When I joined the workforce in 1998, I quickly learned that, in order to survive, I needed to put on emotional armor every single day. For years, I had to leave parts of myself at the door because it wasn't safe for me to bring my whole self in. Like many women of color and people of other marginalized identities, I faced the personal and professional harm of being cut out from social cliques—which are often key for networking and advancement—and the exhaustion from dodging sexist, racist, and xenophobic daggers. And I was one of the lucky ones, because I had managers who empowered me to do my best work, often advocating for new opportunities. But even they were victims of power hierarchies and were ill-equipped to understand the stress of being stereotyped.

Covering (a form of identity camouflage where an individual downplays part of themselves) and code-switching have a profoundly negative effect in the workplace. I've seen too many women and people of color put themselves on guard to the point of exhaustion in order to cope with discrimination. Forty-two percent of women of color, 40 percent of men of color, and 40 percent of women of all backgrounds cited being just that, "on guard," in anticipation of racial or gender bias, according to a 2018 study from Catalyst. Other people responded that they were on guard because they felt they were being devalued due to their physical appearance, disability, age, or religious beliefs.

These employees stay socially distant because they worry about facing scrutiny. Often it's not outright discrimination but rather a lack of interest, lack of caring, and day-to-day exclusions from the fabric of an organization that create this emotional tax. When BIPOC staff are routinely forgotten on invitations to meetings, aren't copied on certain emails, aren't approached about coming to drinks after work, that stings. I've been there. When employees have to expend boundless energy on their defenses to survive in their environment, what do you think happens to their output? To their relationships with colleagues and supervisors? They cannot give 100 percent because they are working from a deficit. They have to spend a large majority of their energy on emotional vigilance, corporate politics, and managing fight-or-flight responses.

As humans, our need to belong is innate. We all want to feel seen, heard, and worthy—that we deserve to be here, wherever that is. Have you ever felt left out, underestimated, or sidelined at work? Maybe it was when you shared an idea in a meeting, only for it to be co-opted by someone else or simply ignored. Or maybe it was when you found out that a new team member with less experience was hired at your level and with a higher salary. I will never forget when I was brought in on a major initiative in my department, only to realize that I was being asked to lead and execute something that I had been previously excluded from for months. My peers had already been in the ideation process long before I was asked to bring in my perspective, despite it being a project that could only be completed by my team. It seemed like including me had been an afterthought. In that moment, my ego deflated and my shoulders slumped. I felt socially rejected.

That isolation and lack of connection is the dark side of corporate culture, and most of us have been both victims and perpetrators. Hypocrisy runs deep: as someone who has been the leader of global diversity and inclusion initiatives, I've been tasked with being the face of diversity programs across many organizations, all while facing my own inclusion battles. I have felt invisible and disposable, my voice muted by white men who had no trouble taking up all the air in every meeting and hallway conversation, their sense of entitlement rarely checked or questioned. But perhaps most painful was the silence and denial surrounding racial privilege and abuses of power that I have experienced from white women who advocated for diversity and inclusion but enforced white cultural norms with respect to dress, appearance, and behavior. These women actively challenged gendered microaggressions but failed to do the same with racially biased and inappropriate behavior.

Barriers to inclusion tend to be invisible to those already thriving in an organization. If you've prospered in your organization, you may find it difficult to accept that systemic and cultural barriers prevent some people from successfully navigating your workplace. The dominant culture either fits you, or you have become accustomed to changing your behavior to fit into the dominant culture. In other words, workplace culture is nearly invisible to you because you don't face the same roadblocks as your colleagues.

You may be asking yourself, OK, I've reflected and have a vision of where I want to go. Where do I begin? Use this book as a guide to start chipping away at the inherent bias in the norms, behaviors, processes, and structures in your organization.

Your Road Map to Revolution

Your road map to **reflect**, **visualize**, **act**, and **persist** is unique to you and will serve you on your journey well past reading this book. I will share practices that can help you drive change. It is up to you to be selective in choosing what will move the needle for your organization and to be disciplined in the execution. Resist knee-jerk responses. Pause and reflect. It is important to pull away from your fight, flight, freeze, and appease responses. Instead, micro-nudges, unbiasing moments, and small behavioral shifts can deliver change. Think of this book as a series of actionable prompts on your journey to culture transformation.

I believe that persistent, reinforced micro-moments of learning and action can change behavior. How we listen, teach, assess, train, embody, and test our courage impacts our success in developing the cultural mindset shift required to dismantle racial inequity in the workplace. It can be done. It may feel overwhelming to want to do everything but not know where to begin. At the end of every chapter, you'll find nudges toward action to help create your own road map to revolution.

- **Reflect and get clear on your ambitions**. Ask yourself: What does it mean to be in relationship to and with people who are similar or different from me? How can I build relationships at work and with external stakeholders to communicate across our values more effectively? Why is this work important to me?

- **Craft your vision statement**. Creating a more diverse, equitable, and inclusive workplace is critical because _____. Refer back to this when you're feeling stuck or fatigued. This will keep you focused, efficient, and effective.

- **Confront your fears**. What are you nervous or uncomfortable about? Will you let that stop you? Embrace courage and know that you're going to make mistakes along the way. That's OK.

- **Focus on your mindset**. Go into the journey with an open mind and willingness to learn and grow. Practice saying, "I don't know." Think about what you can do to educate yourself, model inclusive behaviors, or change your mindset.

- **Understand how deep bias runs in your workplace and the world**. Start by recognizing your own blind spots and assumptions. Question why things are done a certain way and think about how they might be done differently. Rewrite the old rules. Ask: What behavioral changes and interventions will have a greater chance of achieving my desired results?

- **Stop one-size-fits-all training**. Listen to your employees, learn from the data, and ask for what your specific organization and managers need to create a more inclusive workplace. Ask: How can we provide support, surface issues, or push for changes through our day-to-day interactions with others?

- **Build bridges and connections**. Your customers, your team, your managers: What do they need from you to feel seen, valued, and empowered? To be connected to a shared vision and goal? Think about them as you seek to build inclusive teams where everyone feels a sense of belonging.

- **Remember to take a beat**. Look before you leap. Give yourself some grace to reflect before you act.

2

BUILD BETTER TEAMS...PERIOD.

WHY DO WE hire people? Because we need help, ideas, skills, and support to build and grow. But what if we take a step back from the nitty-gritty of the hiring process—a grueling opera- tion that's laden with bias, privilege, secret handshakes, and unfair treatment—and focus on the larger purpose of hiring? As you ap- proach this work, your first thought shouldn't be, "I need to get more Black and brown people on our team." It should be, "I want to build the best and most diverse team." A team that is reflective and repre- sentative of a rich pool of talent inclusive of race, ethnicity, gender, mindset, and more.

People have a hard time hiring people outside of their comfort zone. You can design and implement the most inclusive hiring practices, but if your managers are not willing to champion diversity, equity, and inclusion across the business, you will struggle to attract and re- tain diverse talent. Reactive hiring practices aren't sustainable. Telling people that they "have to hire a Black person" doesn't work, because that language focuses on a binary, quantitative measurement of suc- cess, which only produces short-term, non-inclusive results. Managers like this follow the script once and believe their work is done. The new

Black employee is labeled a diversity hire, is automatically laden with low expectations, and thus is doomed from the start. The working biases and assumptions of the company have not been discussed openly, and this Black hire has been set up to fail. Since this employee has been devalued from the start, they will no doubt fail or quit, bringing the company back to where it started on its diversity goals.

One female senior executive I know who works at a global beauty company was directed by her CEO to hire the sole Black woman being evaluated for the job because she didn't currently have a Black woman on her team. The candidate had a noncompete that prevented her from starting at the company for six months, so the new employee's manager was frustrated that she had been strongly instructed to hire someone who wouldn't be able to shoulder part of her team's workload for half the year. Here's what I told her to do: stop stressing yourself out about hiring this particular candidate to solve for your team's lack of racial diversity and instead put pressure on the recruiters to find a broader selection of viable candidates. This woman was not the best hire at this time because of her noncompete, and the CEO needed to look beyond optics and recognize that there were many other talented individuals with strong professional backgrounds across all racial and ethnic groups that should be considered for this role. When pushed to yield, I say push back.

If a BIPOC hire is brought in only to be socially isolated and treated like they won't rise in the company because they don't "really" belong, they will leave.

I have yet to speak to a *Fortune* 500 company that has not put in place a diversity hiring strategy as one of their first "diversity and inclusion" initiatives. It's often the first move companies make to course correct and attempt to build a pipeline that advances diverse talent into entry-level, management, technical, and executive roles. Companies, both big and small, have diversity representation goals in place. They try to revamp the status quo of hiring by expanding the demographics of their talent pools and changing their processes, and there is an ever-growing list of companies striving to help them remove bias, track metrics, and accelerate progress through technology. I've seen many of these strategies in action, I've seen many of them fail, and I've experimented with many of my own.

Fair and transparent hiring mechanisms are an essential driver of diverse representation, but we're not doing it right. Fifty-seven percent of recruiters say their talent acquisition strategies are designed to attract diverse candidates, yet their processes and results say otherwise.

To desegregate workplaces, hiring managers have to be willing to question their choices at every stage of the process: sourcing, screening, interviewing, selecting, and onboarding. Then they need to move in a different, actively anti-racist direction. If your current hiring practices have shown years of majority-white hires, whiteness has been privileged in your hiring practices. Instead of asking, "Why aren't there more qualified BIPOC candidates?" you should ask yourself, "Why are we allowing this company to be a whites-only space at every level of the organization?"

A diverse team doesn't happen overnight. Culture change takes time, and representation is only one measure of progress. We need to start somewhere. To set yourself up for success, you need clarity on metrics (what you're aiming toward), transparency (how different processes lead to different outcomes), and accountability (who is responsible: The recruiter? The hiring manager? The team leader? The colleague who made the referral? Quick tip: the answer is all of the above).

It's time for a new hiring playbook—a new corporate playbook too.

These next few chapters will tackle the hiring process and suggest both tried-and-tested and emerging strategies to create more opportunity and align your practices with your intentions.

Help Underrepresented Talent Envision Themselves at Your Company

Most companies have a solid hiring process and a stated commitment to diversifying their workforce. More recently, many have claimed to be sharpening their focus on hiring more Black leaders across all levels of their organizations. Companies know the business case for diversity, but for deeper impact you have to align the mission of your organization with your hiring goals. Even if you're not the CEO, you must clearly state to your team what diversity, equity, and inclusion means to you. You must explain why it matters to build a diverse team of diverse leaders. The incentive must be clear and must go deeper than a general passion for social justice or the chance to drive shareholder value. Your team members need to connect to your organization's mission, values, and goals. And the talent you seek to hire needs to feel convinced that they can flourish in a role they can't yet imagine.

Salesforce promotes equality in its diversity mission statement: "We're greater when we're Equal." T-Mobile says, "Uniqueness is powerful." These are beautiful sentiments, and I applaud these companies for promoting this message. But what comes next is most important: after you craft a statement that packs a punch, you must deliver on it. Your hiring mission should amplify your overall values and goals and act as a guide or reminder throughout the process. It should be bold and specific. It should authentically describe what it's like to work at your company from the perspective of those with different career and lived experiences.

For example, Disney's company mission is: "To entertain, inform and inspire people around the globe through the power of unparalleled storytelling, reflecting the iconic brands, creative minds and innovative technologies that make ours the world's premier entertainment company." Their hiring marketing tagline—"Where will your story begin?"—succinctly reminds candidates about the promise of being part of the treasured stories associated with the brand. But what if you haven't seen yourself reflected in those stories before? Well, perhaps being more direct—as in, "Every story matters. Where will your story begin?"—could help candidates see themselves as active agents in telling *new* stories. That's how you get the attention of those who think in terms of their complex identities, values, and passions.

Translate and discuss this with your whole team, not just your hiring team. Word-of-mouth referrals often carry the most weight, which makes everyone a recruiter. Companies that succeed in this bring *all* employees into their mission to increase BIPOC, LGBTQ, and female or nonbinary job opportunities. Ask yourself: How does your hiring mission connect to company goals? Why should everyone on the team care? For Disney, this could look like: to tell better, more authentic and relatable stories, we need more perspectives. For Salesforce, it could be: when our sales teams reflect and create for the communities, voices, and movements of our time, our clients grow.

Common People United, a digital strategy company focused on facilitating community works and activism, translates its company philosophy, "Work that matters," into an HR mission. On its website, the company states: "We absolutely need big thinkers, big personalities, and big movements to see positive change on a national or global scale. We also need small groups of people doing work that matters on a day-to-day basis, and we try to surround ourselves with people who feel the same way." You have a winning recruitment strategy when you connect this to an inclusive hiring mindset that helps prospective candidates see themselves at Common People United as the thinkers, personalities, and movement makers who will be welcomed and allowed to drive change.

If your CEO is not doing this, get them to listen to what achieving racial representation means to you and your business, and how to get untapped talent in your organization. As the tech start-up AppNexus grew, there was a persistent impression that there weren't enough women in leadership. "There were always 'reasons' why," says former founder and CEO Brian O'Kelley, but he wanted to understand the root cause of this leadership gap. Flimsy excuses about a dearth of talent weren't enough. When he was invited to a meeting held by the AppNexus Women's Network, he jumped at the chance to listen in—until the women started talking. O'Kelley was confronted by the women's stories and the reality of their experience at the company. He was peppered with questions about the lack of women on the board and the lack of opportunities for growth. "It was really hard to hear," O'Kelley says. "It would have been so easy to walk out of there and do nothing. But I was the CEO and sitting in that room I had the realization that it was my responsibility to fix."

O'Kelley credits a change in his vantage point for the company's transformation. Instead of focusing on the "why not" (Why aren't we hiring more female leaders? Why don't we have a woman on the board?), he shifted his focus to the "why" (having a female board member will make us more attractive to venture capital firms; putting women in senior roles of responsibility will help us recruit more female talent; when we have women on the team, our sales grow). That mindset soon became contagious throughout the company.

Like O'Kelley's team, you can invite your CEO or senior executives to an employee resource group meeting. Or you could email them, share your thoughts with your boss, ask a question at a town hall, or encourage your boss to hold the higher-ups accountable. It's also imperative to tune in to what is not being said. What are people's fears, blind spots, or obstacles to hiring racially diverse talent? "For years McKinsey has been putting out rigorous international data on the financial performance of companies with diverse leadership, diverse boards, and that those companies outpace and outperform everyone," says Freada Kapor Klein. "So if business was truly rational, they would have seized on that years ago. But it's not rational, and instead it's packed with fear."

When you build an inclusive hiring strategy and mission, if you dig deep enough, at some point you have to ask yourself: Who gets access to coveted job opportunities and stretch assignments? Who controls access to hiring decisions? Who's going to give up their seat at the table to make room for someone else? That's the elephant in the room; that's what everyone is afraid to say. If people in positions of power are invested in the change they claim to wish to see, they will remove themselves from the equation and ensure that those who have been ready to take on these roles are considered to replace them and given the resources and time to succeed. We are increasingly seeing white male board members give up their seats following sexual harassment allegations. Does it need to be only then? In other words, do you care enough to get out of the way for someone's advancement? If you haven't addressed the anxiety that comes with that and the shared responsibility required to make it happen, your diversity, equity, and inclusion strategies are set up to fail.

I've often heard that people don't fear change; they fear loss. When talking about your mission, you need to disarm the fear of loss, fear of being replaced and misunderstood, fear of losing the privilege and power you have taken for granted, and fear of being out of your element. Instead, invite others to be part of the change through a shared sense of purpose and benefit. A scarcity mindset believes that if one person wins, another person loses; an abundance mindset focuses on the limitless opportunities available. This can be hard to believe when the economy dips and threatens job security or when opportunities are in fact limited, but an abundance mindset focuses on the fact that we all do better when we all do better. That's why this work matters.

Confronting Privilege in the Hiring Process

Privilege is a word that's tossed around a lot, but it's important to understand that the privilege you hold because of your race, sexual orientation, gender identity, ability, socioeconomic status, or religion leads to shortcuts to success for you that others, who you may be working with side by side, don't have access to. In short, a white person's professional successes are shaped by systems of privileges that funnel them forward, like having access to white professional networks that come with job references. "I have come to see white privilege as an invisible package of unearned assets that I can count on cashing in each day, but about which I was 'meant' to remain oblivious," writes Peggy McIntosh, author of the essay "White Privilege: Unpacking the Invisible Knapsack." "White privilege is like an invisible weightless knapsack of special provisions, maps, passports, codebooks, visas, clothes, tools, and blank checks."

It's normal to be resistant or defensive about admitting your privilege and access to resources. Privilege is the ability to look away; I'm asking you not to. Tension erupts because privilege threatens two central desires we hold: we want to live in a fair, meritocratic system, and we want to feel like a good person. Because the concept of privilege doesn't fit with these desires, what happens is an attempt to justify your privilege, deny its existence, or distort the dynamics of it. Michael Sandel, professor of political philosophy at Harvard University, coined the term the "tyranny of merit." He urges individuals to take a look in the mirror at their "meritocratic hubris" and stop believing in their success as their own doing while they look down on others who haven't made it.

"How do we have an honest conversation about dismantling this idea that we have meritocracy and that every white man who is in a position of power earned it, because he didn't?" asks Reshma Saujani, founder of Girls Who Code and author of *Brave, Not Perfect*. "We don't touch that or address that, and until we do, we are going to have the same conversation. As a South Asian woman, I acknowledge my privilege, but people assume facts about me that allow my voice to not be heard. I'm often overlooked, or bumped into. I have had my hand raised real high, but no one really saw it. I'm assumed to be smart, but not violent. No one is crossing the street when I come walking down." Privilege is a transient concept—you can be privileged in one room and not the other.

When people are perceived to be different from the majority, privileged culture, empathy and understanding for their potential and contributions is limited. Many Black women have felt pressured to conform to European standards of straight hair because Black people's natural hair has long been considered "unprofessional." Several states and cities have passed or proposed laws banning policies that penalize people of color for wearing natural curls, dreadlocks, twists, braids, and other hairstyles that embrace their cultural identity. However, the racist bias against natural hair and limited standards of professionalism continue to plague our workplaces.

White men and women, for the most part, know their power grants them access, safety, and the ability to claim things that no one will question. But it's easier to deflect blame than to face supremacist views, because you have mostly convinced yourselves that those views are only held by others. Dismantling racism, sexism, and all the "isms" means disrupting the status quo. Anti-racism requires that white people sacrifice their comfort when they see it was created through someone else's oppression. That includes the comfort of moving through majority white spaces. White and BIPOC managers need to believe our diverse colleagues when they speak uncomfortable truths. And all managers need to leverage our privileges—be it seniority, whiteness, heterosexuality, or wealth—for change.

I'm not asking those who currently hold most of the power—namely, white male managers—to be powerless. This is about a redistribution of power. Yes, in some cases you may need to move on to create space, but what would be truly revolutionary is for everyone to use their power for good. Once you can see how systems and structures create inequity on the individual level—both the advantages and disadvantages—then you can start to fix them.

For example, if you are a white male manager, your privilege grants you the power to speak up and act on behalf of others, and research shows that when you do, your words and actions have a particularly effective influence. The raw truth is that advocating for a hire or a new policy has more weight coming from a white senior manager. When a BIPOC colleague does the same, they are held to a higher standard of results. Research from the Academy of Management found that when a white male manager made a hiring decision, it had no impact on his performance rating, even if that candidate did not look like him. But when a BIPOC male manager hired someone who looked like him, he took a hit for it. That's privilege in action.

Use your privilege to:

- **Examine your hiring process with a critical lens toward reducing bias**. Suggest changes to recruitment and hiring systems—how you identify, research, generate, and network with potential job candidates, and how you recruit, select, hire, and make offers to new employees—that have been rigged to keep so many locked out.

- **Diversify your professional network**. Most people are hired through referrals, and most white people have all-white social circles and professional networks. Seek out diversity-focused professional organizations that you could be using for your referrals, and encourage your colleagues to do the same.

- **Be vigilant about identifying and removing obstacles so that racially diverse talent can move through the hiring process fairly and consistently**.

Everything from a job description to your company's LinkedIn profile to your website's career section should reinforce your company's inclusive culture and ethos. Removing bias from hiring practices and opening up job opportunities to people who might not traditionally have had access to them are critical parts of reducing inequities in how organizations operate. Relinquishing unfair advantages in the hiring process is not reverse discrimination. Admitting that we have long factored race and gender into selection processes that have led to white-majority workplaces will not destroy you. Embracing racial progress and confronting white professional norms does not mean that white people are under attack. It's time for us to expand the definition of "us" and refocus our hiring habits toward broadening opportunity, belonging, and equity.

A word about white privilege: White privilege does not mean that if you are white you have not experienced hardship or exclusion. If you were the first in your family to go to college, you didn't have access to workplace navigational tools either. It simply means that you have not experienced racism and that racism has not been a barrier to your access and opportunity. White fragility is when white people experience discomfort when faced with their role in perpetuating white supremacy. The truth is that we all have to get better at sitting with discomfort and not allowing it to block action and change.

Diversity Hiring Metrics That Matter

Measuring the success of an inclusive and equitable hiring process requires more than answering the question, Is this position filled or not? You must evaluate the system currently in place, understand how bias and privilege impact access, set ambitious goals, hold people responsible for achievement, and monitor progress across key recruitment stages. Here are four metrics and practices that you should evaluate.

1. **Who is getting interviewed?**

   Metric: Intersectional diversity (race, gender, age, etc.) of applicants who make it to the interview stage

   If you're seeing low numbers, this may be a sign that you need to reevaluate your recruitment practices, including referral programs, job criteria (such as whether college degrees are really necessary), outreach strategies, and screening processes.

2. **Who is moving through each hiring stage?**

   Metric: Intersectional diversity by hiring stage, also known as pass-through rates

   Continuously monitoring applicant and candidate progress across all hiring stages (sourcing, screening, interviewing, and selection) will make it clear where in your hiring process you lose racially diverse candidates and why. A drop in representation at different stages may indicate a particular failure point in your talent systems and may require a different response. For example, if your initial candidate pipeline has a high level of BIPOC talent and you notice a significant drop after the interview process, that may mean you need to address bias in your interview process.

3. **Who is doing the interviewing and selection?**

Metric: Intersectional composition of interviewers

A balance of interviewers will bring unique experiences to the process and can help candidates feel more comfortable. Have your interviewers been trained in inclusive hiring? Are they using competency-based interviewing techniques? Or are they making decisions based on their own biased ideas about how an ideal candidate should look and behave?

4. **Who is getting hired?**

Metrics: New hires versus existing workforce and new hires versus industry benchmark

Hiring goals give your team a clear metric of how many hires they need to land each quarter. If your hiring rate is high but you see no change in overall organizational diversity, then you need to review diversity turnover rates—or as I call it, the *diversity revolving door*—and reassess your goals.

Set Bold Goals

Demand accountability of everyone, all the time. Without key performance indicators or measurable goals at every stage of the hiring process that are designed to change business as usual, talk of increasing compositional diversity is just talk. Hold your teams and company accountable to your revitalized mission with diversity hiring metrics that can be measured and tracked. The bolder, the better. These should be lofty goals, not a minor percentage increase that produces superficial data that diversity numbers are improving.

Let's stop using dated standards to define success in diversity hiring outcomes, such as overemphasizing the diversity composition of entry-level talent and focusing solely on hiring white women without a recognition of the intersectional barriers for women of color.

In 2018, AppNexus's O'Kelley kicked off the company's annual global customer conference, emboldened by the Women's Network's demands that he do better. O'Kelley looked at the 2017 conference lineup and calculated that only three out of twenty speakers were women, and so established a goal to double that number. "I was so proud at the end of that conference," O'Kelley says. "Not only was it a robust, seamless event packed with great content, I was thrilled that we had increased the number of female speakers. I thought I made a big difference." But then O'Kelley got a call from a colleague. "She told me that the Women's Network was livid because even though there were more women on stage, men still spoke for 90 percent of the time and there was never a woman on stage without a man. I felt like I was punched in the gut. Initially, I got defensive and mad. I thought, 'Are you kidding me?'"

O'Kelley admits it took him an hour to cool down and realize the error in his thinking. He called back and said, "OK, tell me again." He realized that even though the overall representation metrics were a dramatic improvement over the previous year, the measures of success failed to take into account status quo blind spots that assumed men were still the standard. "That's Diversity 1.0," O'Kelley says. "At that conference, I was the best Diversity 1.0 CEO, but the women of my company rightly decided to change the standard, so I failed them as a Diversity 2.0 CEO. Diversity 2.0 is about equity. When I did a conference postmortem with the team, I praised them for crushing every metric we set out, and then told them it still wasn't good enough. We needed better metrics."

So what's good enough? What should be expected? At a minimum, your racial-plus (race, gender, sexual orientation, gender identity or expression, class, ability, age, nationality, religion, and ethnicity) diversity goal should be 50 percent of your total workforce, or at least double what it is now. When setting goals, take into consideration possible growth, contraction, promotion processes, and restructuring plans. Will hitting your goals require massive turnover, or is there a budget for a hiring spree? Will every new hire have to meet one of these representation gaps? While corporate recruitment directives can't legally require that every new hire be female, Black, or Latinx, targets such as these can create a shared sense of accountability for recruitment practices and internal restructurings.

Project Include has for years advocated for setting specific demographic targets in the technology industry. In 2019, Ellen Pao, cofounder and CEO of Project Include, provided guidance to Silicon Valley start-ups and tech companies for setting four diversity and inclusion targets in two years: 10 percent representation for Black employees, 10 percent for Latinx employees, 5 percent for nonbinary employees, and 45 percent for women. They set these targets after reviewing representation gaps across their roster of start-up clients over several years. The aim is to avoid watering down the definition of diversity, which has historically resulted in hiring more white women and maintaining a vastly white workforce. "The most encouraging result we've seen is that hiring teams with gender and race diversity early on creates a flywheel effect that makes attracting, hiring and retaining candidates from all underrepresented backgrounds dramatically easier," reported Pao in a Medium post.

When setting goals, top-down and bottom-up can be equally successful. As an example, the BBC's 50:50 Project, a grassroots effort to reach gender parity in journalism, helped reset the organization through a common goal and voluntary data tracking and sharing. What started as a simple idea introduced in one program in the BBC newsroom unleashed a movement—a revolution! Here's how it started: At the end of each night's prime-time news program, the production team would take two minutes to count and record the gender split of the guests, with reporting taking place monthly. In January 2017, during its first month of counting, the show reached 39 percent women as contributors. Three months later, it hit 51 percent for the first time. Following proof of concept, Ros Atkins, founder of the 50:50 Project, and his team shared instructions, guidelines, measurement templates, and checklists with other programs. In March 2020, two-thirds of teams reached at least 50 percent women in their output, an increase of a third from where they began.

To add this level of impactful strategy to your numbers, consider critical mass theory. While it has been debated in academic circles, I favor Rosabeth Moss Kanter's articulation of it as a threshold to guide organizational transformations. Critical mass is a term borrowed from nuclear physics that refers to the quantity needed to start a chain reaction. In this case, it's the idea that one-third or more representation of minority groups can influence or "tilt" the culture of the overall group. As a guidepost alone it won't solve for unequal treatment, but it can shape your aspirational goals. It is possible to get to critical mass, but it needs to be a widespread, cross-company effort. Otherwise, you end up with a lopsided workplace.

For example, in tech, the BIPOC representation on the marketing, legal, and HR teams is generally higher than in engineering. Those individual groups will boost a company's representational diversity, but you're not going to get rid of biases and barriers across the organization until you've also achieved critical mass in the engineering departments—the core revenue-generating sources of power.

"There is a tipping point in organizations. When between 20 to 33 percent of a company is made up of underrepresented groups, there is the sense of critical mass," says Kapor Klein. "That is transformative, especially when it exists from the top to the bottom in the hierarchy, especially in more prestigious parts of the organizations."

Tackling the Fear of Reverse Discrimination

I am often asked if it's illegal to set a goal tied to representation gaps. Many companies worry about the tension between legitimate efforts to promote representational diversity and reverse discrimination. The aim is not to make hiring decisions based on any single demographic consideration. However, we have long been giving undue recruiting advantages to white men and women in the workplace. That is what we're essentially being asked to rebalance. So, yes, we need to add more demographic diversity to the mix in order to ensure the final selections are representative of the workforce you aspire to build.

Diversifying talent pools is about leveling the playing field so that there is more diversity among those competing for roles. Goals or targets that take into account race, gender, and other protected traits are legal, acceptable tools for combatting underrepresentation. These efforts may be lawful if they (1) are designed to eliminate imbalances in traditionally segregated jobs, (2) do not unduly harm nonminority workers, and (3) serve as a temporary measure to eliminate imbalance and are not intended to maintain a new balance.

That said, this is complicated. I have never met an in-house legal team that didn't fret at the idea of establishing representation goals for placing people in specific jobs. Even if an employer is using an objective hiring assessment, results could be perceived as discriminatory. If you strictly adhere to the results of an assessment, those results could have a discriminatory impact. But if you somehow depart from those practices in the interest of increasing diverse representation in your workforce, it can create a claim of reverse discrimination.

In short, you can ask for BIPOC candidates to apply for roles or be part of the pool you select from, but you cannot tell anyone they have to hire one. There should be an equal pool of candidates to evaluate. You can tweet that your company is seeking to hire diverse talent for an opening: "We're actively seeking diverse candidates for a new account management position," or "We're committed to inclusive hiring practices—apply to be our new creative director." However, diversity cannot be the sole consideration when you are trying to fill a job opening. Under federal employment discrimination laws, a decision not to hire someone because of race, color, sex (including pregnancy, sexual orientation, or gender identity), age, religion, national original, disability, or genetic information (including family medical history) is illegal. Again, you can still approach a friend outside your company and say you'd love some BIPOC candidate recommendations for an opening, and then add them to the mix for consideration based on their qualifications. A good way to avoid discrimination claims is to not discriminate in the first place.

To combat the fear that you're doing something wrong by being specific in your recruiting goals, talk about this with your teams and train them often. Explain the legality of it. Companies like Google and Hewlett Packard Enterprise have long offered diversity recruitment training to ensure all employees are well versed in the dos and don'ts of diversity hiring practices.

Share this talking point: "It's not illegal to focus your talent search when you're trying to correct a diversity gap." There is a difference between committing to hire and promote a certain percentage of individuals on the basis of their race or other factors and committing to interview or consider these individuals for hire or promotion.

What's illegal is making a decision based on a protected class. The challenge is that when you put those practices in place, hiring managers can sometimes game the process by only selecting Black candidates for a specific role, for example. Beyond being illegal, it doesn't set up the candidate for success when they're hired, and this practice can reinforce negative stereotypes. The perception of being the "Black hire" becomes the employee's burden to carry, unfairly. Setting diversity-focused hiring goals is always perceived as tricky legally, but I believe in sharing transparent goals based on representation gaps in distinct areas—say, content creation, senior leadership, and software development—and then applying specific and measurable interventions to address those gaps as we've discussed in this chapter.

When in doubt, always seek the advice of HR or your legal counsel. There's a school of thought that lawyers always stick to the letter of the law, but that's their job. You should aim to build a relationship with your HR and legal partners and work together to create the best workforce. No one wants to get sued, but you also want to make sure you're pushing where you can to address system failures. The irony is that equal opportunity laws were established to create more opportunity for more people, and to protect everybody the same way. It's all in the expectations you set and the operating mechanisms you put in place to reduce harm.

Spelling out a commitment to fair hiring practices, such as your equal employment opportunity statement in job ads, is basic but necessary. Customize this statement and call out that diversity is a priority in all of your language, such as adding, "We encourage people from traditionally underrepresented groups—such as Black, Indigenous, Latinx, Asian, Middle Eastern, and North African talent—to apply." Kapor Capital's job postings are an excellent example. They read: "In keeping with our beliefs and goals, no employee or applicant will face discrimination/harassment based on: race, color, ancestry, national origin, religion, age, gender, marital/domestic partner status, sexual orientation, gender identity, disability status, or veteran status. Above and beyond discrimination/harassment based on 'protected categories,' Kapor Capital also strives to prevent other, subtler forms of inappropriate behavior (e.g., stereotyping) from ever gaining a foothold in our office. Whether blatant or hidden, barriers to success have no place at Kapor Capital."

Incentivize Goal Achievement

Academic researchers Siri Chilazi and Iris Bohnet have shown that behavior change requires transformations along two dimensions: the *will* and the *way*. It's not enough to be motivated to be an inclusive leader or to publicly commit to anti-racism if you do not have the knowledge and the skills to act on that ambition. Goals have the potential to transform behaviors because they provide both the will (motivation) and the way (understanding and skills) to change.

When goal setting, how you incentivize and hold people responsible for achieving the desired outcome can be the difference between success and failure. Accountability is key; there is no other route to success. Goals help motivate behavioral change by promoting accountability and transparency; boosting pride, recognition, and competitiveness; and shifting perceptions of desirable outcomes.

Diversity hiring goals should be a part of every employee's job description and annual performance review and should be factored into compensation and promotion decisions. Meeting the company's diversity hiring goals should be specifically stressed for middle managers and executives whose outsize positions enable them to change company hiring practices.

In five years, Nike has achieved more than 50 percent BIPOC representation through inclusive hiring practices like attaching key metrics to hiring and holding leaders accountable for representational growth in their teams. Now, Nike has its sights set on senior leadership positions and has pledged in the next five years to increase representation of women and BIPOC in those roles, tying executive compensation to the success of hitting those targets.

Linking hiring goals with executive compensation—as Accenture, Johnson & Johnson, Nike, Mercer, and other companies have done—can be equally successful in engaging the whole company. Even if you're unable to influence new hires across departments or you lack the approval for your own hires, you can, as a manager, set your own metrics of success for what you can control. What is the composition of your team and what do you think it should be? When you have an open role on your team, clearly define the opportunity to shift the diversity composition of your business and culture. Be as specific as possible to align your recruitment plans with business needs. Also, think about what other aspects of business you have the ability to "hire" for, whether it's a product vendor, a freelancer or contingent worker, or speakers at a conference.

Next, communicate these targets broadly. Studies have shown that when you share your goals with others, you are twice as likely to achieve them. When you share them publicly, there are millions of people watching and keeping score.

Joe Biden publicly committed to hiring a female vice president (and he did!). Reddit cofounder Alexis Ohanian stepped down from the company's board and, via Twitter, urged his colleagues to fill his seat with a Black candidate. Some parliaments around the world achieve fairer gender representation (at least 50 percent female) through various reforms such as fining parties every year if they don't have gender parity, or by using a "zipper" method, where a seat alternates between male and female leaders.

In 2015, April Reign was watching the Academy Award nominations while getting ready for work. "It struck me that there were no people of color nominated, so I picked up my phone and tweeted '#OscarsSoWhite they asked to touch my hair,'" she told the *New York Times*. It was the tweet that started a movement. In turn, the Academy of Motion Picture Arts and Sciences acknowledged it had work to do to address its membership, which was 94 percent white and 77 percent male. The proof was in the envelope: the 2015 nominations and Best Director snub for Ava Duvernay for *Selma* reflected a supreme lack of diversity in who had voting power.

But a year later, all twenty acting nominations went to white performers again. This is often the case in corporations where hiring initiatives fluctuate given shifting priorities at the leadership level and where there is a lack of focus on retention. At an emergency meeting, the Oscars' board of governors launched A2020, a plan to double the number of women and ethnically underrepresented members in four years. They had to hit these goals; the Twitterverse was watching.

And they did. In 2020, the Academy invited 819 new members: 36 percent were BIPOC and 45 percent were women. To balance the compositional diversity throughout the organization—not just at the bottom—they also added six new governors, three women and one BIPOC.

Besides mandating unconscious bias training for all governors and making a commitment to building an anti-racist and inclusive organization, the most innovative and transformative new measure was a rule set forth for membership: new members will be eligible for a ten-year membership and must remain active in the film industry in some capacity.

This essentially means that aging white men no longer have membership for life, a practice that has for decades reduced opportunities for non-white men and women seeking access to executive and board positions. If we continue to focus our diversity hiring efforts on the entry-level candidates alone, it will be decades before change happens at the senior level. These thoughtfully targeted new measures aimed at tackling bespoke needs of the Academy show that there isn't a one-size-fits-all solution to diversity hiring. Practices have to be tailored to the organization.

According to a McKinsey report on the Black workplace experience in the US private sector, it will take ninety-five years for Black employees to reach talent parity (or 12 percent representation, equal to their current population percentage). You may be asking why companies continue to prioritize investing their capital in semiretired white men instead of hiring racially and ethnically diverse emerging talent. Well, one step is to acknowledge the biases and systems that keep institutions such as the Academy overwhelmingly old, white, and male and create a new system, such as term limits. The Oscars also released new inclusion standards for its Best Picture nominees, whereby a lead actor, subject matter, or percentage of the cast must highlight an underrepresented group. While these standards fall short at transforming an industry whose entire ecosystem is based on sustaining white male power, it's a start to thread diversity into all layers of business. We can all learn lessons from these tailor-made goals to reach critical mass for all aspects of your work life.

Your Road Map to Revolution

People wrongly assume that increasing workforce diversity means sacrificing principles of fairness and merit, because it requires giving "special" accommodations to BIPOC candidates rather than treating everyone the same. I argue that a racially sensitive management team recognizes that fairness requires treating people equitably, which may entail treating people differently, but in a way that reduces systemic disparities. To recruit a more diverse workforce, everyone involved in the hiring process needs to understand the hiring goals, recognize why they matter, and be held accountable for hiring with diversity, equity, and inclusion in mind. Every recruiter knows how painful it is when someone in the chain—the hiring manager, the interviewers, or the leadership—breaks the systems of accountability. The following practices should be the starting point for you and your organization.

- **Gain clarity on your hiring mission**. Explain why building a diverse workforce is an organizational priority. This mission should be bold and specific. Discuss and share it with your team to ensure everyone is on board.

- **Identify how bias and privilege appear in the hiring process**. Despite years of diversity recruitment programs, bias based on hidden assumptions and stereotypes heavily influences who gets access to job opportunities, relationships, and stretch assignments. Measure the percentage of underrepresented talent at every stage of the hiring funnel—sourcing, screening, interviewing, and selecting—to determine what works and what needs adjusting.

- **Design ambitious hiring goals**. To do so, take a look at your current workforce and look for representation gaps. Create bold targets (at least 50 percent growth) based on minimizing those gaps plus your capability for adding head count. Discuss critical mass theory to help your team understand the importance of setting such goals.

- **Discuss the legal dos and don'ts of the hiring process**. How can you be an equal opportunity employer while aiming to correct representation gaps? Offer training for all employees to better understand how to do this.

- **Hold people accountable to your goals**. Tie them to compensation and rewards or other metrics of success. Share them publicly to keep yourself in check.

3

OVERHAUL YOUR RECRUITMENT

S OON AFTER I left Google in 2017, engineer James Damore posted a fiery, ten-page memo to an internal message board that argued women aren't a "personality fit" to be engineers and that the company was not inclusive, especially when it came to the ideas of conservative white men. Threatened by diversity initiatives, this white man was arguing that white men were experiencing reverse discrimination. The full memo was posted to tech blogs and amplified by mainstream media.

This was not the first time the tech giant had been charged with the incongruities of its diversity approach (though perhaps it was the first time from a conservative white male point of view). But this time Google was forced to confront its own inability to effectively address biases and barriers for underrepresented talent while facing internal and external turmoil. If you can organize the world's information, how can you not better reflect it in your workforce? I and others had raised the issues of an ongoing culture of racism and sexism with Google leaders, and now they were very publicly being confronted with their years of inaction.

There's nothing like a PR crisis to put a fire under a CEO and senior leadership team. In February 2020, over three years after that contentious meeting where I presented our diversity hiring strategy, I was happy to see that one of my team's biggest asks came to fruition. Sundar Pichai, the CEO of Google, announced a $10 billion investment in the expansion of data centers across the United States to cities like Atlanta and in southern states like Alabama, South Carolina, Tennessee, Texas, and Virginia to create access and opportunities for a talent pool that has been there all along. In the tech industry, there is a persistent assumption that failures in diversity hiring efforts are a result of limited Black talent. I'm hopeful, in light of the trend toward a more remote and geographically dispersed workforce due to COVID-19, that more companies can follow suit and remove similar barriers to entry for hiring, and that Black professionals looking to break into these fields may no longer have to move to inhospitable tech hubs like San Francisco, which is known for its lack of diversity and unaffordable housing market.

Google took its time to get this right, but the time is now. We all want hiring to be fair and unbiased. But job candidates with less privilege face barriers and biases that make it harder for them to get noticed. Even when they do land an interview, they may not be evaluated fairly. They're often held to higher double standards. This is our opportunity to be anti-racist (thank you, Ibram X. Kendi) in our hiring processes and enact real and sustainable change.

It's time to let go of recruitment processes that yield the same results year after year. Creating a new hiring process from beginning to end, including updating your applicant-tracking systems, is hard work. Don't be afraid to abolish what doesn't work and add what does. In their application flow, the recruitment team at Policygenius, an online insurance company, asks candidates to check off their preferred pronouns and record the pronunciation of their name. That small feature immediately conveys the sense of a welcoming, respectful culture.

Be willing to remove bias from your hiring and recruitment model and refine your process to fit the needs of different groups and individuals. Otherwise, you risk remaining in the status quo instead of sparking a revolution for good.

Building better teams is everyone's responsibility. Pay attention to what matters. We have historically focused on hiring pipelines but not on the deeper issues with workplace cultures, power asymmetries, harassment, exclusionary hiring practices, unfair compensation, and tokenization that are causing people to leave or avoid working in certain industries. No matter your role and level, consider these barriers for underrepresented groups as you take a closer look at your recruiting processes.

Avoid Using Résumés as Gatekeepers

Ah, the résumé, that one-page summary of your greatness. It's also one of the largest contributors to implicit bias in the hiring process. Rampant résumé bias at the screening stage—where recruiters and applicant-tracking systems weed through résumés to find candidates that best meet the hiring manager's job criteria—leads to a wealth of talent slipping through the cracks.

For starters, let's take name bias, the highly documented practice of skipping over candidates who have ethnic-sounding names that don't fit into the traditional white standard of professionalism. A Tamika may get passed over for a Tanya; a Sayed may get passed over for a Sam. Economists Marianne Bertrand and Sendhil Mullainathan found that white-sounding names like Emily Walsh or Greg Baker received, on average, 50 percent more callbacks for interviews than African American sounding names, such as Lakisha Washington or Jamal Jones. Or, as another study has found, Jamal needed eight more years of experience than Greg to be considered equally qualified. That's why African American and Asian job applicants who mask their race on résumés have better success getting job interviews, according to research by Katherine DeCelles and her colleagues. This stereotype-based bias means that from the very first possible consideration, the recruiter or hiring manager already sees someone who—whether they want to admit it or not—they feel is less competent or likely to fit in with the company culture, to meet their "hiring bar." These biased standards for professionalism are based on white norms: white European standards of what work is, what it should look like, and who belongs within those spaces. So a candidate has to spend more energy trying to sound and look like the candidate the company wants, rather than just being the talented individual they are.

I have managed several recruitment teams, so I understand that you can receive hundreds of résumés for every open position, and that in order to get through growing piles of résumés, you need some sort of gut check to make sure that applicants meet key qualifications. On average, recruiters take 7.4 seconds to scan a résumé, according to career website Ladders' 2018 eye-tracking study. In less than ten seconds, the recruiter determines if an applicant is a suitable match based on first-impression information like current job title, company names, universities attended, and potential internships. This gut check, this gray area, is where bias rears its ugly head.

Think about the last time you looked at a résumé. What details caught your eye and helped you decide if this was a candidate worth talking to? Did you fall into the Ivy League, top-tier-university, instant-credibility trap? Many managers do and still believe that hiring Ivy League alums means hiring the best, which in their minds will translate to stellar performance. But, of course, most of the country does not have an Ivy League degree. It's a poor determinant of performance, yet it is perhaps the most consistent exclusionary recruitment practice in both the screening and selection process. When Google increased the number of universities from which they recruited for internships to include non–Ivy League schools in 2014, they significantly increased the pool of talent from historically underrepresented backgrounds, and, no surprise, the group of interns that summer was far more diverse.

Some companies leverage technology to enact fairness at scale. At least 98 percent of *Fortune* 500 companies use applicant-tracking systems to collect and sort thousands of résumés and redact key information or use artificial intelligence (AI) technology so that résumés are scanned for skills, eliminating potential bias. But the process by which résumés can earn bonus points for matching words in the job description or other preselected terms—which eliminates "unqualified" candidates and filters the "best" résumés to the top—is equally problematic.

Wharton assistant professor of business economics and policy Corinne Low, who conducted a résumé audit study, cautions against the reliance on machine scanning: "Firms need to remember that if you have some of these biases, they're going to get hard-wired into the algorithm. You have to think very carefully about how to strip that out."

Here's what will make a difference: stop putting so much weight on résumés. They're not a good indicator of success, as proven by researchers from Florida State University, who found that previous work experience is a poor predictor of future job success and that there is zero correlation between experience and how a candidate would perform on the job and whether they would stay with their future employer. Résumés don't reveal soft skills either, which are a valuable asset in leadership. So why do we continue to use résumés as an evaluation tool? Because it's how we've always done it, and because they provide easy shortcuts for assessment.

In fact, some smaller tech companies—like Compose, a cloud storage firm, and the Better Software Company—have stopped the practice entirely. Similarly, many colleges and universities have stopped requiring ACT or SAT scores because they recognize that performing well on these tests may be more indicative of one's privilege rather than intellect. Instead, these institutions are upping the stakes for interviews. I understand that companies have limited resources and are unable to interview every single applicant, so they try to make it easier to filter people out using résumés. Here's what to do instead.

1. **Put emphasis on the cover letter or a creative pitch**. Cover letters have lost their favor in many industries or are seen as a perfunctory step in the process, but they are the real sales pitch, not a collection of facts about where you were lucky enough to go to college. At Vice Media Group, when we launched the 2030 Project—a fellowship seeking curious and passionate individuals whose career plans had been impacted by COVID-19—one of the most creative pitches was a TikTok video that intrigued everyone about the applicant's potential. Ask candidates to tell you who they are and why they want this job. What will they bring to the table? What's not being said on their LinkedIn profile? What's their real story? *That* is a better indicator of someone's readiness and eagerness for the job than any list of accomplishments.

2. **Use a Q&A platform as part of your application process**. Whether via video or writing, ask a standard set of screening questions. What are the top three questions you would ask in an interview? Use these as a first-round review. Wepow, for example, is a video interviewing platform company that allows you to meet more candidates without having to read mountains of résumés. Candidates can record responses to interview questions in their own time, which eliminates the need to schedule interviews with recruiters. We used it at Viacom for sourcing entry-level candidates and found it to be an effective screening tool to evaluate soft skills, the ability to problem-solve, work style, and more.

3. **Try a skills test or neuroscience-based brain games**.
   Tech companies are infamous for their cognitive interview
   practices, but many others—like Tesla, Accenture, and
   LinkedIn—have worked with a company called Pymet-
   rics, which created a thirty-minute game-playing scenario
   to evaluate a person's cognitive and emotional capabilities.
   Candidates take on puzzles and quizzes that measure a
   person's problem-solving skills, fairness, generosity, and
   other key capabilities customized by the hiring manager.
   It's a relatively painless experience for candidates that
   helps companies select talent based on specific traits required for the job. To detect bias in its questions, Pymet-
   rics continually analyzes answers to ensure that certain
   demographic groups aren't all missing the same answer.

   Another option is to give a work sample test. Assignments
   that highlight the type of work the person will be tasked
   with can offer key insight into their potential performance.
   In journalism, there's a practice of giving candidates an
   edit test, where they are asked to complete a variety of
   tasks, from copyediting a paragraph to brainstorming ideas
   for a new section. Some of these tests are laborious, and
   there are stories of companies using the ideas in future
   projects without crediting the original thinker. But the essence of the assignment—to see the kind of work a candidate can produce, whether it's a creative brief or a market
   analysis—is a useful screening tool. It can also weed out
   candidates who aren't serious about the position.

Stop the Friends and Family Program

Representational diversity hasn't shifted because, in practice,
personal recommendations often outweigh a recruiter's sound
hiring plan. Hiring managers turn to their friends or family for

referrals (per some studies, 70 to 90 percent of positions are filled this way). When that circle looks way too white (75 percent of white people have zero friends of color), you can draw a direct line to who is benefiting from word-of-mouth hires. This is called shortcut bias.

"It is well known that nondiverse, particularly white, employees are far more likely to refer other white employees to their companies," says Cid Wilson, president of the Hispanic Association on Corporate Responsibility (HACR) and former Wall Street executive. "Companies give greater weight to these employee referrals than external applicants because it's the feeling that the employee is a stakeholder of that company and is not going to recommend an employee that won't succeed."

Success in this case is code for "fit," which is an overused, bias-inducing term in the interview process. We refer who we know. We refer who we're comfortable with—that is, people who look, think, and act like us. So ask yourself, what does achieving fit really mean to you and your teams? How many times have you inadvertently made decisions that were comfortable for you but not in the best interest of the team or business? What are the reasons you have told yourself to support your decisions, and are they true?

"Your recruiters just can't compete with that unless there is systemic change that internal recommendations must emphasize diversity-focused employer referrals," says Wilson. "Every employee can join in and help drive this change, but unfortunately very few companies are telling all of their employees to send diverse candidates as part of your referrals," or even requiring it as part of formal referral programs.

One company that does is Pinterest. In 2015, Pinterest publicly announced that they wanted to expand the number of engineering roles to hit 25 percent women and 8 percent from underrepresented ethnic groups, and non-tech roles to reach 12 percent from underrepresented groups. To hold themselves accountable, Pinterest partnered with Paradigm, a diversity and inclusion consulting firm, which implemented strategies like unconscious bias training and diverse interview panels. Paradigm also enrolled current employees in their mission to hit these goals by asking them to be cognizant of who they were recommending for new hires. Were they recommending diverse candidates? Could they start doing that and expand the Pinterest network?

Pinterest employees welcomed the challenge, and in just six weeks referrals from underrepresented communities increased 55 percent. Three years later, in 2018, Pinterest had hit nearly all their goals (they reached 7 percent of engineering hires from underrepresented ethnic backgrounds instead of their goal of 8 percent but succeeded on their female engineering and ethnic background nonengineering goals). Yes, Pinterest had the budget to hire an outside (read: expensive) partner to help them get there, and the takeaways from the training were not groundbreaking, but challenging the employees who call Pinterest home moved the needle.

Another strategy to reduce unconscious bias in the system of employee referrals is to push back on the volume of internship referrals. When I worked at the Disney ABC Television Group, ABC News internship recruiters took great pride in building a robust and diverse pool of top college-level talent. It didn't matter. The intern program manager was handcuffed from selecting the candidates we received from diversity-focused internship partners because the spots were quickly filled internally with "must hires"—that is, those who came as a favor to a sales client or an executive. After an analysis of past practices, these must-hire candidates were revealed to be the majority of historic intern classes. While the active partnership with underrepresented intern groups was there, we were often unable to open the door widely and place these candidates in the internships that would open doors for them.

To fix this, we enabled managers to hire more diverse interns by capping what I called "the Friends and Family Program" at 10 percent of the total number of intern hires. I let policy be the buffer. When we established and shared these new norms, we more than doubled the representation of diverse talent from the prior year. Reducing the interns-as-a-favor protocol was a real, concrete step the company took to improve hiring outcomes. This is an action every manager can implement now.

One other way to immediately create more equity in your intern class: pay them a minimum wage or small stipend. College credit doesn't do the trick. Offering paid internships will allow you to attract more candidates, especially those who cannot afford to work for free. The US Labor Department has passed laws to protect interns (and others) from unpaid roles, specifically stating that the employer cannot derive immediate advantage from the activities of the intern. Pay up. It's the right thing to do.

Attract Diverse Talent Like You Mean It

In 2019, the PGA partnered with Jopwell, a career-advancement platform for Black, Latinx, and Native American students and professionals, to collect feedback on perceptions of the golf industry and career access and opportunities. Jopwell discovered that there wasn't a lack of interest in golf from these groups. Rather, two-thirds of respondents shared the perception that golf isn't an inclusive or diverse industry. That, coupled with a lack of awareness of open roles (27 percent of respondents) and access to contacts in the industry (26 percent), created a major barrier to entry. However, once respondents were told explicitly that the PGA of America wanted to create a more diverse workforce and broaden its hiring reach, the likelihood of applying went up from 46 percent to 64 percent, according to Jopwell and the PGA.

To break down these barriers, the PGA launched a job awareness initiative. They actively promoted the PGA WORKS program, a fellowship for people from diverse backgrounds, on social media. They increased the visual representation of BIPOC golfers and talent on their website. And they launched strategic partnerships with media companies like *Black Enterprise* to attract new audiences. The result? The PGA saw a direct increase in applications from under-represented communities and continues to partner with Jopwell as they work to diversify the golf industry, says Jopwell CEO Porter Braswell. Additionally, PGA and Jopwell partnered to create a joint photo collection to increase the visual representations of BIPOC in golf. That collection has been viewed over one hundred million times, and the photos are reused throughout the PGA's website. As my former Google colleague Suezette Robotham used to say, "We need to help people see themselves here."

The pre-applicant stage of the talent-acquisition process is perhaps one of the most important. If you want to attract more diverse candidates, you must build a robust and transparent talent-focused marketing strategy that enables candidates to see themselves in your roles, hallways, and meetings.

Look at your careers page: What are you saying? Can prospective candidates see themselves in your organization? If they can't right now, don't lie to them about it. When I was global head of diversity staffing at Google, I was asked to consult on a career website redesign, specifically to ensure our recruiting language and approach would land well with diverse talent communities. I'll never forget a particular planning meeting where we were asked to consider the Facebook career page for competitive intelligence. The site boasted a rainbow of employee photos. I had to scroll to the bottom to see one white guy, Mark Zuckerberg. Now, I know the stats on Facebook. I appreciated the intent to promote inclusivity, but you must tell candidates the truth. Yes, it can be through an aspirational lens, but it also has to reflect reality—false advertising simply won't work. Candidates are savvy. They will dissect what you're showing them and question your language and stories, what's included and what's omitted. So be bold, be inclusive, and be honest.

This goes for universities as well. I remember being asked to pose for marketing photos when I was a student at Bucknell University in the nineties. Here we were, a group of friends who were Black, South Asian, and Asian, and they added a white guy, also a friend, for good measure. We were tickled pink when we saw the shiny brochures prominently featuring us. But we also thought, "Oh boy, we're not fooling anyone. Once they are on campus they'll know just how white everything is."

So before you diversity-wash your website, ask yourself: Why should someone want to work for you? Your employee value proposition (EVP) is a succinct crystallization of what makes your organization a desirable place to work. Relevance, distinctiveness, credibility, and authenticity are the key qualities of a strong EVP. Bonus: these qualities generate better candidates. Make sure you are promoting your company's most desirable EVP qualities honestly. "We provide safe working environments for all employees" sounds like a minimum; it does not captivate. "Increasing diversity, equity, and inclusion in hiring, compensation, promotion, and workplace culture is our top priority." Now that's how you attract the best and brightest.

If you aren't the kind of place where underrepresented talent wants to work, no amount of outreach will help. You have to start at the top. Are your company's diversity, equity, and inclusion objectives and values publicly available? Does the employment brand reflect the lived experience of employees and the communities they work in? Does it signal to diverse communities that they would be welcomed and valued in your organization? Do current staff of color feel valued and groomed for success to the point where they feel confident recruiting more BIPOC staff into a racially welcoming environment? Are you building genuine partnerships and relationships with the groups and communities where diverse talent thrives? And how clearly can any of your peers and colleagues articulate to a candidate their career path once they join the organization? If you can't answer these questions—or feel that your organization is lacking here—before going out to look for talent, think again, regroup, share your thoughts with HR, and then get out there.

If you want to understand the perception of your company but don't have the budget for a consultant or staff for a task force, try data-driven survey tools, like the Muse's BrandBuilder, that can uncover your EVP by asking for your employees' stories about working with your company. Another idea: survey current and prior BIPOC applicants. What do they think the company stands for? What influenced their decision to apply? What do they think would be the biggest opportunities and, conversely, barriers for success? We can't build a better recruitment model until we start asking better questions.

Four Recruiting Don'ts

1. **Don't use the phrase "diversity hire."** It's racist. Also, try to avoid saying you want to hire "more diverse talent," and instead be specific about your representational gaps and the strategies to close them. Don't say, "We need to hire more BIPOC employees." Instead, say, "We have hired too many white people in x department or function and need to address that imbalance by hiring y number of Black or Latinx or Asian or LGBTQ (insert the demographic background that addresses your gaps)." This will help paint a clearer value proposition and acknowledge the elephant in the room—the lack of diverse representation in your organization—that pops up when you say "diversity."

2. **Don't reference inequitable data, and don't blame the pipeline of qualified applicants**. That ignores the historical inequality and institutional roadblocks that have left BIPOC out of elite colleges and elite companies to begin with. Instead, set benchmarks that reflect where you should be and where the country and your industry are headed. By 2040, according to the US Bureau of Labor Statistics, the majority of the US workforce will be ethnically diverse, with women of color accounting for a significant share of that growth. The post-millennial generation (Gen Z) is on track to be the most diverse and best educated yet.

3. **Don't fail to look internally**. Is anyone ready for a promotion or expanded responsibilities? Can you use an open role

---

71

as an opportunity to provide a growth experience for someone whose strong performance or potential has gone unnoticed?

4. **Don't take a check-the-box approach**. That is, if you fail to contextualize and acknowledge the interconnected barriers to this work and simply go after surface-level changes, you will be at this again and again.

Change the Spec

Racial bias in hiring starts with the job description. Hiring managers often complain that their recruiters are not bringing them enough qualified diverse candidates. This is the point when I will likely ask a clarifying question: What does "qualified" mean to you? The answers I often receive are muddled, defensive, and rarely consistent with what the job description laid out. We must redefine "qualified" or even eliminate it from our vernacular. Qualified is subjective when there are no checks and balances on bias. Qualified puts an emphasis on past accomplishments instead of potential for future success. Qualified is a lazy and unclear statement used to defend decisions without sound logic and reflection.

One way to welcome traditionally underrepresented applicants is to paint the big picture of a role rather than relying on a checklist of specialized skills, degrees, or years of experience. Focus on what the candidate can expect to do day-to-day, essential components of a role, and what their impact will be. I've seen recruiters and managers screen for qualifications that are proxies for must-have qualities, when they're really nice-to-haves (for example, asking for ten-plus years of experience). Some examples of core requirements:

- **Masterful project manager**: has the ability to manage multiple projects at once and communicate across a wide variety of stakeholders with often uncoordinated expectations

- **Analytical and data driven**: strategic thinker who uses data to tell a story and provide clearly articulated insights

Recruit for *those* key capabilities. Write your job descriptions with *that* language. And screen consistently for those qualifications.

The more you rely on "this is how we've always done it" approaches as a shortcut, the more you compromise on the diversity of experiences, perspectives, and approaches on your team. There's nothing wrong with preferences or conventional approaches, except when they become embedded expectations that only you are aware of and that you can change at your whim. Candidates who are more like you or who are from similar networks are more likely to pick up on those cues. Conversely, candidates who are less like you are less likely to read the playbook in your head.

First impressions matter. Your job descriptions must feel compelling and, most important, accessible. It's all meaningless if underrepresented candidates aren't applying to open jobs in the first place. At Vice Media Group, we put a lot of energy into redesigning our recruiting process, and that included updating our external branding and ensuring our job descriptions more accurately described what success looks like in each role, regardless of gender identity, race/ethnicity, or any other identity. We don't always get it right, but we apply discipline to this process by regularly auditing our job descriptions, process, and hiring outcomes.

A big part of this is just being more thoughtful about the word choices you make. Avoid buzzwords and clichés like the plague! Words like "rock star" and "ninja" have been proven to signal a male-dominated culture and be racially insulting. Likewise, using highly corporate language is often a signal to members of underrepresented communities that they won't thrive, because that language has gone largely unquestioned in predominantly white, male workplaces. You must be mindful of the effects of incredibly subtle language differences in how you position your role descriptions. For example, when you describe a position as *managing* a team, research shows that you increase the likelihood of a larger number of male applicants. For *developing* a team, there's a strong likelihood of increasing the number of female applicants. But *leading* a team is more gender neutral, helping you get the largest, most balanced, and most qualified set of applicants for your open role. In science, technology, engineering, and mathematics (STEM), language around "genius" is terribly gendered; math skills are learned, not something men are uniquely born into. To attract more women to STEM fields, Harvey Mudd College launched a marketing campaign that focused on applicants' potential for growth rather than expectations on ability. The fact is that if someone doesn't have inborn skills, they can learn them. Of course both are important, but how you message it changes the outcomes. Do your homework and improve on this important practice.

Amazon engineers have built an internal wiki page with alternative phrases to help remove unconscious bias from the workplace. "Brown bags" should be replaced by "learning session" or "lunch and learn." Other terms like "blacklist/whitelist" and "grandfathered in" are also considered to be racially biased and should be replaced with more acceptable phrases like "blocklist" and "exempt from regulations." Similarly, Twitter engineers have shared a list of coding terms they'll swap out to be more inclusive, many of which are used in database-related job ads. For example: "whitelist" changes to "allowlist," "blacklist" changes to "denylist," and "master/slave" changes to "leaders/follower, primary/replica, primary/standby."

Another tip: use a job description text analyzer that has a proprietary list of racially biased words and flags them in your job description for easy replacement, including with recommended bias-free language. Textio is an augmented writing platform that gives real-time feedback about both the gender balance and the overall impact of job ads. The tool's data shows that job listings with strong equal-opportunity language fill 10 percent faster on average across all demographic groups. In an increasingly competitive and distributed talent market, every bit of edge helps.

When done right, in just a short amount of words, job descriptions have the power to attract a more diverse pool of candidates. This is where you can tell the story of the job, make your company feel like an exciting place to work, and use language that feels accessible to all. Organizations have gotten so much better at writing exciting job descriptions. When I first joined Viacom, some of our job descriptions were so bland and standard that I often thought, "Who would want to work here?" So we partnered with our communications team to teach us how to apply the same level of energy and enthusiasm they applied to our brand and business narrative. This small change helps people see themselves in an environment consistent with the company brand and is far more helpful at attracting a rich candidate pool that is excited about joining you for what you have to offer.

Write job descriptions with that type of openness and eliminate any descriptions that mandate a certain number of years in a specific industry. For example, instead of saying *x* years working at an ad agency, write *x* years of experience building creative campaigns with clients. Avoid limiting language like only accepting those with college degrees, those with *x* years of experience, or those whose work experiences are all within your exact industry.

Broaden your reach, and you'll broaden your talent pipeline.

Go Where the Talent Is!

In 2020, Wells Fargo CEO Charlie Scharf announced the company's goals to double Black leadership and align compensation with diversity, equity, and inclusion efforts. Cue the applause. But then, during a call with employees, he reportedly said that he understood there is "a limited pool of Black talent to recruit from." And there it is: that ubiquitous and offensive statement from the top that excuses leaders from hitting their diversity, equity, and inclusion goals and doing the work necessary to source and evaluate candidates fairly. Institutionalized racism puts white people in self-segregated social, educational, housing, and employment circles to the point where they don't notice that they are constantly moving through all-white spaces.

There's not a lack of talent; there's a lack of effort. When I hear, "We can't find any Black engineers," "There are simply no Latinx coders," or "The other [read: non-white] candidates were stronger," I see excuses for lazy sourcing. What if you were in sales and you told your boss, "I can't find a company that is willing to advertise with us." Would your boss just shrug and say OK? No, they would question your methods, ask you to analyze your results, find out why companies don't want to work with you, and then encourage you to adjust your pitch and approach. You must do the same for recruiting diverse talent.

Seeking out racially diverse candidates by securing referrals from diversity-focused organizations is a good step for diversifying the candidate pool. You can find historically underrepresented people with the right competencies and skills for the job. I've hired BIPOC executives for nearly every role imaginable. Sometimes I lean on my network, sometimes on the network of others, but I have never been unable to find an extremely talented and qualified candidate from an underrepresented background. We are everywhere, really.

Talent is equally distributed; opportunity is not. Companies can and should dedicate resources for diversity hiring. Many have and continue to do so, but the programs that have been most successful don't silo the effort. At Google, for example, we had a team of sixty recruiters dedicated to sourcing predominantly Black and Hispanic software engineering candidates. That number might seem large, but it simply wasn't enough, especially when considering that the entire sourcing organization consisted of more than three hundred people tasked with building a global talent pipeline across all of Google. There was no way my relatively small team could deliver that scale by being solely responsible for finding Black and Hispanic software engineers.

We would often come into conflict with other teams when it came to who could claim "credit" for finding the candidate first (oh, the gaming risks of key performance indicators), because sometimes the non-diversity-recruitment-focused sourcing team would want to claim credit for helping to close the Black or Latinx candidates. Of course they should! Everyone should share in the win. But is it really a shared win when only one team is dedicated to that outcome? I made the decision to decentralize my diversity sourcing team, placing those recruiters with subject matter expertise on hiring Black and Latinx talent inside each hiring group to build up everyone's skills and ensure everyone would have skin in the game to diversify candidate pools. I fundamentally believe that everyone needs to be able to recruit with an inclusive mindset and skill set and be held accountable for process and results.

The Ford Foundation has been committed to social justice since its inception, and that culture has led to diverse representation across every level of the organization. "One of things I admired most was the HR department," says Bird Runningwater, a former program associate at the foundation who is now a senior director at Sundance Institute. "Even back in the nineties when they were hiring for positions, diversity was the first and foremost goal. They used headhunters, they sought out people, they sifted through applications, they interviewed people, and if they didn't find a diverse candidate to fill the position, they started over." They didn't throw in the towel because it was hard.

This is time-consuming work, I get that. Especially when you work at a small nonprofit or are a recruiter in a start-up where hiring needs and recruitment tactics rapidly change before, during, and after a round of funding. When you don't have the capacity and support to be proactive in your search, that's when you must tap your network to do some of the work for you.

But what does your network look like? When you share a job posting on your LinkedIn page, who is seeing it? Hiring managers should not just audit their networks. They have to actively research, share, and recruit from racially diverse communities and organizations. Similar to eradicating the Friends and Family Program, you need to broaden your networks and organizational affiliations and question your assumptions about go-to job sites and platforms. Otherwise, you will always reach the same people. I've had recruiters beg me to ask managers to stop hiring from their alma maters. I once told a head of sales, "I know you had a good experience at Brown, but about 80 percent of your staff are Brown alumni. You can't complain to me about not having diversity on your staff when you're forcing my team to hire from an almost all-white pool." At first, he resisted. He had an emotional connection to Brown that biased him positively toward their graduates. But when we stopped sourcing from Brown and other similar schools, we found equally talented, if not more talented, racially diverse candidates. Sure, they were not versed in Brown shorthand, but that was not a requirement for the role, and certainly not for engaging with the many non-Brown-graduate clients they were trying to land.

Look harder and consider who you're asking for help. Start within your company, inclusive of employee resource groups and partner organizations and influencers. Then look outward. Get creative (and don't be afraid of some gentle stalking) when looking for diverse communities who may not currently consider your company or industry as a potential employer. If your industry is vastly white, you can look to related industries for BIPOC talent. For example, book publishing should be attracting candidates from journalism, magazines, online media, book awards, bookstore staff, advertising, literary agencies, literary scouts, TV, film, and more. I've followed hashtags on LinkedIn and Twitter that are associated with communities of interest and have encouraged my teams to post job announcements targeted at those participating in them. If you're recruiting for an engineering role, research or ask BIPOC engineers which job sites, organizations, and clubs they follow and make sure you're building pipelines from those networks.

When Trevor Noah was hiring for *The Daily Show*, the vast majority of agents sent only white clients. At first he worried that Black writers didn't want to work with him, but then he met with some of his Black comedian friends who revealed that they never heard about the opening because they didn't have agents. They didn't even know the opportunity existed! Talent agencies are notoriously white, and they have operated as the primary gatekeepers across Hollywood for far too long. So Noah had to actively ask everyone who he thought might know a Black comic to refer people his way. It's easy to assume that every comedian has an agent, but it's simply not true.

Similarly, when Issa Rae asked executives why there were no BIPOC available to work on her show, she was told, "We can't find Black makeup artists." "That is just the most ridiculous statement ever," says Lucinda Martínez, who led HBO's brand marketing and HBO Max. Martínez told me that once HBO gave Rae the job of showrunner, she did what they couldn't. "People of color have no problem finding people of color," she says. "She hired Black makeup artists, creative services, you name it. When you hire more people of color, they open the door for others." And the product is better. Projects like Ava Duvernay's *Queen Sugar*, the Oscar-winning *Moonlight*, and Rae's comedy *Insecure* are revered for the ways they've revolutionized how people of color are shown on screen. Queer cinematographer Ava Berkofsky is credited for using lighting practices on *Insecure* that embrace color within all skin tones, no longer using standard models defined by white skin. Berkofsky was brought in after previous cinematographers' dated tactics just blasted light on Black talent. The result of her work shows Black faces that are not only legible, but strikingly illuminated.

You have to welcome diverse candidates through the door. The hiring process suffers from lack of creativity and default bias statements. It makes my skin crawl when people say, "I want to hire more diverse talent, but I don't want to lower the hiring bar." That's biased and, frankly, insulting. That comment indicates that you are assuming that racially diverse talent lacks the same intellectual capacity or even work ethic as you. That comment also fails to consider that we have been reducing the standard of talent for years to hire well-connected yet mediocre white men, and no one is calling that "lowering the bar."

It's offensive when leaders like Michael Moritz of Sequoia Capital talk about "not lowering their standards" when trying to hire more women. Improving diversity is not about lowering any bar. I'm asking you to raise the bar for fairness in access and opportunity.

Your Road Map to Revolution

Recruiting is all about finding the best talent, and there are many ways to open the door to a richly diverse applicant pool. First, confront your bias, which shuts that door often before you even realize it. Second, expand your talent pool. Stop relying on the same employee referrals from the same Ivy League schools or companies. And finally, launch an authentic marketing campaign for your jobs and company to encourage more people to take a chance on you.

- **Reduce bias when recruiting**. Question your first impressions when reading a résumé or meeting someone who doesn't look like you. Name bias exists. Shut down your own sneaky inner voice.

- **Stop relying on résumés as gatekeepers**. Instead, look to other, less biased ways to assess talent, like standardized interview questions, cover letters, work sample tests, and more.

- **Stop the Friends and Family Program**. This will limit recruiting from the same talent pools and same referral sources and create more opportunities for more people. For accountability, set goals around employee referrals that help meet representational diversity goals. On the flip side, set limits to the number of "must hires" allowed, particularly when hiring for interns.

- **Revamp your company website and marketing language to attract more candidates**. Show what diversity, equity, and inclusion means to you and what it looks like in your organization in everything from your job specs and career sites to your social media. Job seekers want to see themselves represented in the organization they wish to join.

- **Rewrite your job descriptions**. Beware of the "this is how we've always written it" organizational trap. Biased wording sends a subtle message and can influence some not to apply. We all have a tendency to conflate requirements and outcomes with our preferences and conventional approaches. Gain clarity on the must-have requirements for the role and what you're willing to be flexible on, and reword your job description inclusively. There's a reason why some job ads distinguish between must-haves and nice-to-haves. Be consistent.

- **Expand your talent pool**. Go where the talent is and engage in targeted networking and pipeline building. Seek out diversity-focused organizations for referrals. If your industry is mostly white, start to widen the pool by recruiting and hiring from adjacent industries. Focus on transferable skills rather than experience within your specific and homogenous industry.

4

MAKE BETTER HIRING DECISIONS

AS IF RESPONDING to a traumatic event, hiring managers are often inclined to fill open positions immediately. Who could possibly make a good decision under those circumstances? You rationalize yourself into shortcut decisions meant to lessen the burden on you and your teams. You recycle the old job description and follow the same patterns of recruitment that led you to your last hire. But here's the major flaw: you did not unpack how your recruitment practices produced racial inequalities with that hire, and you haven't yet with this one. Instead, pause and reflect on what core values and skills are needed or lacking on your team, what this new hire can contribute to your team's strategic growth or cultural transformation, and how much wider a net you need to cast to ensure you have a diverse selection of talent to choose from. Consider all the possibilities.

If I had a magic wand, I would slow down the hiring process. Rushing leads to "stick with what you know" candidates and bad hires. When I've pushed back on hiring the same type of employee over and over again, sometimes a hiring manager will plead, "Just this once. I don't have time to interview more diverse talent." Or they may say, "Let's just fast-forward this candidate. I know him and he's a good fit." Cue the eye roll.

Making a bad hire is both expensive and dangerous. It will cost you culturally and economically. Sixty-nine percent of employers said their companies were adversely affected by a bad hire last year, according to a recent study by CareerBuilder. Forty-one percent of those businesses estimated the cost of a bad hire was over $25,000; 24 percent said it cost them more than $50,000. Bad hires can also lower morale and cause other people to leave.

Honestly, I've made my share of bad hiring decisions that, in hindsight, have caused heavier workloads and emotional distress. When I've reviewed my decision-making process, I've found the reasons inextricably tied to timing pressures, power differentials, uncertainty, and unwillingness to acknowledge my own biases. There were times when I let senior leaders' biased opinions sway hiring decisions despite my reservations. There were times when I erred on the side of potential and not the experience necessary for success in the role. And there was a time when I hired someone without fully vetting feedback I had received from informal references. This feedback referred to immature patterns of behavior and decision-making that came to light in the hire's performance almost immediately. We handled it initially through coaching and eventually through a mutually agreed resignation but not without losing significant time, resources, and emotional energy.

We don't spend enough time thinking critically about the micro hiring decisions we make every day (like where we post roles and who we ask for referrals), the patterns of bias in decision-making, and the inefficiencies of our hiring processes. We tend to focus on the end result—who was hired—and not the millions of choices that were made along the way. We take for granted that hiring decisions continue to be controlled by predominantly white men in power. We operate under the misguided notion that inserting a series of steps in the recruiting process will instantly yield fairness. When it comes to executive hiring—the roles that truly shape the moral, legal, reputational, and talent imperatives of an organization—we rarely question that those decisions are being mostly driven by the C-suite and handpicked from among a few privileged candidates.

We have to admit that determining someone's future output and competencies based on a series of interviews and other skills tests, no matter how well structured, is hard. What makes it harder is a false claim of measured reliability, when in fact the hiring bar is raised and lowered at will all the time. Even in a company that has built a structured recruiting method and introduced AI or other technology tools to cut against biases and reduce prejudice, the ultimate decision will always rest with people crammed with biases and cultural blind spots. Paradigm, a diversity, equity, and inclusion consulting company, has found that 98 percent of organizations already have a candidate pool more racially and ethnically diverse than their current workforce. But most companies dismiss candidates who do not fit the current professional mold because of a discriminatory caste system inherent in their culture.

Revamping your methods of assessing and interviewing candidates will reduce the abundance of bias and hasty hiring. You can level the playing field by ensuring traditionally underrepresented candidates are fairly considered at every stage of the process. It may take more time, and you may have to help others confront uncomfortable truths. But it's worth it.

Once we commit to making better, less biased, and forward-thinking hiring decisions, we can begin to chip away at the imbalance of power in our organizations.

The Right Hire or the White Hire?

Bias is everywhere; there's no question. Our brains make millions of assumptions every day based on past experiences or socialized ideas, which lead to bias. Implicit bias and pattern matching are transmitted through hiring systems—which leads to highly competent, qualified, and diverse candidates leaking out of the pipeline—and it continues throughout the career cycle, influencing promotions, economic prosperity, and psychological safety. When you consciously or unconsciously penalize people for bringing their full selves—the clothes they wear or the way they talk—to work or the interview table, you perpetuate a cycle of prejudiced behavior and damaging outcomes.

At Google, we found that stripping out names in the screening process did move more female engineers through each stage of the hiring process: screens, on-site interviews, and offer acceptances. However, that was not the case for Black and Hispanic software engineers. When we experimented with taking out names in the early screening processes, we found slight improvements for BIPOC but would again see the number of candidates reduced at the later stages of the process when they were face-to-face or on the phone with interviewers. So why did white women get a lift from stripping that information but BIPOC didn't? I believe it's because we couldn't eradicate the effect of racial bias in the interview process.

Consider someone who comes in for an interview with an accent that is hard for you to understand. Research shows that our brains instinctively reject the extra work, and with it the person. Why does that matter? Because it can be easy to disregard, pass over, or discriminate against a candidate because you can't get past their accent. One of my favorite quotes from the movie *A Walk in the Clouds* is, "Just because I speak with an accent doesn't mean that I think with an accent." In this simple statement, the character Alberto Aragón demands that his distinctive style of speech be recognized as a sign of his cultural and language heritage, not a limited intellectual capacity. We all deserve that. Yet those who are deemed meritorious are often those whose accents fit within a traditional white standard.

Iris Bohnet, author of *What Works*, has found that there are 150 unconscious biases, from confirmation bias to familiarity bias. They seep into every aspect of life. Biases can deeply disrupt the interview process, particularly when it comes to race. If you are a white person who has no friends of color (a study by the Public Religion Research Institute found that 75 percent of white people have social networks that are entirely white), how likely is it that your discomfort with a BIPOC candidate during the interview is a reflection of your segregated social circles? Furthermore, studies show that white people struggle to accurately read emotions of Black people and will perceive Black faces as automatically angrier than white faces. If you're shocked to hear this, shake it off. You can start fixing your hiring model by interrogating your biases and questioning yourself and others when BIPOC candidates are dismissed for being "cold," "angry," "loud," "fake," or "awkward," or for other racially coded reasons. What is the factual basis for those interpretations?

"We haven't yet found a way to eliminate our tendency to default to bias," says Kenji Yoshino, author of *Covering* and Chief Justice Earl Warren professor of constitutional law at NYU School of Law. "But we do know how to change default behaviors in moments of heightened awareness to shift from exclusive to inclusive behavior. Look at the #MeToo movement and how college students have shifted from sexual harassment bystanders to upstanders. Five years ago, if you saw someone leaving a party drunk, you probably would have just looked the other way. Now the default reaction is that if you see something, it's your responsibility to make sure that person is OK. The awareness in one moment can lead to habit-changing action in another."

Reviewing résumés without names attached to them and sourcing from untapped talent pools are good and needed steps, but these efforts won't go very far if white leaders can't get over their fears and prejudices about BIPOC talent. For instance, Black candidates who happen to be more direct in their style of communication can get dinged for being too confrontational, while those who are white with a similar style are seen as being straight shooters. I once questioned a colleague's assessment of a Black male executive for a top leadership role. We had a clear mandate to hire a diverse executive, and here was a highly credentialed leader who had served in multiple executive leadership roles. My colleague's reason for not moving this candidate forward: "I've heard that he's got sharp elbows." My response was, "He's a tall, Black man who has risen to the top ranks in predominantly white organizations. I'd be surprised if he hasn't turned off a few white people. I could say the same about the other white men on the slate. Why are you not raising the same concerns about them?"

Unconscious bias training for everyone active in the hiring process is your first line of action (or rather, defense). These trainings are an opportunity to understand how subjective decisions are based on the decision-maker's perceptions and to be more conscious of hiring bias. I have led enough of these interventions to know that they can serve as a valuable foundation—not a systemic solve—for uncovering how to reduce bias and prejudice in hiring decisions.

Prejudice doesn't disappear because you acknowledge it. It disappears when you are willing to combat your own sneaky inner voices. That takes time and practice. Yoshino has a formula to create new habits: trigger > routine > reward. The trigger is the awareness of your bias. The routine is what you do about it. And the reward comes when you do something positive. For example, a BIPOC team member tells you that they feel diminished by you because you constantly interrupt them (trigger). You set out to pause when you feel inclined to interrupt women and BIPOC in your next meeting (routine). Women and BIPOC team members share positive feedback about how much they enjoy your team meetings and are able to produce far better ideas and solutions (reward).

At Vice Media Group, we developed a hiring playbook. This step-by-step road map for an inclusive and equitable hiring process helped our interviewers become more objective evaluators. We outlined the process and expectations at each stage of the hiring process and tasked recruiters with reviewing the process and expectations with each search. Along the way, we learned that bias existed at both the behavioral and structural levels. That is, we had to get better at questioning decisions based on preset ideas of what an ideal candidate should look like and test our own procedures and norms, such as requiring college degrees and years of experience for roles where these were not an indicator of success.

The most powerful action I know to combat bias is to call your perceptions and assumptions into question, again and again. After you receive a résumé, speak with a candidate, or interview someone, ask yourself objectively about your first impression. Write it down if it's helpful. If you thought "underqualified," ask yourself why. What was it that made you think that? If you said "intimidating," ask yourself why. Push yourself harder to see farther. That's what will get you in the right movement-making mindset.

Test Time

To help your team understand the impact of bias on brain patterns, ask them to take the Implicit Association Test from Harvard's Project Implicit. It is a simple online exercise that measures associations between concepts, stereotypes, and evaluations that reflect attitudes and beliefs that people may be unwilling or unable to state. Meaning, you can purport to be "woke" and work to behave without prejudice, but your automatic associations could show that you (like many others) still associate Black people with violence and women with being in the home.

When I first took the test, I felt a deep sense of shame. The test told me what I didn't want to hear: that I have a preference for younger people and light-skinned people. This was an incredibly embarrassing result for me, but it shows that bias and stereotypes lie in all of us. Once you understand what your baseline bias is, you can begin to address it. For a more scalable approach, try Eskalera, an employee engagement platform that has created an inclusion index and curriculum approach to make participants aware of their diversity, equity, and inclusion strengths and development areas. It provides them with tools and activities to continue learning, growing, and training—much like any other skills-based practice.

Taking these tests won't save or heal you. What they will do is help you come to terms with how these biases impact your day-to-day interactions and decisions, recognize situations where you are more prone to the influence of bias, and minimize its influence. "The problem is not seeing color. It's what you do once you see color," says Vernā Myers, chief diversity officer at Netflix.

Push for More: More Candidates, More Interview Prep, More Accountability

A series of experimental studies published by the *Harvard Business Review* found that whatever demographic group composed the majority of a finalist pool was likely to be chosen as the favored candidate. Thus, when two out of three candidates were white, a white candidate was significantly more likely to be chosen; likewise, if there's only one woman in your candidate pool, there's statistically no chance she'll be hired. Instead, the authors of that study found that when they added "just one more woman or minority candidate" to the pool of finalists, the chances of hiring slightly increased. For example, when two out of three candidates were Black or Hispanic, a Black or Hispanic person was more likely to be selected.

It makes sense. By increasing the commonality among candidates, you eliminate the "only" effect in the hiring process. By counteracting this effect, it is less likely that a candidate will be judged for criteria outside their control (like ethnicity, sexual orientation, and gender). A critical mass of candidates from underrepresented groups eliminates the psychological instinct that you're taking a risk or sacrificing something for the sake of diversity.

Interviewing mandates—meaning you must interview a certain number of people who check a certain ethnicity or gender box—have risen in popularity. I've referenced the NFL's Rooney Rule, established in 2003, which required teams with head coaching vacancies to interview at least one BIPOC candidate. Since then, they've upped the requirement to two, and several tech companies, like Amazon and Uber, have followed suit with diversity interview mandates. These goals can be effective but cannot be leaned on as the sole tool for increasing workplace diversity. What happens after the interview? What systems are you putting in place to reduce inequities in hiring outcomes?

Revisit your motivations in Chapter 1. Creating equal opportunities for all genders, races, abilities, and identities should be the baseline, and it's also about the bottom line. The connection between financial performance and diversity is difficult to prove because research has only established correlation, not causation, between the two. However, there is ample evidence that diverse organizations are more successful at recruiting and retaining talent, especially diverse talent, and teams that include different viewpoints or thinking styles boost intellectual potential and produce more and higher-quality intellectual property, such as patents.

Ensure that you and those who make hiring decisions—from screening to final selections—are equipped to objectively evaluate a candidate's skills, knowledge, and potential to succeed. At Greenhouse, a recruiting software company, they focus on three areas for interview training: the rules, unconscious bias, and logistics. The rules cover what to ask and what not to ask (legally) and the best ways to respond to tough questions. They then cover biases, the need for a structured hiring process to tame them, and how they have shown up in past hiring decisions. And finally, they set expectations for the process.

The more you can prepare effectively for a successful interview and decision-making process, the more fair and just your hiring process will be.

1. **Be disciplined**. Set aside time to prepare before and debrief after the interview.

2. **Prepare**. Review the job description, candidate profile, and key questions with a focus on the areas of importance to the role and team.

3. **Put yourself in their shoes**. Make time to get to know the person, not just the candidate. Ask about their expectations and be transparent about the process and discussion as appropriate, and always test your biases.

4. **Debrief while it is fresh**. If part of a panel, debrief immediately, even if just for five minutes. Separate intuitive feelings from objective data. Compare candidates against concrete, objective criteria—I can't say this enough. Share your feedback with the recruitment team.

Ask for This: A Structured Hiring Approach

A structured hiring approach is a step-by-step plan that applies a fair, consistent lens to hiring that begins when the role is first approved. It's a data-driven strategy that sets a list of clear, objective criteria to evaluate all candidates, uses a deliberate process and an evaluation rubric applied consistently to all candidates, and ensures hiring decisions are based on evidence, not subjective relationships. Here's a sample:

1. **Kickoff Meeting**: Recruiters and hiring managers discuss team composition, the aspirational mix and culture, job parameters, and roles and responsibilities.

2. **Scorecard Definition**: What technical or operational skills and capabilities do you need on the team? What may be other

dimensions of success, such as communication, collaboration, or problem-solving? Use a quantitative rating system—such as a five-point sale—to reduce bias versus relying on open-ended questions.

3. **Interview Planning**: Who is doing the interviews? How will you prepare them to ensure they are consistent in their assessment criteria? How will you consciously intervene to lessen the impact of bias?

4. **Candidate Evaluation**: Ensure everyone is clear on the hiring attributes you will use to make a final decision. Create an opportunity to question the process versus leaning on preconceived notions of success. Evaluators support their ratings with explanations and specific examples.

The degree of structure in interviews is significantly related to the degree of bias in outcomes. Unstructured interviews provide interviewers with wide discretion in terms of which questions are asked and how their responses are evaluated, and as such can result in biased evaluations of candidates. In contrast, structured interviews limit the discretion of interviewers and thereby the degree of bias they can exert in the process.

Combat Bias with Consistency

It's crucial to improve interviewing practices and decision-making across the board so that talented people are not being subtly shut out or excluded from the process. The subjective nature of the interview process makes it difficult to evaluate candidates without preconceived ideas, default perceptions, and subconscious expectations. Based on past interviewing and hiring experiences, our brain patterns influence our thoughts and predict future outcomes. For instance, you might think, "The last time I hired a Black video producer, he didn't turn out to be the rock star I thought he was" (judgment bias). Or, "I am so happy we hired Modupe, who worked at Netflix, because I love talking about movies with her" (halo bias). There's also the horn effect concept, whereby we attribute negative characteristics to an individual due to perceiving an undesirable quality. For example, "Every José I have met has been dull. This José already strikes me as boring." You can't fight these feelings—they exist—but you can establish protocols and strategies to thwart them from having too much power.

One of the most successful ways to do this is to build decision-making teams that allow for more diverse perspectives, robust feedback compilation, and richer candidate experiences. There should always be more than one person interviewing and evaluating a candidate. Final hiring decisions come down to hiring managers and those who influence their decision-making, and some companies like Google have transferred the power to hiring committees to help introduce diverse perspectives and reach more objective decisions. Assembling an interview team with a diversity of experiences leads to less bias.

There are two ways I've seen this executed. One is where the team interviews a candidate as a panel at once or in smaller groups over the course of a predetermined interview cycle. I've seen this process work best when hiring for entry-level talent or high-volume roles like sales representatives and software engineers, and at small start-ups who need to hire fast. This practice is a time saver and will allow for a fairer evaluation by allowing everyone to hear the same questions and responses. To streamline the process, each interviewer is prepped and assigned a particular capability or question. The benefit of this model is that it eliminates subjective circumstances (a distracted interviewer, or an interviewee who is fatigued from six previous interviews), but it can be very overwhelming for a candidate. Be mindful that being the only person from an underrepresented group in a room or a Zoom with all eyes on you can be intimidating and lead to performance failures.

The other method is sticking with a more traditional interview process where two to three finalists meet with three to five interviewers, with one being the hiring manager. Regardless of the interview process, ensuring the process is consistent—including asking each candidate similar questions and treating internal and external candidates the same at each stage of the process—should be the top priority. That's the takeaway: consistency. Consistency can cut through institutional barriers for traditionally underrepresented talent.

In both situations, your interview team should reflect a diversity of skills and responsibilities to round out the panel's perspective and enhance the candidate's experience. The team must be assembled thoughtfully, with each member having an equal voice and welcoming diverse opinions. You should also be intentional in selecting a mix of backgrounds for your panel—at a minimum, include more than one woman or nonbinary person and members of other underrepresented groups.

A solid interview team should include

- a direct peer;

- a cross-functional peer;

- someone who will report directly to the person; and

- the hiring manager.

When my team was hiring for *Refinery29*'s editor in chief role, we designed a diverse interview panel that included a cofounder, hiring manager, two peers (one cross-functional), two mid-level employees, and two junior-level employees. We set clear and shared expectations about the unique perspectives each would bring to decision-making. We also let the candidates know who would be interviewing them and why. The aim was not to misrepresent our diversity. We were honest and transparent about where we were as a company and what we aspired to be.

If you know it's critical for someone to meet a BIPOC in the hiring process, make that happen, but be thoughtful of not overburdening or tokenizing your one Black engineer and requiring him or her to be on every interview team. At YouTube (owned by Google), Susan Wojcicki encouraged the recruitment team to think creatively and audaciously about hiring more Black and Hispanic software engineers. One of the recommendations was to ensure Black and Hispanic candidates would "see themselves" at YouTube by including a Black or Hispanic YouTuber in every interview process. But if you have less than ten Black and Hispanic software engineers in the entire organization and you're interviewing eight people a day, they won't have time to do the jobs you hired them to do. Plus, this policy didn't take into account that only a portion of these BIPOC engineers were qualified to be part of the interview process; most hadn't received interview training and had limited interviewing experience. Instead, the People Ops (the term Google uses for HR) and business team tasked with diversity initiatives opted for a creative solution, whereby Black and Hispanic candidates would, at a minimum, meet a BIPOC YouTuber for lunch or coffee during their interview cycle.

Even small start-ups can systemize the hiring process and get everyone eager and excited to be a part of the interview panel. When the Cru, a peer mentorship platform and community founded by Tiffany Dufu, was hiring for a director role, the COO, Katie Rogers, enrolled a few key members in the process. Here's the email she sent:

Hi team,

We've got a healthy candidate pipeline for the x role (thank you for spreading the word and sending in referrals!) and we're going to start scheduling interviews in the next few weeks.

I've listed all of you as a part of the interview panel—candidates will always speak with me for at least a 30–45 minute phone screen before they make it to the next round with you all. As a part of this process, I've created a score-card so that everyone is clear on what they'd be testing for in their time with candidates. This is all to make sure that we're getting different perspectives without asking redundant questions while also ensuring we're hiring the right person for this role who can get the job done. If you don't feel good about testing for what I have listed for you—no worries! Just talk to me about it so that I can ensure we're testing for each of these in one way, shape or form.

At a start-up like the Cru, where there are less than fifteen people on staff, every new hire is significant. Founders set the DNA of their organization with their first ten to twenty hires. Culture dynamics start at day one and get cemented over time with each new hire. Dufu takes this process very seriously and recognizes that without new perspectives, there is no innovation, and rightly so. Recently, when Dufu shared her enthusiasm about hiring a new team member with a potential investor, the investor's first question was, "Where did they come from?" "I knew they were looking for the name of the company this person used to work for so that they could gauge the pedigree of the hire, but I decided to share what was far more important: 'They came from being an expert in the human condition. They came from grit, self-determination and hustle,'" she says. "If we're going to build new platforms that unite us and enable us to move our lives forward, we can't hire the same ole Silicon Valley prototypes who built the old ones. We'll have to do the work to recruit incredibly talented people who have a fresh lens on the world."

Don't Interview for "Fit." Interview for Function, Potential, and Culture Add.

Dufu's approach is a refreshing take on the more common practice of hiring people with a specific background like the investor was expecting (Ivy League, prestigious former company). The attributes Dufu cited—grit, self-determination, and hustle—are much better indicators of success than one's arbitrary acceptance into a top-tier college. The conventional or traditional hire is not always the safe hire, and the person with a less name-brand background who went to a state school (which is the majority of the country) could be bringing in a wealth of skills that are missing from the company. That type of gatekeeping is a form of affinity bias.

Affinity bias or "like" bias is the concept that if you meet someone that you identify with, you might be more willing to push them through the process even if they don't score as high on key capabilities as another candidate. It is also the tendency for people to hire people like themselves. They figure that they fit the model of company success, and so someone with a similar background would also fit. It's the most apparent way the hiring bar gets lowered or raised.

It's easy to gravitate toward what looks familiar and to attribute positive qualities to that which feels comfortable. After all, in typical circumstances, these are the people you interact with for the majority of your day. It's nearly impossible to *not* consider these questions during an interview: Will I get along with this person? Would I enjoy having dinner with them after work? Is this person going to have a nice rapport and easy time with the other members on the team? We all want life to be easy, and no one wants to manage "difficult" employees or colleagues, but this line of risk-averting thinking is what creates a homogenous, exclusive workplace. These are questions to ask yourself when evaluating a friendship, not a future employee. Too often, this means folks make the mistake of hiring based on likability and affinity rather than proven skills and results.

Often masked as culture fit, this dusty concept leads to racial and other biases in the hiring process. Too often, BIPOC workers are denied a role or advancement because they are not seen as a good culture fit by white leadership. As Ellen Pao points out in *Reset*, a group of people with different backgrounds and worldviews may seem to be a bad culture fit in that they may be slower to come to agreement, but conflict is not always a bad thing. When decisions are tested by different views, they are strengthened. If everyone is hired to have the same worldview, it's easy to create a disconnected bubble. Further, dismissing someone because they lack culture fit is often a coded way to suggest that a candidate has not assimilated into white culture or the white standards of professionalism of that particular workplace.

As we seek to bring diverse hires into our workplaces, we should be intentional about enhancing organizational culture and not just striving for optical diversity. Instead of culture fit, aim for "culture add," which helps assess whether a candidate will enhance your culture through explicit performance values rather than implicitly biased cultural values. (Hint: this also applies to existing employee evaluations, which we'll discuss in Chapter 8.)

Culture add helps center the contributions each new hire makes to your teams. Consider these questions:

- What is our current culture and how does it reflect our values and behavioral principles? What is missing?

- What core values, behavioral principles, and organizational practices do we need new hires to know about and match?

- What aspirations do we have for strategic growth and cultural transformation, and how will a new hire contribute?

Success is bringing on someone who is additive to your culture, someone who brings a different experience and background while adding to your organization's mission and values. If there is something about a candidate that doesn't sit well with you, like their attire or communication style, that's not a reason to ding them immediately. Consider your answers to the previous questions, challenge comparisons to exclusive, white professional standards, and center on the value these candidates will offer to the teams that you are part of, and to your larger organization.

Background Check Q&A

Q. *Should companies be vetting folks before they are hired for making public racist, sexist, or homophobic comments on social media, or for having been sued for sexual harassment? Are online searches to check for these things legal and useful?*

A. Unquestionably, vetting job candidates is a critical component of the decision-marking process. Recruiters and hiring managers should conduct thorough due diligence on all candidates, especially executive hires, as part of their standard screening practices to ensure they're not hiring sexual harassers or individuals with records of ongoing and recurring acts of racism and discrimination. If you haven't already, you should seek legal counsel when building a fair screening policy that addresses the standards and values by which you will assess all candidates.

It can be complicated to police online posts. A freshly hired editor in chief resigned from a publisher before her start date because of racist tweets that surfaced from when she was a teenager. Does being a teenager give her a pass? Does it depend on what she said? You have to establish sound criteria for what you're assessing and reviewing to be able to explain the why and only screen out based on substantiated and substantial findings.

Ask Better Interview Questions

While it is hard to change how our brains are wired, it is possible to change the context of hiring decisions by training interviewers on how to shape their questions to get the information they need. Your best strategy against falling into the "fit" habit is to develop preset interview questions that speak to the candidates' abilities to perform consistently against predetermined performance metrics and organizational values. Accountability and analytics reduce bias, but data is a double-edge sword. You're still hiring human beings and should ask them better questions to understand who they are.

Research has shown that managers who conduct structured interviews with a combination of behavioral and situational questions have more successful outcomes than those who do unstructured interviewing. Behavioral questions ask candidates to describe prior achievements and match those to what is required in the current job (e.g., "Tell me about a time...?"). Hypothetical questions present just that, a job-related hypothetical situation (e.g., "What would you do if...?").

Consider asking these questions:

- When you need to learn something new, how do you approach it? Where do your ideas come from?

- Tell me about two people you have worked with whose lives you positively impacted. What would they say if I called them tomorrow?

- Tell me how you build relationships. How do you make connections with people you have less in common with?

- What excites you most, and conversely, what scares you the most about this opportunity?

These questions can help find the sparkles in your talent pool beyond the standard problem-solving abilities. Always remember to follow the story: What did you do? How did you do it? Why did you do that and what were you thinking? What was the result? What did you do next? After your interview, ask the receptionist, recruitment coordinator, or even security, "How was the candidate's interaction with you?" How people treat strangers speaks to whether they act with compassion and respect.

These questions can help you assess what has shaped the candidate's career decisions, relationships, and openness to different perspectives. The goal is to create a conversation that leads to revelations about their character and competencies, not a rehearsal. This should also help you spot skills in nonlinear work histories. People don't have career paths; they have growth paths. Companies like Kapor Capital have begun considering "distance traveled"—that is, where a job candidate came from and how many obstacles they had to overcome—as an important measure of work ethic and resilience. We need to get better at thinking about what useful skills candidates may have gained from unusual, nonlinear experiences.

We can try to get at those behaviors during the interview process in a way that's agnostic to background. You don't want to fall into an assumption trap, believing that only those who have worked at another start-up are qualified to work at yours because they know what it's like to work in that environment. That doesn't speak to potential. If you're interviewing for project management skills, ask about how someone managed a project from start to finish. Those skills could have been gained in a previous role or through coaching or launching a personal website.

When you can take your time throughout the process, when you have the space to ask questions about a candidate's values, how they show up at work and in their lives, their quirks, and their talents, you can make better hiring decisions. "I want my team to develop relationships with people," says Keesha Jean-Baptiste, senior vice president and chief talent officer for Hearst magazines. "They should meet them, get to know them, and go into the process with a full understanding of who these individuals, these multifaceted people are, so that you're coming from a place of support when you're hiring, rather than thinking, 'OK, I'm checking the box now.'"

At Hearst, Jean-Baptiste is creating a set of interview questions to help gauge a candidate's mindset around diversity, equity, and inclusion behaviors, which the hiring manager, recruiter, and other interviewers would ask to hear the answers from multiple perspectives. For the mindset piece, the interview question is, "What have you done or put in place to augment diversity initiatives at your workplace?" Jean-Baptiste says, "It's a reality check to make sure that we're bringing in people whose values align with where we are trying to go." Note: This question should be asked of all hires, regardless of racial or other type of background. There should be expectations that values are aligned for hires in all positions, even those whose job descriptions aren't focused on diversity, equity, and inclusion work.

Inclusion Q&A

Q. If I'm asked in an interview about our company's diversity, or, more candidly, if the candidate would be the "only," what should I say?

A. Legal teams get worried if you're talking about hiring someone because of their demographic characteristics. It may sound obvious, but you shouldn't say we have a problem with hiring Black people so that's why you're here. Instead, be honest about the state of diversity in your team and organization and your aspirations to diversify. Say, "My team's current demographic composition is x and y, and I would like to change that to be better aligned with our growth strategy, our mission, and our purpose." Be honest. I am always up-front about our gaps and our opportunities; there is no way of sugarcoating it. I told a recent hire that she would be the first Black woman on the leadership team. As an executive of color, this was not her first rodeo. However, it was important to emphasize the weight and relevance of her position and what we were actively doing to hire more racially diverse talent at all levels. Candidates of color will understandably approach a job that specifies that the company is looking for diverse talent or where the candidate will be the only BIPOC with a sense of trepidation. They worry about being tokenized (the "only") and the pressures that come from that experience. They are also naturally concerned that hiring managers may feel that they've checked the box and don't have to hire any more BIPOC team members. This can be immensely stressful.

Not speaking the truth about what they will encounter on their first day and beyond is a disservice to the individual and the mission you're trying to deliver on. Be honest if most of the team is white or if the candidate would be the only Black or BIPOC staff. Explain that you are genuinely committed and will follow through on hiring more BIPOC so that no BIPOC person is the only one on a team. Say this, and mean it. The point is not to say that we want to hire you for diversity, but that we recognize we have gaps, and your skill set, voice, and lived experience would be additive to our organization. Make it clear that you see them for who they are and will ensure others do the same.

Standardize How You Debrief and Decide

Now it's time to compare notes. In an ideal world, if you're going through a structured process, you bring everyone together who was on this job-filling journey to determine if the candidate should move forward. In order to be effective at this stage of decision-making, it's important that each person is comfortable actively weighing in on decisions and is able to do it transparently.

Ideally, the first review should focus on the core responsibilities of the role: What are the must-have skills or talents? At Google, the hiring committee would review interview feedback and then determine if the candidate was a pass or go. We would look for outliers: Why did someone give the candidate a low (or high) score on cognitive ability? Is that feedback valid or could it be attributed to bias? Research from Lean In's 2020 report *The State of Black Women in Corporate America* shows that when a specific person monitors for this, evaluators are less likely to base their recommendations on subjective factors, such as a candidate's culture fit or personality.

Google's review committee added an extra layer of scrutiny. It was a necessary pressure test that would sometimes result in changed decisions. Is there recency bias, favoring the candidate just interviewed versus the one interviewed two weeks ago? Are we certain that we assessed the candidate fairly? If not, let's add another interview to test if that changes the outcome.

Putting this structure in place and creating steadfast rules of assessment eliminates the personal pressure that is often felt in the hiring process. You must have a clear, consistent framework for decision-making, including determining who makes a final decision and whether stakeholders or other team members are allowed votes, vetoes, or recommendations. Identifying the decision-making process and the level of diversity at all stages is also important. Be mindful of referrals. In many industries, most hiring still comes through referrals. I can't tell you how many times a white male senior colleague has strongly fought for a candidate who did not meet the role's qualifications but who happened to be a referral from a friend. Then there's the founder or client who asks ever so graciously, "Can you take a look at this person?" Or, "Can I add this person to the mix, as a favor for a friend?" The structure protects you and empowers you to remind someone that their request, a symptom of privilege, will not unduly impact the outcome.

Other questions we should ask regularly: What perspectives are we missing by hiring for homogeneity? What backgrounds and viewpoints are we missing? Can we hire to fill those gaps, to ensure we build a diverse team who will bring in a broad range of ideas and perspectives? Now imagine adding: if the final candidates across multiple slates remain disproportionately white, we will revisit decisions to ensure finalists are equally competitive and always include one or more BIPOC candidates. And: if timing pressures are impacting decisions, we will tap into a budget for temporary workers to ensure we make sound and lasting hiring decisions. Now you're putting measures in place that will help you reach your goals.

At the end of the day, there is no perfect formula for hiring. Despite countless science-backed technical solutions that say otherwise, it is nearly impossible to make a 100 percent unbiased hiring decision, but putting structures in place and nudging your people toward better habits adds a level of fairness in a process that often has too many inconsistent influences. Getting more underrepresented candidates through the door will require rethinking your applicant pool, job qualifications, bias in access to interviews and assessments, and hiring-manager training. Change won't always happen fast, but the more aware you are of your perceptions and actions, both conscious and unconscious, and the more you begin to take steps toward repairing them, the closer we will come to equity in the workplace.

Try This: Self-Reflection Questions to Mitigate Bias

Proactively addressing biases is key to a more accurate assessment of future performance and function. Self-reflection and bias confrontation is hard, but it is one of the most important responsibilities that a hiring manager can have. After you meet with a candidate, jot down your answer to these questions:

- What is it that your team really needs? Can the candidate fulfill those needs?

- Why would you hire them? Why wouldn't you?

- If the candidate is not successful a year from now, what would you suspect the reason might be?

- What questions would you still like to know about the candidate before making a final decision?

- Test if you're having an automatic feeling or judgment about this person. If you're having a negative reaction, what is it that this person is bringing up in you that is making you struggle? Are you under particular stress, pressure, or high cognitive load that may negatively impact your reaction to this candidate? Does the candidate remind you of someone in your life or from your past?

- Have interviewers used coded language like "cold," "opinionated," "bossy," "sharp elbowed," or "thick accent" disproportionately in reference to female or BIPOC candidates? Do these comments refer to the skills required for the role, or do they reflect gendered and racialized biases interviewers may hold about these individuals?

- Will the candidate be additive to your culture and actively support diversity, equity, and inclusion? During interviews for the current UN secretary-general, male and female candidates were asked whether it was time for there to be a female secretary-general. The final candidate was a man, but as part of the process he had to convince the interview panel that he was the feminist for the job.

Be honest with yourself and your answers.

Your Road Map to Revolution

Pay close attention to how your organization recruits and assesses talent at every step of the recruitment and hiring process. Ask yourself these questions: How can I influence who is hired at my organization? What role can I play in deciding which candidates are considered or how the process runs? If you help evaluate candidates, insist on reviewing a diverse slate. If we continue to make the same organizational mistakes of only hiring, listening to, and advancing people we know and we feel comfortable with, we risk alienating not just our current team but our future one as well.

- **Continually examine bias throughout the hiring process**. There's no autopilot here. When you become aware of bias, disrupt it. Call your perceptions and assumptions into question, again and again.

- **Require inclusive interviewing training for all**. Ensure that those who make hiring decisions—from screening to final selections—are equipped to objectively evaluate a candidate's skills, knowledge, and potential to succeed. To be effective, this training needs to teach employees to counteract bias in specific scenarios.

- **Push for more candidates**. Everyone wants to get a new hire in the door quickly, but find the confidence to ask for more candidates, even when you're getting pressure to fill a seat. Don't accept excuses like "But there's no qualified talent," or "Those are the only applicants we received." It's necessary to create a more diverse workforce.

- **Standardize the interviewing processes to keep assessments fair and balanced**. Consistency is key. Have standard questions to ask and a scorecard for all interviewers to use for assessment.

- **Designate a selection criteria check**. Have an HR representative or a member of the team be responsible for making sure evaluators remain focused on the criteria for the role. Research shows that when a specific person monitors for this, evaluators are less likely to base their recommendations on subjective factors, such as a candidate's culture fit or personality.

- **Watch for affinity bias or the horn effect during interviews**. That's when you either connect with someone because they went to your college or also love to play basketball, or when something bad about the candidate grabs your attention and you can't move beyond it. You cannot let these factors guide your final impression. Instead, suss out why the candidate's skills or qualities would add to your organization.

- **Shift your focus from culture fit to culture add when evaluating candidates**. Success is bringing someone who is additive to your culture. Aim for culture add by assessing whether a candidate enhances your culture.

- **Ask better interview questions**. Ask open-ended behavioral and hypothetical questions to understand a candidate's potential, separate from his or her background. Talk about how they problem-solve and build relationships. Ask what their colleagues would say about them.

- **Standardize how you debrief and decide**. This is when you bring everyone together to compare notes and determine if the candidate should move forward. Be ready to push back on feedback with thought-provoking questions (e.g., Why did you feel that way?).

5

NURTURE A PEOPLE-FIRST CULTURE

YEARS AGO AT Disney, a new chief of staff, a young woman of color, was making the rounds getting to know leadership. When we met, I was immediately captivated by her curiosity and precision. Then she asked me a question that totally caught me off guard: "Who is your best friend at work?" "I don't have one," I replied, disappointed in my answer. I had cultivated good relationships over the years, but I couldn't pick one best friend who I truly trusted. I didn't have a colleague I could freely share my concerns, doubts, or fears with—where I didn't need to feel on guard as a woman of color or worried that my truths would cause them to betray me or ignore me.

My disappointment wasn't solely about not having a best friend at work but rather that the question made me confront the feeling that I had never felt fully welcome in my team or in the broader organization.

Culture can mean a lot of different things. It is how we acquire ideas, beliefs, and values. Organizational culture is not Ping-Pong tables or free lunch; it is how things get done and how perceptions are shaped. Its language is how people feel. It's if they want to be at work;

if they enjoy working with their colleagues; if they feel safe, seen, and valued; and if they have a best work friend. Every single person on a team, from the most junior staffer to a senior executive, contributes to a company's culture. And it's up to managers to take it from being invisible to visible. What you say and do on a day-to-day basis creates culture—every comment you make, every uncomfortable moment that goes unaddressed, has a ripple effect. This is the energy you put forth and the substance of how people engage and interact.

Work culture is formative work; it rewires our brains and shapes how we think. Toxic environments are not always caused by severe, headline-making issues but rather by ongoing racist expectations and microaggressions that occur on an individual level. See, for example, "My manager touched my dreadlocks in a team meeting." Or, "I am constantly accused of being angry or animated when I'm simply making a point that I strongly believe in." These actions may not represent the totality of these individuals' characters or perhaps seem limited in scope, but they often have larger consequences, informing workplace norms and often leading to a culture of mistrust, harmful work experiences, and systemic exclusion of whole swaths of people.

Managers are the linchpins in organizations. You cast the longest shadow. When you consistently and visibly demonstrate the value of creating and sustaining inclusive workplace cultures, others will follow.

"While I do believe that culture has to come from the top and it has to be centralized as a tenet of the company's mission, your lived experience is defined by your direct team and your direct leader," says Sherice Torres, vice president of marketing at Facebook. In other words, inclusive culture-building can't be delegated. Your focus should be on what's happening in the middle, where the real sore spots reside. The often soul-crushing cultures, systems, and structures that consistently exclude BIPOC employees are nearly impossible to survive when you don't have a manager who supports you, or worse, is the source of your misery and frustration.

As a manager, you're consistently given myriad tasks without the necessary support to do your best—like being a leading expert in diversity and inclusion, acting as a therapist, and taking responsibility for the results of challenging industry conditions. In order to continue delivering at the pace of change, you need the right tools and personalized support to develop yourself, then do the same for others. We can't push an organization forward if we're not empowered to push ourselves forward.

Enabling your success also requires that you work toward creating workplaces characterized by safety, dignity, and respect for all workers. That you carve out time and space to reflect on your industry's culture and the ways workplace norms and habits have traditionally locked out or pushed out people of color. It further requires that you recognize your responsibility to respond to cultural conversations by stepping forward, not shrinking away, and that you rally your peers to push for change themselves. This chapter helps you build your management skills with a focus on inclusion, belonging, psychological safety, and anti-racism.

Lead from the Beginning

A massive mistake leaders make is laboring over the hiring process and forgetting about what comes after the offer is accepted: what it's like for people to work here. When you understand your workplace's belonging gaps—the gap that exists between your existing culture and your desired culture—and the fractures in your culture, and when you've done the work to create an inclusive workplace, you're less likely to be in a constant "solving for diversity" mode. I've been called in to help with damage control too many times to count. The first ask is typically a diversity training of some type, generally unconscious bias or allyship. When I dig deeper for the underlying conditions that led to the request, I often find a series of precipitating blunders that could have been avoided. An innocuous request is too often code for "we've been called out for our lack of diversity, toxic workplace culture, biased product campaigns, or all the above—and we need your help."

New hire onboarding is often an afterthought, when in fact this period is the essential introduction to a company's culture and a critical component of a strong diversity, equity, and inclusion strategy. How you welcome new hires sets the tone for inclusion. *Don't overlook this transition period.* Eighty-six percent of new hires make a decision to stay with a company long-term within the first six months of employment, according to the Aberdeen Group, a market research company.

Beyond handing out ID cards and filling out tax forms, onboarding is a pivotal moment for making employees feel included from day one. Think about when you've started at a new company and found yourself twiddling your thumbs, not knowing who to talk to or what to do. It's a horrible feeling, right? Your first day of work is one of the most disorienting experiences. You question everything. It's as if you're a foreigner walking into a place where you don't understand the language, the norms, the customs, or the politics.

At these moments, new hires look for guidance on what to do and how to do it. Where's the bathroom? Who has power? What are my team's daily rhythms and rituals? Should I speak up or not? How are meetings run? Who can I trust? Do we stab each other in the back? How do I get things done? What is rewarded? The other moments when you're this intensely curious are when you first get promoted to become a manager or a senior executive. These times you ask: What does success look like? What do I want my teams to say about me? How do I want to grow as a leader? Do I have the right people? That's why it's so important to invest your time in setting new team members up for success.

Your job is to decode all this for your new hire. What you do and say reduces the chances that your new hire will feel left out and disconnected and sets the tone for being at ease in a new space, feeling safe and welcome to show up as the best version of themselves, prepared to navigate a new environment. Buffer, a social media engagement platform, starts the employee onboarding process as soon as a new hire officially accepts the position. A highlight of the process is the buddy program, whereby the new recruit is assigned two "buddies" who help guide them through the first six weeks via regular communication and check-ins. This dream team consists of a role buddy (a peer who intimately understands the new hire's role and responsibilities) and a culture buddy (someone who can translate the company culture). The benefits are enormous: the new hire has clear points of contact and inside knowledge of the company, the buddies have an opportunity to network and increase their mentoring and leadership experience, and the company sees an increase in employee engagement and retention for all parties.

When I hired a Black male executive years ago, prior to his joining the company we spoke at length about the racialized tensions he would have to navigate on his team and across the organization. Over the course of the hiring process, we built a strong rapport and trust, and I committed to clearing a path for him. We mutually agreed on what would be needed in terms of buy-in from colleagues to ensure he would be properly welcomed and set up for success. This bridging needs to be done with care. Not all Black hires need or appreciate a path being paved on their behalf. Interventions must be tailored for each hire, along with mutual trust that each hire receives individualized support in addition to support that is racially sensitive. This is not about walking on eggshells around Black team members but rather about creating conditions for their success and the success of their teams and organizations.

I intentionally identified one of the most tenured white male executives as his "orientation buddy." In preparation for their engagement, I said this: "Here's what I need you to know. He is a Black man being asked to lead a team of all white women. During the recruitment process, I have found him to be one of the most affable individuals I know, but we have to be prepared for the racial fears that his mere presence will cause many on this team. He is well aware of the imagined threat he poses in an all-white environment. This is not the first time he has been the only executive of color. For far too long, he has had to make himself likable to reduce the anxiety of others. I know you want him to succeed just as I do. I will support him and engage in transparent conversations with his team about racial stereotypes. My ask is that you, as his buddy and a skilled navigator of our organizational culture, provide him with the tools he will need, give him the internal credibility with leaders and his team through your visible support, and serve as his leadership shield when his ability to lead is questioned. Because it will likely be questioned. I'll partner with you throughout the entire process, and I ask that you let me know if you experience any discomfort in this process as well. It's better that we lay everything on the table now because, as James Baldwin has taught us, 'nothing can be changed until it is faced.'"

His buddy was an exceptional partner. He immediately credentialed him across the organization by bringing him to senior meetings and amplifying his achievements. He shouldered the political and social risks when the Black executive's mistakes—common for leaders learning to navigate new workplace cultures—were raised as red flags. While I did engage the leaders of his team in a conversation about white fragility, we never quite shut down the racial anxiety of his all-white female team. In the end, the dominant culture rejected him, and he had a short tenure. In retrospect, we should have offered bespoke training or had more intentional conversations about how to work together in a racially sensitive way. While we continued to excuse poor behavior of white male executives across the organization, this Black executive's actions and failures were put under much more scrutiny than those of his white peers. And it was a shame.

There is an emotional tax that is levied on Black women and men throughout their careers. Catalyst's report found that when people feel psychologically unsafe, they are less likely to take professional risks and speak up at work. Only 56 percent of Black employees were vocal about important or difficult issues in the workplace, compared with 74 percent of white employees. The workplace has socially ostracized and silenced the ones who have the most to be vocal about. Having sponsors, allies, and buddies can help set you up for success and clear your path, but it will take a one-and-all approach to sustain a people-first culture.

Create an Inclusive Onboarding Experience

What's your company's onboarding process like? I remember my first day at Viacom when I was hired as head of talent acquisition. Along with two fellow new hires, I had to attend the standard orientation program. They played a video about Viacom, and honestly, it was uninspiring. It didn't match the energy I knew was emblematic of the organization; it didn't make me excited to work there. I wanted that moment to affirm my decision to join the organization—we all do. We look for cues to whether we belong in the photos on walls, in the images on company materials, and in the faces of the people who greet us. That's where you can step in.

To onboard your new hire into your systems and culture, ask yourself:

- How can we make our environment help new employees feel welcomed and valued up-front?

- What does this person need to succeed in their first thirty, sixty, and ninety days?

- What do I know about them that is vital to understanding how they work, and who else in the company should know those things?

- Who should be their point person for day-to-day questions and who should be their buddy, an established member of the organization who can help them reduce stress, avoid missteps, and encourage them to feel safe to engage and add the most value?

- Could my or the organization's idea of professionalism un-intentionally make BIPOC employees feel uncomfortable or forced to code-switch or downplay their differences? For ex-ample, are Black women being silently shamed for wearing their hair naturally?

- What can I decode about our organizational culture, lan-guage, and internal politics to make it easier for this employee to feel like an insider?

Little details matter too. I knew that one South Asian male ex-ecutive was concerned that he would not have sufficient vacation days to visit his parents in India twice a year as he had always done. When negotiating his compensation package, we added more vaca-tion days to his employment contract and balanced it out by reduc-ing other fringe benefits that were less important to him.

Make a strong impression by customizing the pre-onboarding experience. Recruiters should pass on all relevant information to hiring managers and the teams responsible for onboarding to ensure all the right things are considered for new hires. For example, if a candidate requires special accommodations such as wheelchair accessibility, ensure your orientation is set up to welcome that can-didate seamlessly into your space. Ask for your new hire's preferred workspace setup, whether in the office or at home. Track religious holiday schedules so that if you're delivering orientations during Ra-madan, for example, you do not offer those new hires water or other items commonly offered without consideration for cultural prac-tices. Too often, people are left to their own devices to figure it out.

And for those who may not have previous institutional knowledge or formal training in office politics, it's a sink-or-swim scenario.

Beyond getting administrative tasks out of the way, help facilitate a faster ramp-up time for your new hire by sending a personalized welcome email at least a week before they join. This should speak to how much you and the company value their presence and future growth at the company and include a new hire reading list, including HR documentation (handbook, benefits, etc.), a glossary or example of company terms, a current road map or strategy for their team, resources on how to get involved to make the workplace more inclusive, and examples of how the team works together, including communication styles. If this looks like an exhausting list of things to do, don't overwhelm them. You can space this out through their first week. The point is to provide them with the navigational tools that they will need to feel settled and informed.

Prepare your team too. Adding a new member will inevitably change dynamics. Prepare them ahead of time by clearly defining the new hire's responsibilities, reporting lines, and handoff processes, if any. Set the expectation of building an inclusive and welcoming environment.

When the new hire arrives, communicate shared purpose and ninety-day objectives, with check-in moments to receive and give feedback. In each check-in ask: What questions can I answer for you? What do you need to be successful? How can I support you?

Integration Exercises

I've found these integration exercises to be effective in transitioning leaders and team members into new roles.

Create a team user manual

Bring the team together and ask everyone to fill in a template that sheds light on how each member of your team likes to work. For example, if someone needs quiet to think, they may decline your invitation to co-work in a coffee shop. It's not about you; it's how they work. This can foster stronger communication and eliminate misguided assumptions and bias. These questions will require time to reflect and may also be difficult for those who have felt sabotaged or undermined in other work settings. It's not enough to ask the question; you have to be responsive and deliver your teammates the tailored support that they need to do their best work. The beauty of this shared document is that it can be sent to any new hire well ahead of their start day to begin to better understand their team. Some prompts:

- Conditions I like to work in (e.g., I need a quiet environment)

- Times/hours I like to work

- Best ways to communicate with me (e.g., Slack will get you the quickest response; I prefer texts for emergencies only)

- Ways I like to receive constructive, corrective, and possibly difficult feedback (e.g., face-to-face so I can talk through it; via email so I have time to think and calm down before responding)

- Things I need (e.g., time to reflect on new ideas; authenticity)

- Things I struggle with (e.g., I need to understand a greater purpose; it takes me a while to trust people)

- Things I love (e.g., brainstorming; working alongside others; experimenting with new ideas)

- Other things to know about me (e.g., I'm inspired by x; I don't drink alcoholic beverages)

Create a team-building experience

Are there things you wish you knew about new team members but were too afraid to ask? Consider a facilitated session. To ensure anonymity, a facilitator asks team members to answer a few questions: Where do you want to grow this year as a manager or individual contributor? Where do you want to grow this year as a team? What's hanging you up right now? What are your preferred ways of absorbing and learning new information? How can your new leader support you?

The facilitator compiles the answers and shares them with the new leaders. The new leader privately reviews them with the facilitator and reflects on responses. They agree to answer all the questions and concerns of the team. Note that some questions or comments may not be answerable. For example, "Why were you selected?" or "When will the organization be done with restructurings?" Typically, the new leader's answers stimulate further areas of discussion for the team. I've found these exercises to be successful in accelerating bonding in the early days of forming a team, especially as these discussions can debunk the stories in our heads that keep us from honest relationship building.

Send a thirty-sixty-ninety-day survey

It's never too early to assess employee sentiment in your organization. Start as soon as someone begins the onboarding process, then continue to collect information about engagement at your organization and analyze the data across demographic groups. This will serve as your starting point to identify strengths and areas of opportunity for your organization or team. To engender trust, you have to be committed to transparency and action. If team members don't experience the changes they ask for in these surveys, they will not complete them. Head to Chapter 7 for more on transparency and accountability in surveys.

Facilitate Stronger Connections

Building connections requires that you demonstrate respect and care for all your team members. Before you offer inclusive team-management programs, you may want to participate in racially sensitive management training. There's nothing more anxiety inducing for a BIPOC employee than the thought of being one of a few people of color in an inclusion training. We worry that white people will talk about their whiteness in weird ways. That they will try to compensate for their discomfort by either ignoring us or making racially insensitive comments, such as, "I understand what you're saying. My wife is Latina." Or, "The way you've overcome racism is so inspiring."

Consider how your everyday actions (or inactions) affect the formation of your culture and your propensity for inclusion. While they may seem like small and inconsequential moments—having lunch with the same person every day, or assuming that a BIPOC employee is an introvert when they're actually lonely—all add up to long-standing systemic inequities in the workplace. Those are barriers to inclusion.

A basic building block of nurturing an inclusive culture is to be willing to make room for others. Start to think more consciously about how you connect and engage with your colleagues. When making a decision about whether to invite someone to coffee or to join your project or to represent the organization, try an exercise of substitution, where you substitute one person for another, and ask yourself: Would I still feel the same way? Would I still respond the same way? Check yourself and ask: Why do I feel that way about someone? Do I have a tendency to identify what's wrong with someone instead of what's right or possible? What keeps me from stepping out of my comfort zone?

Proximity and personal interactions lead to stronger social bonds, according to research from Lucille Nahemow and M. Powell Lawton. Be intentional in breaking out of your bubble, like ensuring that your calendar reflects your stated priorities. How about inviting a Black colleague to coffee, finding out their interests, and then setting up an introduction to broaden their professional network? This can't just be about white people helping and educating themselves by being friendly with BIPOC staff. Those interactions ask BIPOC colleagues for their time, time that could be used for promotable work. If you are asking them for their time, make sure you're offering them something in return as a professional gain. How about seeking to mentor a Latinx colleague new to your organization?

Make a commitment to attend one work event about a racial or other identity group different than yours once a week—for example, events hosted by employee resource groups or diversity-focused industry events—or schedule lunch with a coworker different from you. Whether you are a white or BIPOC manager, be sure you are setting aside time regularly to cultivate BIPOC staff. Make sure you are attuned to each staffer's unique needs, so that you know you are clearing a path for their success and advancement. Then add these actions to your calendar as you would any recurring meeting. It is also important to create a workplace environment where BIPOC colleagues have a sense of belonging, which means honoring, celebrating, and considering differences. If a team member is an observant Muslim, be considerate about their prayer times and fasting during Ramadan. Be mindful of phrases and colloquialisms that trivialize the existence and culture of Indigenous colleagues, such as "powwow" and "tribe."

As a manager, try to keep an eye on team interactions and workplace friendships. Social networks can enable promotions and provide professional opportunities, but BIPOC staff on predominantly white teams are often socially isolated. To be a BIPOC professional is often to be alone on a business team or within a company. Who on the team is well networked, and who appears to be flying solo? Compound that isolated feeling with the known loneliness and invisibility concerns of many remote workers, and a BIPOC team member can feel additionally deserted on a remote team. Most humans can recognize when someone is pulling back from a crowd, but signs that someone on your team is isolated could include: they only talk about work and make no room for small talk, stop offering input, skip optional meetings, eat lunch alone at their desk, keep their office door closed, don't show their image on video calls, or don't seem to connect with other colleagues.

It's unfortunately common for BIPOC to have been undervalued, stalled, underpaid, held back for advancement, belittled, sabotaged, undermined, and pushed out of majority white organizations. They are often bringing that added weight and trauma into a new work-place and may be coming in on edge, on guard, and slow to trust. If you suspect this is happening, take time to speak with the person privately. Before you launch into solutions, ask directly about how they are feeling about the work environment. Then ask if they would be open to suggestions for more support, whether it's connecting them with an affinity group, a BIPOC mentor, or paid mental health services that can help unpack microaggressions.

Additionally, as their manager, make a concerted effort to create moments for idea sharing and cross-team communication. Seek out (but don't mandate) intersectional perspectives in processes, projects, and initiatives and facilitate conversations. Think about ways to promote collaboration across your team. It could be as simple as moving your desk structure and swapping seating. It could look like assigning different team members to projects or pairing up team members who would not normally work together as project leaders. Roanhorse Consulting, an Indigenous-women-led think tank, encourages co-leadership. "The idea that one person is supposed to know everything is antithetical to how I grew up and was taught by my community, which is that we all have gifts to give," says Vanessa Roanhorse. "So instead we have created a think trust, or a group of people who share the responsibility of making choices, and lean on each other." This type of nonhierarchical and nontraditional (and therefore different from a white standard) structure could have some profound benefits, like allowing for more creative solutions from multiple perspectives and building that vital team trust.

Create opportunities for social interaction that are not just about funny memes, happy hours, and team outings (though those are good too). Open channels with an intersectional lens for employees to connect with one another—for example, community groups—and to voice concerns and bring forth ideas. (Note: be prepared to act on those concerns and ideas. That's Chapter 7.)

To combat social isolation, Culture Amp experimented with a Slack-bot called Donut that pairs up employees on a virtual coffee date. Every three weeks, participants receive an automated message that starts a chat between two randomly selected employees. Conversation starters were shared, but the aim was to create a setting where you didn't have to talk about work. "The focus was to foster a sense of connectedness," says Stacey Nordwall, people program lead at Culture Amp. It worked. After two years the program is still going strong. She says there are close to one hundred people in the dedicated Slack channel at any given time, sharing photos of their meetings and a quick recap of what they talked about so everyone can learn more about each other.

That said, forced pairings can also go awry if they feel like a time waster. Maybe try a few rounds, and if people are clamoring for more, do more. But don't automate anything regularly just because people are afraid to tell their boss or peers that something is wrong. It's important to also give thought to how you structure pairings aimed at building connections. For example, in a dinner party you would pair people who have something in common, like an interest or hobby. To avoid the awkwardness that is inevitable in forced pairings, I've found that offering prompts—such as "Is there a specific moment in your career that has shaped how you think or go about work?" or "The biggest misconception people have about me or my role is . . ."—can help break the ice and lead to meaningful conversations. For a broader set of questions, check out the Proust questionnaire, named for the French novelist who favored this type of game to understand the true nature of an individual. Some questions include: Which talent would you most like to have? What is the trait you most deplore in others? What is your idea of perfect happiness?

Beyond everyday connections, learning about one another's racial identity, culture, and heritage leads to a stronger team community. One of my favorite team-building questions is "What was your favorite childhood meal and why?" I love to see how often people who grew up with vastly different cultural and socioeconomic backgrounds can find an instant connection through foods of their past and present. It's important to normalize difference but not at the expense of those who bear the burden of being different.

Build Empathy Muscles

The best workplaces are built on trust and respect. Here's a basic formula for building it: authenticity + consistency + empathy. People trust you when they believe they're interacting with the real you (authenticity), when they have faith in your fairness over time (consistency), and when they believe you care about their feelings, needs, and success (empathy). Miscommunication, assumptions, omissions, fear, misdirection, bias, and silence destroy workplaces, and they disproportionately harm BIPOC workers.

To fuel workplace connections, Dr. Brené Brown cites the four attributes of empathy from nursing scholar Theresa Wiseman:

1. Try to understand another's perspective.

2. Be nonjudgmental.

3. Try to identify another's feelings.

4. Communicate back the emotion you see.

The first step can be the most challenging when you can't fully understand what it's like to walk in another's shoes. Workplace exclusion is often unconscious, passive, and fueled by a lack of knowledge about what someone else is dealing with. Do able-bodied employees consider that it may be difficult for a wheelchair-using coworker to attend a rooftop lunch meeting when there are no accessible ramps? Probably not, and without understanding what it's like to live as another, those exclusionary practices get repeated. When you seek to know and connect with the people you work with and your consumers, you become more conscious about inclusion.

Privilege-exposing exercises can help. In "White Privilege: Unpacking the Invisible Knapsack," Peggy McIntosh relies on situational context to present a deeper understanding of one's lived experience. To visualize your privilege, McIntosh lists a series of statements to agree or disagree with:

- If I should need to move, I can be pretty sure of renting or purchasing housing in an area I can afford and in which I would want to live.

- I can be pretty sure that my neighbors in such a location will be neutral or pleasant to me.

- I can assume that I won't be perceived as angry, incompetent, childlike, or helpless because of my body.

This exercise can be expanded to reveal white privilege and norms in the workplace. Here are some examples:

- I'm not often interrupted or spoken over during a meeting.

- Coworkers don't confuse me with others of the same race or ethnicity.

- I've never been misgendered or had to correct my colleagues' assumptions about my personal life.

- I've never felt that I had to hide a central part of my identity at work, such as my sexuality, gender identity, disability, immigration status, or mental-health status.

- My manager or my team members have navigated challenges similar to mine.

- I have family members or people in my network who I can ask for advice about my career goals or industry.

- In general, my performance reviews are focused on my work and not my personality, race, culture, or "style."

- I grew up participating in activities, like golfing or skiing, that are common work outings.

- If I make a mistake, I can feel confident that my colleagues won't attribute it to my race.

- I have not been called in to state an opinion on behalf of my race.

- I can feel confident that when I walk into any business meeting, I will be surrounded by people who look like me and who share my background.

- I don't worry that if I express my opinion strongly at work, my colleagues will assume I'm falling into a racial stereotype or that it may be read by others as "angry," "hysterical," or "emotional."

Your answers are important, but thinking about how other team members would answer these questions is even more vital. Who is agreeing with these statements? Who is not? What are the unseen advantages and disadvantages when it comes to getting access and being noticed and evaluated in your workplace? When we give verbal feedback, are we focusing on the behavior, or are we labeling the person? From setting the seats at a meeting to developing the agenda, who or what dictates those actions?

Privilege walks, an exercise that physically illuminates the power of unearned advantages and opportunities, can be helpful in exposing how privilege manifests at work. The idea is simple in concept: all people start from the same line, but they have to take a step forward if they answer no to questions like "Did your parents ever had to work more than one job to support your family?" or "Have you ever been the only person of your race in your department?" They take a step back if they answer yes. It's not only about seeing who ends up where at the end, but rather the process of discovering the many factors outside your control that define where you end up. The first time I did this exercise, I was an executive at Google. By the end of the "walk," I was positioned behind most of my executive peers, most of whom were white or Asian, and closer to my Black and Latinx colleagues. It was a moment of truth for many of us about the silent racial advantages and disadvantages across our teams.

Another activity that enables individuals to assess their privilege is "privilege for sale." In this activity, individuals are given a specific amount of money along with a list of privileges that they can choose to purchase. For those given smaller amounts of money, decisions are often made quickly based on limited resources. For those with larger pots of money, I've seen teams wrestle with existential questions and real-life scenarios that can be jaw-dropping and eye-opening. It can be a highly engaging way to examine what privileges you may have and take for granted.

A downside of these activities for BIPOC coworkers is that privilege is being exposed for white colleagues' benefit and education, but at our cost. Many BIPOC have been pressured to code-switch and cover up their differences from their privileged white colleagues in order to make their coworkers feel more comfortable. Some BIPOC staff can be retraumatized by memories of past struggles that their colleagues are only now seeing. Before considering this or any other exercise in discussing racial privilege at work, think about the feelings of BIPOC staff first. BIPOC team members should be given an opportunity to discuss and run through these exercises, and if any BIPOC staff don't feel comfortable participating, that should be discussed beforehand.

I have worked with senior leaders (mostly white men) who, upon engaging in an exercise to write their own "outsider story"—that is, a moment when they have been an outsider and how that made them feel—have been brought to tears remembering moments when they felt the sting of exclusion. Perhaps they grew up with a lisp or stammer or were teased for being poor or fat. The outsider story technique is used to get majority leaders to shift perspective and build empathy and understanding about others, helping them shape their workplace inclusion narrative. It's important to note that the term "diversity" does not become a catchall for any kind of difference or hardship. If a company's idea of diversity is so broad that a "diverse slate" of candidates can, by their definition, still maintain a whites-only majority, that's a problem. The purpose of this exercise is to help us understand each other through our stories.

Empathy alone won't eliminate exclusionary practices, but it can help sensitize individuals to the struggles that others around them may be facing, thus informing more considerate decision-making. For example, supporting remote work is a primary value of BetterUp, a personalized coaching platform. Yet because all major meetings were held in the company's San Francisco office, remote workers felt detached from the workplace culture and less included. To fix this and build empathy and understanding, CEO and founder Alexi Robichaux established remote weeks, where the whole company worked remotely to understand what it's like to be the person on the video call. Now, post-COVID, we all understand what it's like, but at the time, there was a disconnect between the two teams. They now realized that certain activities that were mainstays during design meetings simply did not work in a remote experience. This test not only increased the teams' understanding and awareness of one another but led to redesigning the structure of meetings.

A day-in-the-life experience can also help bridge understanding. Ford Motor Company has an empathy training program where new engineers strap on a weighted suit to simulate the experience of a pregnant driver. They try to change the radio station and switch gears while their bump bumps into the steering wheel. From this activity, the engineers physically understand the challenges of an eight-months-pregnant woman.

You can also seek out a situation where you're the only one like you in the room at a cultural event, place of worship, or social gathering. This works in virtual spaces as well. Cortney Harding, founder of Friends with Holograms, a virtual reality/augmented reality technology company, created a simulated VR experience to put viewers in the shoes of marginalized people at work. The scene was a typical meeting laden with microaggressions (getting talked down to), micro-invalidations (being ignored), and bias and blind spots in action shown via thought bubbles. "One of the first people to see this was a white guy who was a manager at his family's business," Harding says. "He came in skeptical and did the experience and when he took off the headset, he said, 'That wasn't a conversation, that was an emotional experience.' He then spent an hour unpacking the concept of privilege." The manager subsequently changed the way he ran meetings when he went back to the office the following week, stopping interruptions and making sure he called on equal numbers of men and women. This immersive storytelling and interactive experience is an impactful way for leaders to experience workplace exclusion and practice emotionally charged conversations.

For some of you, this feeling of exclusion is your daily experience, so please skip this. But for others, when doing one of these exercises, take note of how it makes you feel and try to view ideas through different perspectives.

These exercises are meant to help managers unpack how privilege works in everyday situations, why it's hard to see, and why understanding privilege matters for effective allyship and sponsorship. When aha moments happen throughout these exercises, you become empowered to drive change not out of guilt but out of responsibility.

Raise Your Awareness

To truly absorb anti-racism teachings, people need to come to terms with their own racial discomfort and racial missteps and see how they have been holding racism in place. This goes for white managers and BIPOC managers. I've seen BIPOC managers who manage BIPOC staff the way they wish they had been managed.

And I've also experienced BIPOC managers who have been particularly cruel and abusive toward BIPOC employees, often replicating the same management mistreatment they suffered while moving up the corporate ladder. This can be particularly devastating for BIPOC employees who see themselves reflected in their manager.

For any organization, that means that leaders need to educate themselves about race as a sphere of identity, prejudice, and privilege and understand how it impacts BIPOC employees emotionally, mentally, and physically. Admitting you don't know something is the sign of a confident, capable leader. Tap into that quest for knowledge and continue to look for sources to help you better understand privilege and power and how to use that to inform your own behavior. Make it your job to understand how race, unconscious bias, and systemic inequities manifest in your workplace. Question how your experience might be different if you didn't hold the identities that give you privilege, such as your race, class, religion, ability, gender, or sexual orientation. That might look like noticing how often your colleagues use racially insensitive language or when biased language creeps into the promotion decision-making process.

Do your research. If you are white, don't lean on people of color to tell you what to say or do. It's not the marginalized person's job to teach you about how they have been denied access and opportunity, held to harsher standards, or been subject to unfair punishment. Think about how you would want someone to support you, and what you would not want them to say or do. For BIPOC managers, while our education system rarely offers the resources and language we need to combat systemic racism, we can always do our own research to back up our advocacy. BIPOC managers can also be better allies across communities of color. Black, Latinx, Asian, Middle Eastern and North African, Indigenous, and other communities can learn more about each other's specific struggles and sensitivities so that we can build stronger coalitions and collaboration. I know, for me, vision and intent haven't always been enough. I've had to deepen my knowledge and capacity for conflict management to better deal with workplace injustices.

When you do talk to others about the obstacles they face in the workplace, start by requesting their permission. If it's granted, approach this conversation with humility and a learning mindset. You may ask these questions:

- I'm curious about what women, BIPOC, and other underrepresented employees in this organization find most challenging day-to-day—things that I may not notice or that I may have looked away from before. Would you be comfortable sharing some of what you experience?

- If there was one thing you wish your white colleagues would do more of to improve the experience of women, BIPOC, and other underrepresented employees in this organization, what would it be?

- If there was one thing we could stop doing every day, what would it be?

- If you were giving me advice on how to really show up as an inclusive manager, leader, or colleague to make our workplace fair and welcoming, what would you say?

Raising your level of awareness means that you have to recognize that not all members of an underrepresented group experience the workplace the same way. You have to stay attuned to the unique experiences and intersectional identities of your team members. For example, women of color are particularly marginalized and silenced in the workplace. I was once advised by a white male manager to act with the same level of "swagger and attitude" that he brought to a meeting to be taken more seriously. He was convinced that he was offering me golden advice, but, in fact, it was horrible. Instead of placing the burden on himself and the other white male team members to do a better job of listening and collaborating, he placed it on me to act like him. I smiled sheepishly and nodded my head. For one, I thought his behavior was irritating and disrespectful; it would never fly in my Latino household. I also knew that, because I was a young Latina, that same behavior would read as overly confident, cocky, and condescending. And while he was allowed to behave that way, I couldn't afford that risk. I didn't have the confidence then to tell him that, but you should know that is a truth many of us bear.

I have facilitated fishbowl activities, where groups are separated into an inner or outer circle to discuss ideas of identity, belonging, and shared experience. Those in the inner circle have a discussion about a particular question or topic; those in the outer circle listen. The intent is to practice being both a contributor and a listener in group discussions. I've been part of powerful fishbowls, focused on diversity and inclusion in the workplace, that were divided into BIPOC and white groups. White members in the middle circle tend to struggle with discussing their privilege and power. And when it's the white members' turn to listen, they often have emotional outbursts when they hear the harrowing stories of their BIPOC colleagues. I've heard a range of responses, including: "I never realized that the language I take for granted in meetings causes you harm on a daily basis." "I'm ashamed that I have taken the privileges of being white for granted." "I didn't see that I had been inflicting harm on my colleagues." "I'm just realizing now that I'm not the police here. I need to figure out how to call people in, not shut them down." It's one thing to read about racism, and another altogether to listen to your peers speak about the emotional and psychological labor involved in compartmentalizing their identities while in the workplace and in your presence. You must learn about and acknowledge the subtle and systemic discrimination that privileges white workers and impedes BIPOC workers if you intend to change those conditions.

Don't Be Afraid to Name It

Words have power. You know it when an unsolicited compliment brightens your day, or when a careless comment still stings hours later. Through our language, we have the power to reduce stigma, build accountability, and affirm our shared humanity. Fostering inclusive workplaces requires that we pay attention to the language we use. It also requires us to extend grace to ourselves and others to make mistakes, learn, and then do better.

In every role I have held as a diversity, equity, and inclusion leader and consultant, I have been "advised" to use more palatable language. "Instead of racism or oppression, perhaps you could say 'implicit bias'?" "Could you just share the racial demographic data as white versus other? We want to avoid showing the low racial counts." In this case, legal teams are concerned with offering any data that could be used against the company in active lawsuits. And, most recently, "Is it possible to not use the words 'systemic racism'? It causes a level of discomfort that we believe will take away from your powerful message."

Really? Systemic racism, bias, and white male privilege are embedded deeply and widely in our society, and a two-hour workshop or keynote won't stop the weaponization of white womanhood, the complicity of Latinx and Asian Americans in anti-Blackness, the disregard of Indigenous, transgender, and disabled communities, or the persistent stereotypes and racial conflict that prevent interracial understanding and collaboration. There is no quick fix, and using evasive language does little to address the matters at hand.

Language matters. The words we use and the perceptions and images they evoke have a profound impact on how we perceive each other. "Words carry weight, and sometimes that is baggage— cultural, personal, historical," says Dr. Jennifer Sandoval of the University of Central Florida. The United States has a long history of using coded language—the practice of substituting terms describing racial identity with seemingly race-neutral terms—to disguise explicit or implicit racial animus. Coded language is "illegal immigrant" for people from Latin America, "bossy" to describe women who are assertive, or "thug" to describe men of color who aren't necessarily doing anything criminal or violent. This language fosters anxiety and dehumanizes BIPOC. It can also mask discomfort and disconnection. In the workplace, discrediting a Black woman as "angry" or "challenging to manage" is another way to uphold white male standards of professionalism at the expense of anyone who doesn't fit that category. Subjective, coded language isn't just words. How people are perceived and how their performance is reviewed affects who is selected for high-profile assignments, who is promoted, and who is pushed out. Reflect on whether the language you are using has racist or derogatory connotations by asking yourself the following questions:

- What words and phrases do I use that indicate an immediate racial stereotype or negative image of a group?

- When describing a group of people, how can I describe them without using racially coded language that masks my discomfort or disconnectedness from them?

- When in an environment where racially coded language is being used, how can I explain what's really going on and openly discuss how to work through bigoted fears?

We have to name the root cause of the problem—racism—and be willing to reflect on what we downplay and why. We further need to be intentional about the words we use to promote a space of belonging and inclusion for all. It requires us to address the intentional and unconscious racist comments that BIPOC and other marginalized groups have to deal with on a daily basis. White workplace norms were built over decades and function as intended—to preserve white culture and concentrate power in the hands of white males. When these coded terms are unpacked and myths debunked, resist the urge to dwell in fear and shame. Embrace the truth.

Confronting our own privilege, access, and opportunity can be challenging, but it is necessary. One of the notable changes I've witnessed in the wake of the racial unrest following George Floyd's murder is that people now say the words Black, racism, and white supremacy. They no longer whisper these terms.

Instead of focusing on what *not* to say, focus on what to say. One rabbi suggests an exercise in which white people start saying "white" when they talk about their day. Don't just say, "I spoke to our son's teacher." Say, "I spoke to our white son's white teacher." Don't just say, "I bumped into our neighbor/friend/colleague today." State, "I bumped into our white neighbor/friend/colleague today." "I saw a great movie/read a great book/heard a great song about a white couple coming to terms with their issues." Become conscious of whiteness as an everyday practice, in order to see how white supremacy and the exclusion and marginalization of BIPOC have been normalized.

Additionally, look at the hidden meaning of what you're saying. Statements such as "As a woman, I know what you go through as a racial minority," "When I look at you, I don't see color," and "I can't believe this is still happening" are insulting and unhelpful. Researchers classify phrases like these as micro-invalidations, which are "communications that exclude, negate, or nullify the psychological thoughts, feelings, or experiential reality of a person of color." The effect of being told that "we are all humans" or that "all lives matter" is to negate the unique way people of color live in oppression. When you are using such words, particularly jargon or commonly said phrases, question yourself. What do you mean by that word or phrase? Does using it share your meaning or does it hide your meaning? I have been guilty of hiding meaning through my choice of words in an effort to make something more "palatable," but true change cannot happen unless we say what we really mean.

Speaking the language of inclusion is important. As a cisgender, heterosexual woman, I've had to get smart about language and the stigma and barriers faced by my LGBTQ coworkers. I've made an active choice to ask people for their pronouns. I've yet to meet someone who finds it disrespectful. (Note: Please don't use the term "preferred pronouns" when you ask for someone's pronouns. It makes it sound as if using someone's correct pronouns is optional, when it's really a way to acknowledge a person's identity.) I've put Post-it notes on my speech scripts to remind myself to use my pronouns in my introductions, and I display "she/her/ella" in my social media to signal to transgender and nonbinary people that their pronouns will be respected. I'm a fierce and imperfect ally who has to work at it, every day.

Do your research (the terms are always changing) and, when in doubt, ask. Your intent as you enter emotionally complex conversations will have a much stronger impact than whether you say Hispanic, Latina, or Latinx. Be ready to ask questions to learn the right words to use—and be open to being corrected. If you make a mistake, apologize and reflect on your error so you can correct it next time.

Along the way, you will discover that the Inclusion Revolution requires you to break free from corporate speak and begin to recognize the racial systems that protect biased and inequitable language, actions, and behaviors. If you're willing, you may find yourself challenging your peers to push for change alongside you. For white people, simply acknowledging that you have benefited from something that has seriously damaged someone sitting next to you is a good first move. What comes next is an ongoing process of building shared understanding, respect, and, hopefully, trust.

The Hidden Meaning of Language

One of my favorite sources of the hidden meaning of language is Rachel Cargle's Instagram page "The Great Unlearn" (@thegreat unlearn). In it, she edits and dissects white people's comments that she receives to offer "some critical language and a more critical lens as you engage in these conversations in your own spaces." Here's an example:

The statement:

"Yes, systematic racism is real, but lots of white people who seem #blessed are dealing with their own childhood traumas and abuse."

The analysis:

"Yes/But," also known as "whataboutism," is a variant of the "tu quoque" logical fallacy that attempts to discredit an opponent's position by charging them with hypocrisy without directly refuting or disproving their argument. (source: Zimmer, Ben. WSJ, 2017)

The statement:

"Although you are correct, I wish you would have not marked out her name. Her intentions don't seem to be malicious."

The analysis:

She is leaning on the idea that intentions hold more weight than the impact. I use what I was taught: If you accidentally step on someone's foot, you don't ever say, "Oh stop crying, that wasn't my intention." You apologize, acknowledge the pain you caused and walk more carefully and intentionally.

Your Road Map to Revolution

You can design and implement the most inclusive hiring practices in the world, but if the rest of your organization and talent systems do not change, you will still struggle to attract, welcome, and retain racially diverse talent. Instead of just worrying about hiring BIPOC talent, focus on being the kind of manager who treats all team members equitably and with respect. When you lead with an unbiased, people-centric mindset, the rest falls into place. Increasing belonging is powerful and compelling, and also complex to operationalize. Start by paying attention to when the workplace might not work for others.

- **Assess your onboarding process**. What's the first impression you're making for a new hire? How can you customize the experience for each person to set them up for success? This is not about access to email, but access to others who will be vital on their professional journey. A buddy system can be incredibly effective.

- **Personalize your onboarding process**. Beyond administrative tasks and personal preferences, are there cultural, religious, or ability needs that must be considered? What will help this person be most successful? Ask them!

- **Facilitate stronger connections**. Create stronger team bonds in an authentic and results-driven way, whether it's through structured conversations or spontaneous sharing moments. Look out for employees who may feel isolated from the team and provide avenues of support.

- **Build empathy muscles to establish trust**. You can do this through privilege-exposing and day-in-the-life exercises to understand what the work environment is like for others. Also consider VR experiences that allow you to see what it's like for marginalized employees at work.

- **Recognize the impact of your words**. Understand that words come with meaning, that what you say is not always what you mean, and that you may be interpreted differently and held accountable for any harm. Normalize asking for pronouns and notice when you use coded words. On your journey to conscious communication, you may make some slips. It's only natural. Don't let it stop your progress. Learn from it and try again.

6

SET PSYCHOLOGICAL SAFETY IN MOTION

W HAT MAKES A perfect team? In 2012, Google set out to find the answer. Would it be bringing together the smartest people? Those who have similar work styles? A diverse mix of backgrounds? After months of research, they came to this conclusion: "The 'who' part of the equation didn't seem to matter." The most successful teams, the ones who hit their goals and seemed to have the strongest bonds, shared key behaviors like showing empathy for each other and taking turns in conversations. They all expressed a feeling of psychological safety, which allowed them to share more ideas, have impactful debates, and work together to achieve the best results.

People on these successful teams lowered their walls and felt safe to do so. That's the premise of psychological safety: it's the belief that you won't be punished for making a mistake or sharing your opinions, whatever they may be. In today's rapidly shifting workplace landscape, it is critical to have and engage the voices that can question the status quo, call out potential issues, and be heard without the risk of being punished. That should be a given, right? Not quite.

141

In an ideal world, every one of your team members and colleagues feels safe and comfortable to share their raw truth and speak truth to power, but that vulnerability doesn't always come easy—especially for BIPOC, junior employees, or those who are most risk averse and afraid of losing their jobs. If you sense this—and, frankly, even if you don't—you must prioritize creating a culture of psychological safety that empowers and encourages people to speak their truth. When you create safe spaces at work where employees can speak up, they believe their voice is welcome and that your team and organization are worth dedicating time and energy to. Amy Edmondson, who identified the concept of psychological safety in teams in 1999, describes it as creating a space where new ideas and concepts are both encouraged and accepted. In other words, psychological safety keeps people engaged, productive, and motivated.

Creating a culture of psychological safety starts with trust, and trust starts with you. Take a step back to rethink how you engage with your colleagues and teams and how you respond to their experiences. Whether it's starting conversations about white fragility or holding department meetings calling out racially charged incidents when they happen, you can send a powerful message as an ally in a position of influence.

You can also codify a new set of behavioral expectations that foster psychological safety. Doing this will lead to strong business performance, suggests research by McKinsey. Once these are in place, offer trainings that reinforce key principles, including open dialogue to explore disagreements and talk through tensions on teams; cultural awareness, to better understand norms in different cultures; situational awareness, to develop a better understanding of what is going on around you and its implications for how people are treated; situational humility, my favorite, which encourages a growth mindset and curiosity; and sponsorship, to functionally equip managers with tools and techniques to enable others' success.

Vulnerability Can Lead to Radical Participation

If you educate yourself about common workplace microaggressions, you can be more vigilant and do more to support BIPOC colleagues. For example, Black women in particular are often silenced through tone policing, where their comments are dismissed merely because of a white listener's feelings about the way they were delivered. Comments such as "You're being too sensitive," "It was just a joke. Calm down," or "I don't know why you're making such a big deal about this" make Black women doubt the legitimacy of their own reactions, judgments, or feelings about racial slights. You can prevent and delegitimize this behavior in the moment, or later in private, by saying something to the perpetrator like, "I love a good joke, but that was not a joke" or "It may not have been your intent, but your comments were inappropriate and hurtful."

One of my superpowers is my depth of empathy and my willingness to be vulnerable with my teams and colleagues. This plays out behind closed doors when I'm able to quell discord between team members, to discern subtle shifts in teams and culture, and to draw out the quieter team members. But these same leadership skills have also been dismissed as weakness. Some find my methods of infusing inclusion, transparency, and a racial lens in my management practices a threat to a workplace culture that has traditionally been skewed toward the success and dominance of white leaders.

Vulnerability doesn't diminish my capacity to lead; it enhances it. BIPOC staff are not a threat to white people's professional success. Finding ways to help BIPOC staff feel safe leads to the entire company's success. It makes no sense to isolate certain staff members to the point where they don't feel safe to make creative and meaningful contributions. The best teams trust each other, and to build trust, a manager must allow for vulnerability and create safety for everyone.

How can someone be candid and vulnerable with you if you're not vulnerable with them? Entering conversations about race, inequity, and exclusion as a white person can feel bewildering, scary, and antagonizing. Say so! If you are a BIPOC manager, it's important that you assert your boundaries. It's OK to pull a leader or workshop facilitator aside before a discussion and say, "I don't want to be called upon to represent the Black experience during the discussion."

Share your experiences—the good and the not-so-good—honestly and vulnerably with your teams or colleagues. In my experience, they will be thankful for the opportunity to have a real conversation where they, too, can become comfortable sharing the uncomfortable. You may start your conversations by admitting your nervousness or expressing your intentions. One past consulting client of mine, a white woman, did this when launching a diversity business council: "I want to begin by sharing that I'm an introvert and these conversations make me really nervous. I mostly worry about disappointing you. My hope is that we can create a safe space for everyone. I also want to acknowledge that I'm sure that there is a lot that I don't know and ask for your grace as we navigate these uncertain waters together. Above all, please don't let me be narrow in what I expect or do."

Powerful, right? I could see everyone in that meeting, mostly BIPOC and junior employees, breathe a collective sigh of relief. They put their walls down. Any previous apprehension or misgivings were put aside temporarily. She replaced criticism with curiosity, admitted her fears, and encouraged feedback. The group was ready and willing to listen and share. What followed was a productive, engaging, and illuminating conversation about the path forward, where all employees were able to openly discuss the barriers they faced in building the workplace that they deserved.

That was a winning moment, but I'm not going to sugarcoat how hard it is for people to drop the superficial office talk and have a real, honest conversation. The questions you need to ask of those on your team—What is preventing you from feeling like you belong? How easy is it to discuss difficult issues or problems on your team?

How often have you experienced unwanted conduct, such as bias or bullying?—can be painful for all.

Getting people to open up is challenging when it's not anonymized. It's important to note that vulnerability can be harder for BIPOC employees who have experienced the sting of racial stereotyping. Managers should be aware of racial imposter syndrome, which gives rise to feelings of self-doubt and makes BIPOC employees afraid to reveal what they don't know. This can also hurt their ability to learn and grow, so you need to find ways to draw them out and make them feel safe and supported when they make mistakes.

I get it. There are things I say now that I never would have blurted out twenty years ago. At a recent executive meeting of mostly white men, we were discussing the leadership traits we believed were necessary to accelerate our company's growth. The group seemed to quickly form consensus on a "benevolent dictatorship" leadership style for centralizing decision-making.

For me, this conversation was hugely uncomfortable. I grew up with grandparents and an entire community who survived a thirty-year brutal dictatorship in the Dominican Republic. As a result, I'm heavily inclined to question many of the institutions and leaders we put our faith into. In that meeting, I felt safe enough to speak my truth. I said, "Most people don't know this about me, but I have an uneasy relationship with people in authority, and this language causes me emotional discomfort. Further, there is a racially systemic root to this. I don't think we should run this company like any kind of dictatorship." Hierarchies benefit white people, and the workplace is built in a hierarchical way. If the executive ranks are all white and all the BIPOC are junior staffers, there is no way a "benevolent dictatorship" is going to be racially inclusive. A dictatorship is never a good business model when you acknowledge that good ideas can come from people at any level. Now my boss and my peers know my truth, and I created a space for others to speak theirs. I felt a responsibility to share a different point of view that could lead us toward a more inclusive leadership approach. And I could do it because I felt safe. I didn't feel that there was a risk of losing respect from my peers or losing my job.

Why did I feel that way? For one, I am in a senior executive position and confident when standing my ground. But it was really about trust. I knew that I had earned my team's trust. And that I didn't need to convince the team and my boss with anything more than my truth. Fear is real, but trust is what allows for conversations that build meaning and create connections. When our brain senses safety, it activates a signal to trust and open up. As a result, we are more open to share, discover, and collaborate, all leading to higher levels of partnering, trust, and a sense of belonging.

Another spark for inclusive conversations is to host panels, lunch and learns, speaker forums, and other event series centered on previously untouchable topics. The tech company Asana launched a Real Talk event series to share others' lived experiences, such as a panel of Latinx engineers across different tech backgrounds from Google, Slack, Airbnb, and Threadloom who discussed the impact of cultural identity on their careers. These events are common and can energize teams. I say, hold as many as your business will permit. The key is to not let the information fall flat, but rather to use these discussions as an opportunity to launch additional conversations with your direct reports. What did they think about what they heard? Have they had similar experiences? What other topics would they want to talk about?

Keep these conversations going. Leaders can build psychological safety by creating the right climate, mindsets, and behaviors within their teams.

Psychological Safety: Do You Have It?

In his book *Think Again*, Adam Grant notes that psychological safety begins with admitting our mistakes and welcoming criticism from others. He goes on to further codify what it is and what it isn't.

When you have it:

- Seeing mistakes as opportunities to learn
- Being willing to take risks and fail
- Speaking your mind in meetings
- Openly sharing your struggles
- Trusting in your teammates and supervisors
- Sticking your neck out

When you don't:

- Seeing mistakes as threats to your career
- Being unwilling to rock the boat
- Keeping your ideas to yourself
- Only touting your strengths
- Fearing your teammates and supervisors
- Having your head chopped off

Foster a Speak-Up Culture

Psychological safety for BIPOC employees starts at the top of the organization. Treating all staff the same does not acknowledge the social and economic inequities BIPOC may have faced before they joined the organization. In our search for an equal playing field, we may end up losing sight of the unique needs among BIPOC and white communities. That is, a BIPOC employee early in their career may need you to reduce more obstacles to their success due to racial and structural bias. If it's a norm for a white, male executive to use swear words, yell, be combative, and tease as a form of hazing and camaraderie, that needs to be reexamined. In his recent memoir, Barack Obama said he found this specific behavior from his senior white male colleague to be invigorating but didn't realize that when he wasn't in the room, those same behaviors made women and BIPOC staff uncomfortable. Valerie Jarrett called him out on this, and Obama spoke privately to Rahm Emanuel and other white male leaders to say they needed to knock it off; their work style was intimidating their team members.

Start by role modeling and reinforcing the behaviors you expect. Every time you seek out and act on opinions from junior colleagues of color, you send a powerful message of inclusion to your teams. Every time you publicly acknowledge a racialized misstep—such as calling one of your Black employees the wrong name by mistake—you signal to others that it is safe to do so. This further empowers your senior leaders and managers to overcome their fears, identify where they're falling short, and take steps to be a more effective advocate.

Employees are more likely to exhibit inclusive leadership if their managers exhibit these behaviors. For example, do leaders in your organization seek out opinions that might differ from their own on a regular basis? Do your managers treat others with respect? When staff challenge a manager's ideas, how does the manager react? Are they defensive, or do they listen and incorporate different ideas?

Modeling good habits can help recapture the immediacy and companionship of working in an office together. When kicking off a project, talk about how you expect your team to work together and explain that the process matters as much as the result. Be respectful of other people's ideas and comments, even if you disagree. Saying, "That's a helpful perspective" or "I'm really glad you brought up that point" proves that you welcome fresh ideas. Challenging ideas. Nonconformist ideas. Psychological safety is not about rewarding individuals and teams that only share what you want to hear. The goal is not to secure your comfort; it's to create a climate where people can speak up and challenge ideas without fear. It's equally important to act on team members' good ideas and corrective suggestions. Don't just listen for show. If your teams don't believe you'll incorporate their ideas, they won't contribute.

It's time to welcome challenging conversations about power, privilege, access, and opportunity. Both white and BIPOC managers can be so afraid of making a mistake or saying the wrong thing that they don't say or do anything. White colleagues are often ill-equipped to talk about race and unwilling to address their own complicity in systemic racism. I've often heard white managers say that they are reluctant to engage in conversations about racism because they fear being slapped down. On the flip side, BIPOC are afraid of deepening racial divisions and worry about their own personal safety and job security if they raise racial tensions. Much too often, employees simply want to know that their managers care. Instead, they are often left with a vacuum of acknowledgment or a sense of shame about what they're experiencing at home or at work.

The real enemy of inclusivity and equity is silence and inaction. Asking questions—of yourself and others—and listening deeply can help you overcome uncomfortable silences, social distance, and awkward exchanges. You will come out of it more empowered, motivated, and inspired to start looking at your colleagues, policies, and practices in a new light.

A speak-up culture doesn't happen overnight. A culture of fear exists because of well-founded concerns. Your job as a people manager is to create a supportive space where your team members will feel listened to and understood. This requires that you show real care and respect for your people and that you're willing to listen to raise your understanding, not to fix a problem or convince others of what you believe. It further requires you to open yourself to what your colleagues have to share and be willing to challenge your own assumptions.

Show commitment to progress for each of your team members by not letting fear hold you back from creating a safe team environment where every employee can thrive.

How much space do dominant voices take up in your organization? If your colleagues say their voices are not being heard in meetings, turn the spotlight on them, use your own voice to amplify the ideas of those who are continuously sidelined and silenced. Female aides adopted this amplification strategy in Obama's White House to avoid having their voices ignored by the predominantly male room. When a woman spoke up, other women would repeat her point or idea, giving back credit to the original speaker, according to the *Washington Post*. This forced the men to listen and rendered them unable to steal credit for the idea. "We just started doing it, and made a purpose of doing it," one former Obama aide told the *Post*. "Obama noticed, and began calling more often on women and junior aides." Amplification pacts work. I've known colleagues who buddied up and committed to publicly backing each other, so that if one of them spoke up against a microaggression in a meeting, they knew their buddy would amplify their words. It is essential for allyship to exist across gender and race; men can ensure that they repeat and credit women's ideas, and white people can commit to speaking up if a racist microaggression occurs in a meeting.

Ask yourself: In what ways am I behaving like a domineering leader and not so much like one who sparks the initiative and imagination of my entire team? How can I actively improve access to decision-making meetings? How do I challenge coded language and behavior when certain identities take up more space than others, physically or verbally? When was the last time that I amplified the voice of an underrepresented member of my team with a "plus one" or by saying, "That's an important idea. Let's hear more"? How do I decide who talks in a meeting?

As a manager, you should refrain from dismissing or tuning out ideas that don't align with your own. I am mindful of ensuring my team feels heart and regarded in decision-making, even if I don't ultimately use their suggestions. Often I will say, "I haven't heard from Tatiana or Walter, who are closest to this work. Did you have anything to add?" Some people are introverts and don't like to speak up, but those who have been systematically and consistently ignored in meetings, been mansplained to, or had their ideas stolen may need a supportive manager who gives people the option to contribute.

The Four Stages of Psychological Safety

Another way to look at psychological safety is along a continuum of four stages, developed by social scientist Timothy R. Clark, in which human beings feel (1) included, (2) safe to learn, (3) safe to contribute, and (4) safe to challenge the status quo—all without fear of being embarrassed, marginalized, or punished in some way. Moving through these four stages enables individuals and organizations to create higher levels of inclusion, collaboration, innovation, and belonging. If you and your team feel all four, you will see a rise in confidence, engagement, happiness, and performance.

Stage 1. Inclusion safety (connect and belong)

Inclusion safety allows us to operate without fear of rejection, embarrassment, or punishment and boosts confidence, resilience, and independence. When we create inclusion safety for others, regardless of our differences, we acknowledge our shared humanity and reject false theories of superiority.

Stage 2. Learner safety (learn and grow)

Learner safety means we feel safe to engage in all aspects of the learning process: asking questions, giving and receiving feedback, experimenting, and making mistakes. It's important to note here that BIPOC have good reason to fear harsher punishment for making mistakes compared to their white colleagues. As novelist

Celeste Ng put it, privilege is about who is allowed to make mistakes. When we sense learner safety, we're more willing to be vulnerable, take risks, make mistakes, and develop resilience in the learning process. Conversely, a lack of learner safety triggers the self-censoring instinct, causing us to shut down, retrench, and manage personal risk. Managers need to ensure that all staff, including BIPOC staff, know that there is a company commitment to their success and that, as appropriate, mistakes will be met with support, not punishment.

Stage 3. Contributor safety (be heard and make a difference)

When contributor safety is present, we feel safe to participate as a full member of the team, using our skills and abilities in the value-creation process. We lean into what we're doing with energy and enthusiasm. We are encouraged to draw out our best efforts. What does this look like? A sense of autonomy, guidance, and encouragement in exchange for effort and results.

Stage 4. Challenger safety (better outcomes)

Challenger safety provides the support and confidence we need to ask questions such as, "Why do we do it this way?" "What if we tried this?" and "How might we?" It allows us to feel safe to challenge the status quo, without the risk of retaliation or damaging our personal standing or reputation. It allows us to overcome the pressure to conform and gives us a license to innovate and be creative. This includes safety for BIPOC to speak up when conventional wisdom or a traditional practice is biased or racist. As a manager, you should know that this might make team members feel defensive and uncomfortable at first. Good managers will thank people for speaking up and course correcting.

Be an Intentional Ally

"Early in my career, I had a hard time contributing in meetings," writes Fran Hauser, author of *The Myth of the Nice Girl*. "I had a boss who would call me before a meeting and say, 'Fran, in today's meeting I am going to ask you to give everyone an update on the restructuring.' This gave me time to prepare my thoughts and contribute in a way that felt comfortable to me. Before long, it became natural to speak up and I didn't need a prompt." Tom Carmazzi, CEO of manufacturing corporation Tuthill, asks employees to write their thoughts on index cards and stick the cards to the wall to give everyone a chance to share their opinion without having to raise a hand. It's equitable anonymity, which creates safety for honest feedback.

Back in the early part of my career, I joined a client meeting at Moody's. As we were going around the table, getting to know each other and sharing stories about our childhoods, a senior analyst turned to me and asked, "Daisy, answer me this. Why do all Dominicans play baseball?" I instantly felt my stomach sink. I felt minimized by that cultural cliché and embarrassed that I needed to respond to it in front of my peers and clients. I stumbled for a bit and weakly said, "Well, some of us become credit analysts." The table laughed, and we moved on. Or so I thought.

A few days later, I debriefed Nicole Johnson, our team's manager, who happened to be an openly gay white woman. I mentioned the exchange as part of my review, and the discomfort that I had felt. I was worried at first, but to my surprise, she instantly expressed a deep sense of empathy and jumped into action. She called for an investigation by HR, which I didn't even know was an available resource, and took immediate steps to ensure that senior analysts and managers would never make insensitive and inappropriate comments like that again. Teams were trained on cultural sensitivity; the senior analyst received coaching and offered a sincere apology to me.

To be fair, it was awkward. But it was the jolt the team needed to place more attention on power differentials and cultural insensitivities. It was a start and a positive model for me and others of what we should expect from our leaders. My boss, Johnson, modeled allyship by disrupting a seemingly harmless social exchange. By advocating for me and seeking a resolution that would not leave me feeling isolated and unsafe, she helped me see the agency I had to effect change for myself and others.

Not everyone is as courageous as she is, but we all can learn to be. Her allyship came with solidarity and action.

When Freada Kapor Klein was asked to speak on a diversity in tech panel at the MIT Sloan Tech Conference, she said, "Great, have you asked underrepresented people of color to be judges? Because if it's not a diverse team, I'm happy to give up my seat. I don't participate in events where it's all-white anything." This is common practice for Kapor Klein. Actions and statements like this from allies shift behavior and expectations.

Being an ally means more than just recognizing your privilege and agreeing that people from traditionally underrepresented groups should be valued and accepted. It means normalizing speaking up against passive-aggressive racist statements, calling attention to the emotional and psychological labor of marginalized groups, and learning from your mistakes. Being an ally starts with empathy.

Allyship that doesn't come with solidarity and action is performative. Critical theorist bell hooks tells us, "Solidarity is not the same as support. To experience solidarity, we must have a community of interests, shared beliefs and goals around which to unite.... Support can be occasional. It can be given and just as easily withdrawn. Solidarity requires sustained, ongoing commitment." In fact, solidarity is about sacrificing your own comfort and convenience for that of others. If you see your team members (including BIPOC) making statements that are racist, sexist, or ableist, overtly or subtly, shut it down. Stand up in those moments. You're in a position to create a safe space, and it is your responsibility to do so. Take that responsibility seriously.

The disconnect in what allyship means has led to a complicated feeling when it comes to the term. Research by Lean In and Survey-Monkey shows that more than 80 percent of white women and men say they see themselves as allies to colleagues of other races and ethnicities, but less than half of Black women and only slightly more than half of Latinas feel they have strong allies at work. Your team members can smell performative allyship and virtue signaling a mile away.

Allyship can look and feel like many different things based on your starting point and what you're trying to achieve. It's important to have a shared understanding of allyship, because, without it, attempted allyship can add unintentional harm or insult to the groups you hope to support. This disconnect points to something fundamental: wanting to be an ally doesn't mean you are an ally. There are no certificates or capes for allies. If you have to name yourself an ally, you should question why someone doesn't recognize you as one.

For some, it may be about fulfilling a desire to be seen as a good person. For example, you act on behalf of others, particularly friends or colleagues you see being hurt or disrespected. Others think of allyship as bringing justice or equity into the world. They see working to correct systems of oppression as a moral obligation.

Allyship is:

- **Not self-defined**. Allyship should validate the marginalized, not those practicing allyship. You can't give yourself an ally badge. But you should frame the work this way: "We are showing support for x. We are using our privilege to help y."

- **Not an identity**. Allyship is a continuous process of learning and building relationships through trust, consistency, and accountability. There's not one book to read or box to check when it comes to allyship.

- **Action through solidarity**. It's easier to say you're an ally than act like one. You should address issues alongside those who face marginalization, not in front of them paternalistically or behind them timidly.

- **Self-aware**. An ally is keenly aware of how their own history impacts their attitude, beliefs, and behaviors. This requires an understanding and acknowledgment of your privilege and power.

An accomplice—a sister term to ally—takes risks and makes material sacrifices to actively challenge the status quo that has been designed to benefit them. An accomplice will advance fairness and equity while working within organizational power structures. These terms are not interchangeable but are both key to understanding the role you can play in advancing inclusion.

My favorite term to use is "upstander." The term, coined by diplomat Samantha Power and shared widely by global nonprofit Facing History and Ourselves, refers to someone who speaks out and stands up for justice on behalf of others. It calls for reflection, compassion, understanding beyond oneself, and, perhaps most important, courage. An upstander pays attention to the news so they're not uninformed about how the lives of their employees and colleagues are impacted by forces outside the workplace.

There are slight differences to these terms, and you can choose to be an ally, accomplice, *and* upstander. Cultivating the role you choose, and the time you choose to exercise it, will help you build more racially inclusive and welcoming workplaces. That means being willing to notice and interrupt racially charged behavior, such as constant interruptions or dismissive language in a meeting or workshop, emailing someone's manager to let them know their team member is doing a great job, or asking probing questions during a performance review to challenge bias in feedback.

Mitigate Microaggressions

Great managers protect their employees from racial toxicity and enable them to do their best work. If you are a manager who acknowledges the need for greater diversity in your workplace, you also have to acknowledge your workplace's racial inequities and past harms when it comes to race. This requires an examination of your personal and organizational history. Why are most of the people that you've hired white? Have you prioritized retention and upward movement of BIPOC staff? White managers should seek to understand their own history—what they have inherited and what they have perhaps unwittingly replicated—and reflect on whether they have actively or passively maintained a racially segregated norm. BIPOC managers also have to consider whether they have—unintentionally or out of fear—prioritized white colleagues' comfort in ways that make life more difficult for other BIPOC who are coming up in the company. If managers are unable to be brutally honest with themselves, they won't be able to help create and sustain a welcoming workplace for all.

You gain strength, courage, and confidence when you know who you are relative to others. The mirror may reveal that your own behavior and the practices that you have been upholding are not connecting to your values. You may consider yourself liberal or social-justice oriented, but now your data may reveal contradictions. A natural tendency is to ignore what you see, withdraw, explain it away, or deny it. But you need to face it. DeRay Mckesson, civil rights activist, says, "Protest is telling the truth in public." Part of holding up a mirror is facing ourselves, doing something about it, and not letting that reflection fade away. We can use our words and our actions in the service of revolutionary protest to tell the truth, force a response, and set into motion change that won't be undone.

Have you ever been left wondering whether a vaguely insulting comment at work is an expression of racism, sexism, ageism, or ableism? "Wait, did she ask for my ethnic heritage because she wants

157

to get to know me or because she doesn't believe me to be American?" For BIPOC, that is a very familiar, tiresome, and distressing feeling. We live in a racially charged American culture that has socialized giant taboos around race and normalized harmful racist stereotypes. When these comments offend, upset, or hurt you, you're left worrying that confronting the microaggression may lead to defensiveness, denial, and worse, gaslighting. The sting of stigma is harshest when you're left to fend for yourself.

Microaggressions are "the everyday slights, indignities, putdowns, and insults that people of color, women, LGBTQ populations, or those who are marginalized experience in their day-to-day interactions with people," according to Dr. Derald W. Sue. They can be expressed verbally or through body language. Imagine a white woman clutching her bag when a Black man enters an elevator. There are degrees of intensity within microaggressions, from micro-invalidations (subtle denial of a person's feeling, experience, or thoughts; "I was only joking") to micro-insults (comments that demean or discredit; "She's so bossy"), to micro-assaults (explicit attacks; "That's so gay"). They can make a workplace feel hostile and toxic and can impact performance, relationships, retention, workplace culture, and company morale.

Whenever I've been the target of a microaggression, my rule of thumb is to collect my thoughts and emotions before addressing the aggressor, respond assertively and with "I" statements. "When you restated my comment in the meeting without giving me credit, I felt undermined." "When you referred to me as articulate, I felt as if you assumed that I shouldn't be." "When you confused me for the other Latinx person in the room, I felt as if we were both invisible to you." If you've witnessed a microaggression and are not part of the group being marginalized by the comment or action, do not speak on their behalf. This could be unintentionally dehumanizing and belittling. Instead of saying, "You offended them," you may say, "Here's why I'm upset or hurt by your comments."

To be clear, it is not the responsibility of women, BIPOC, or members of marginalized communities to make workplaces micro-aggression free. But there are ways of responding that can lead to constructive conversations and outcomes, if both parties are willing.

Proactive interventions and diversity training programs that are part of a well-structured diversity, equity, and inclusion road map can help get ahead of toxic behavioral patterns and mitigate microaggressions. A facilities management company hired a vendor to train in-house diversity peer counselors who could volunteer to mediate conflict arising from microaggressions. This was meant to create a safe place for positive change, outside of HR, for when microaggressions need to be corrected but don't arise to HR levels of discipline and termination. BIPOC in a company may prefer using this option, as they may be fearful of reporting to HR. Often the BIPOC in the company are junior staff, and the people demeaning them are—sadly—their bosses. If you consider trying a peer counselor program like this, you should compensate the peer counselors for taking on this responsibility beyond their normal job descriptions.

Tailor your training to the unique issues of each industry, organization, and team. One global law firm hired Steps, a drama-based training company, to design and deliver a program to ensure every partner understood how their behavior supported or hindered an inclusive environment. Steps interviewed staff members of color—across all divisions, departments, and seniority levels—and asked them to provide anonymous examples of microaggressions and systemic racism in their workplace. Steps then presented their findings in a video, anonymizing the stories and using actors to dramatize the scenes. One scene showed a white partner struggling to have a conversation with a Black associate. The partner was well-intentioned and wanted to be supportive, but the fear of doing or saying the wrong thing likely kept them from providing the kind of support their Black colleagues needed to grow and develop.

Actors would stay in character, and the moderator would allow staff to question the actors about how they felt during the scene. The scenarios showed the kinds of interactions the company engaged in every day, to demonstrate how discrimination had crept in. For many staff members, it was revelatory. "People have no idea of the impact of what they do and what they say," says Liz Jones, USA country head of Steps. "It's so often unconscious and unintentional. Most people don't come to work with the specific motive of making your day miserable. They come with a positive intent. That's why these exercises are so impactful, because you can see the impact of a wrongly placed word or tone. It makes you think, I wouldn't want anyone to feel that way."

Company initiatives like this can encourage agency and action from people at all levels. They alleviate the pressure on managers to design from scratch. They help leaders imagine what they can do to demonstrate equitable and inclusive leadership. And they help everyone hold the entire organization accountable for high performance in equity and inclusion.

Are your employees hungry for more ways to help but aren't sure where to start? That could be an opportunity for education, either building local team plans or curating a broader learning program to help employees and leaders explore their personal identity development, understand their unconscious bias, and build empathetic cultural competence. I designed Vice Media Group's management training programs to build awareness and confidence so that managers could create psychological safety, trust, and a sense of belonging for their teams.

Then, employees across the globe quickly started reaching out individually to ask for more "DEI training." To help increase employee engagement despite limited resources (I couldn't train everyone at once), we created a self-directed Inclusion Corner program in our learning and development platform, where employees at all levels across the globe could log in to take the latest diversity, equity, and inclusion training, explore topics of interest, and share feedback on what worked or what they would like to learn. Over the first few months, we added courses on personal identity development, empathetic cultural competence, Black history, and more. All offerings aimed to be applicable in the workplace and in day-to-day life. For example, we offered bespoke resources about how to talk about racism with your children and bystander intervention resources to stop anti-Asian, anti–Asian American, and xenophobic harassment. We encouraged teams and community groups to take the training together to help enhance the experience and shared completion stats with leaders to give them a sense of what learning areas they could focus on with their teams. We committed to expand our library to include global cultural competence and other identity-based modules. When you hear about a microaggression—whether it's calling someone a fiery Latina, deadnaming someone (calling a transgender person by their birth name, as opposed to how they identify now), or asking a Muslim woman if she ever takes off her hijab—use that as an opportunity to educate. Tailor your courses to what's happening in your workplace.

One note: if you've committed a microaggression, pause and remind yourself that you're not a bad person and that a good person would commit to making things right for the person harmed. Then, immediately acknowledge the other person's hurt, genuinely apologize, take responsibility to educate yourself, and take steps to make things right. This is not about living in shame or pressuring the harmed person to forgive and forget so that you feel better. Making real amends is key. It's important to note that managers of color also make mistakes and inflict insults and invalidations on others, and this is equally unacceptable. This is part of your learning path.

If you can identify yourself in the examples in this section, this is a time for radical self-reflection and committing to challenging your internalized biases and how they influence your interactions. Commit to doing the work to become a true workplace ally and challenge the racially harmful behaviors you see within your professional and social circles. You can prevent microaggressions and positively influence the decisions and actions within your teams.

Kick Covering to the Curb

I can't tell you how many times a coworker, client, or other leader has said to me in a rather surprised tone, "You're so articulate!" or "Wow, you hold yourself so well." Why is it such a shock that a senior Latina executive speaks and behaves in a professional way? The implication is that people who look like me aren't supposed to talk and hold space like an executive. The assumption is that the corporate environment isn't designed for people who don't fit the white, professional, polished world. BIPOC are routinely called unprofessional whenever they make white colleagues uncomfortable. For BIPOC employees, there's always been an implicit understanding that these organizational environments aren't designed for people like us.

It's easy to navigate a workplace where everyone looks like you, hangs out in the same places as you, speaks like you do, and considers how you dress and accessorize to be the right, professional way. Environments like this lead to what Kenji Yoshino, an NYU law professor, has coined "covering," the practice of downplaying who you are to survive in a workplace. Covering is different from the closely related code-switching, which is when a person quickly switches between different cultural, racial, and social situations with the appropriate language, style, tone, and level of formality. Covering is hiding your differences to fit in in a straight, white, male-dominated workplace culture.

I have often fallen prey to covering and have spent years unearthing the variety of ways in which I and other women of color have been professionally discouraged from bringing the full breadth of our talents to work. There were constant reminders, implicit or not, from my white peers that a misstep could end my career or confirm negative stereotypes about other Latinx professionals. Covering is a sign of a non-inclusive culture, and it's felt deeply. More than

63 percent of all marginalized groups report covering (with 83 percent of LGBTQ employees acknowledging it), while even 45 percent of straight white men do. Even straight white men have shared that they can't speak up when colleagues make misogynistic comments, because this toxic form of male bonding is the predominant social currency at work. Former hedge fund trader Sam Polk famously wrote about Wall Street's "culture of brutal conformity" to misogyny and the bro culture that forced the disrespect and exclusion of women. It makes you think, what mold are we all trying to fit? And isn't it a problem that so many of us feel that we don't?

When Tiffany Dufu, the Black female author of *Drop the Ball* and founder of the Cru, was early in her career as a nonprofit fundraiser, she was frustrated over not having received a promotion she felt she deserved. In an effort to find out why so she could learn and grow, she consulted one of her peers who offered this rationale: "She told me that I wore too much gold," Dufu says. "I was dumbfounded and angry. Soon after, I went to a conference and noticed for the very first time that none of my nonprofit fundraising peers were wearing the amount of jewelry that I was. In fact, pretty much every woman was simply wearing studs in her ears, possibly a ring, and one piece of costume jewelry. I quickly recognized that I did not fit the norm. I also want to acknowledge that it took a lot of courage to blurt out what she was thinking when she didn't have the cultural competency to explain herself in a more effective manner. Remember, I was explicitly asking for her feedback as a board member. It was unfortunate that she did not have the words to say what I needed to hear, but I am grateful that she said something. Otherwise, I wouldn't have made the observation about my adornment later at the conference and I might not be in the leadership position that I am today." Here's what Dufu wishes this peer could have said:

Tiffany, you've chosen a career in which your primary role is to engender trust from high-net-worth individuals whose backgrounds are different from yours. Unfortunately, because of stereotypes that are not your fault, they'll make assumptions when they first encounter you, so how you present yourself matters. It's not fair and you shouldn't have to do this, but you might want to think about ways that you can show up less distracting so that they more quickly recognize your incredible intellect, storytelling, and passion for your cause.

"Soon after that conference, I decided that I would sacrifice my jewelry but that I would never sacrifice my natural hair. No matter how I'd need to evolve my professional look, my crown would always remain my glory."

Dufu learned to adapt without losing herself, but she shouldn't have to. Talented women, BIPOC, people with disabilities, LGBTQ people, religious minorities, and other marginalized groups are much too often pressured into sacrificing who they are in order to fit into an organization that has been designed exclusively for others (i.e., white, heteronormative employees). Your gender, racial, religious, and cultural identity should not be considered a source of shame and something to be minimized. It is your magic! No one should have to spend all of their physical and emotional labor figuring out how to navigate workspaces so that they can survive.

And yet, here we are, in the same compression chamber that sucks the oxygen out of our capacity to lead and our ability to exist as humanly fallible. Companies fail to focus on the root problem: the policies, systems, and processes that use a white standard of professionalism and measure everyone else negatively against it. You can't perform at your best when you're constantly modifying or playing down who you are, including your appearance, body language, abilities, and communication style. Yet we rarely take into account the additional burdens we place on underrepresented talent who have to hide parts of their identity to fit in at work. BIPOC staff have their judgment regularly questioned and have to hold back their true feelings, all because white workplace norms constantly signal to them that they don't belong.

We tend to think of organizations as transactional and professional, yet the racialized norms that define professionalism are no longer apt for the modern workplace. You must assess who your company culture was designed to accommodate, and who gets left out. You must create an inclusive culture where everyone is valued and diversity of perspectives, thoughts, and experience is welcomed, embraced, and celebrated. Ask yourself: What stories are we telling? Are we working with BIPOC, LGBTQ people, and members of other marginalized communities and putting inclusion and equity at the heart of our work, both publicly and privately?

Start by having a candid conversation about covering at work. Covering is about minimizing authentic elements of your identity, personality, or circumstances in order to fit in. For some of us, we feel that we have to hide our culture, class, health, tattoos, accents, and so on. We need to talk about this. Giving yourself, your leaders, and your team members permission to share real stories—where you grew up, who you love, what you worry about—will enable you to see each other through each other. A few tips: (1) check in with your team and acknowledge that you are on this journey, (2) provide extra support for those who need it and especially those who may be afraid to ask for it, and (3) give folks a sense that you get it and care.

You can also launch policies that encourage people to show up as their authentic selves. In its benefits package, Capital One began covering costly gender reassignment surgery, which signals to employees that they can bring their whole self to work every day.

No matter how well-intentioned your diversity, equity, and inclusion efforts may be, they will always fail unless you eliminate your cultural bias toward white supremacy. And what does white supremacy look like in the workplace? Let's talk about some of the unwritten rules that favor whiteness at work.

Tone policing

Imagine presenting a solution for reducing bias in hiring and performance processes and the response you receive from the listener is: "Your points would resonate better if you sounded less emotional" or

"I wish you would say that in a nicer way." I am no stranger to tone policing. I have had countless experiences of being tone policed as a woman ("Calm down") and as a Latina ("You come off as too passionate"). Who is allowed to get angry, who can express excitement or frustration, and what are "acceptable" forms of those emotions? Who gets to define what a professional way to speak or write is? The bias of white professional standards, whereby women and people of color are made to feel uncomfortable or ashamed for raising valid concerns, manifests in tone policing across every organization.

To create a more impactful dialogue that prevents tone policing, ask yourself these questions: In what ways can I focus on what the person is saying and not solely on how they are saying it? What else do I need to know in order to develop a well-rounded understanding of what my colleague is trying to communicate instead of dismissing or avoiding what they are saying? And before addressing someone's tone, ask yourself: Am I responding to being shut down or silenced, or am I trying to put someone in their place? How you prepare to respond makes all the difference.

White comfort and white fragility

This can come in the form of "color blindness," or an avoidance of conversations about racial or gender inequality, bias, and injustice. Statements such as "I don't see color" or "I can't believe this is still happening" are unhelpful, frustrating, and upsetting for BIPOC. When called out for saying or doing something racist, a white person might become defensive, blame the person for raising the issue, or justify what was said or done that caused harm—often denying that they are part of the problem. Avoid making statements like "I didn't mean that" or "You're overreacting." They are not comforting to people of color, and these phrases invalidate their pain and do nothing to make things right. These responses only serve to prioritize the white person's feelings over the person of color's feelings.

Perfectionism

White people know that, for the most part, when they make mistakes, it won't be attributed to their race, it won't be assumed to reinforce a stereotype about their race, and it won't be used as a reason to avoid hiring more people of their race. This is not true for BIPOC employees.

As the saying goes, perfection is the enemy of the good. Inclusive leaders promote a culture of appreciation, reflection, and accountability. They empower team members to take risks and bring their authentic selves to work while also helping organizations to innovate and capitalize on new business opportunities. These are not mutually exclusive.

I'll never forget when, a few months into joining Google, Danae Sterental, a young Latinx woman of Venezuelan descent, asked me for coffee. When we met, it was instantly easy and comfortable. She had one of those bright, warm smiles that lit up a room. We connected over our shared heritage and experiences at Google. A few weeks later, she shared a blog post she wrote about our meeting. In it, she mentioned being so consumed by emotion after we said our goodbyes that she cried the minute the elevator doors closed. She noted that I wore a white dress and heels, had long flowing hair, spoke Spanglish, and greeted her with a warm hug and kiss. This was the first time that she saw herself reflected in a senior leader. Prior to meeting me, she wrote, she thought she needed to sacrifice her culture, her looks, and her identity to succeed in Silicon Valley. Meeting me changed that for her. She finally felt what it was like to be seen at work—"You can be it, if you can see it"—and there was no going back. She has since received her MBA from Stanford and launched her own consultancy helping start-ups build thriving cultures. She's going to change the world being her full, authentic self and helping others do the same.

Four Ways Covering Shows Up at Work

"Covering" is used to describe how underrepresented groups go to great lengths to minimize the perceived stigmas of their identity in order to fit in. In *Uncovering Talent: A New Model of Inclusion*, published by Deloitte, Dr. Christie Smith and Kenji Yoshino take a deep dive into the widespread occurrence of covering at work and the impacts on inclusion.

They identify four axes of covering.

1. **Appearance based**: how employees alter the way they naturally present themselves in order to fit in

2. **Affiliation based**: how employees might go to extra lengths to avoid the stereotypical behaviors associated with their group

3. **Advocacy based**: how employees might avoid standing up for their group in order to fit in

4. **Association based**: how employees might minimize association with others from their group in order to fit in

---

Your Road Map to Revolution

Well-educated, well-intentioned, open-minded, kindhearted people often move along their lives, severely underestimating the impact of their racialized actions and privilege. Racially sensitive management demands much more effort, courage, and determination than simply doing things the way they've always been done. Deepen your own understanding, skills, and tools for listening and supporting your team. Welcoming challenging conversations, admitting your own mistakes, and being willing to course correct can lead to radical employee growth.

- **Set the right tone from the start**. Ask better questions and build an environment centered on trust. Start conversations that matter, but don't expect to receive all the answers. Vulnerability can lead to trust and engagement. It is the missing ingredient in workplaces; model that behavior.

- **Promote and model values of respect**. Model open dialogue and respect for others' ideas in meetings and among team members. When kicking off a project, talk about how you expect your team to work together. Be respectful of other people's ideas and comments, even if you disagree.

- **Foster speak-up culture**. Become a more effective ally by amplifying the voice of everyone on your team, especially those who feel the most silenced. Try amplification pacts, where meeting attendees agree ahead of time to support one another's ideas publicly.

- **Mitigate microaggressions**. Recognize the impact of microaggressions on your employees. Intervene when you see transgressions, and ask your peers to join you in intervening. Use "I" statements: I feel this. That comment made me feel that. If you were responsible for a painful comment, apologize.

- **Be sensitive and empathetic with your actions and words**. Ensure that in difficult conversations, you are focusing on the content of the message rather than the delivery. For example, go to BIPOC employees directly and privately with actionable, non-personality-based feedback.

- **Encourage a culture where covering isn't required**. You can't perform at your best when you're constantly modifying or playing down who you are, including your appearance, body language, abilities, and communication style. Stop using a white standard of professionalism.

- **Motivate people to take action**. Research shows that people's mindsets are impacted by those around them, so you can multiply your impact by catalyzing others around you. Connect with peers to share learnings, ideas, and resources and hold each other accountable.

7

TUNE IN TO THE WHISPERS AND SCREAMS (AND EVERYTHING IN BETWEEN)

DEATH BY A thousand and one papercuts" is a term that comes from an ancient form of Chinese torture known as *lingchi*, where a person is subjected to hundreds of small cuts until the end. It's a dark but accurate metaphor for what happens in workplaces across America: the heavy accumulation of seemingly small indignities. It's shutting up and shutting down to survive.

The truth about the lived experiences of people at your company often lies right beneath the surface. It floats in whispers and in knowing looks. More recently, in raised voices confronting privilege and demanding change through social media platforms. But the weighted feeling of having your dignity and power taken away from you over and over again remains. Over the course of my career, I've made my way into leadership rooms by silencing my feelings, making myself smaller, and tiptoeing around dismissive behavior. Accumulating credentials while I made myself seem less threatening. It felt like carrying a five-ton weight. And I have not been alone. Our collective silence is deafening.

To build an inclusive and equitable workforce, and to get ahead of murmurs and exposés, tune in to the whispers in your workplace. Pay attention to what's going on behind closed doors and out in the open in conference rooms or video meetings. To do that with a racial-equity lens, you need to recognize that while racial inequity affects all people of color, different racial and ethnic groups have vastly different experiences and it's important to understand them. It's OK to seek understanding about the experience of Black, Latinx, Asian, and Indigenous employees on your team. The goal is to equip yourself to talk about and wrestle with the impact of race effectively, and not in "race-neutral" ways.

I've worked in human resources for the majority of my career, and I can say with near certainty that office gossip often bears some truth. Often those rumors are spread offhandedly as happy-hour chatter or light warnings—"Everyone knows he's a creep" or "She's totally racist"—without deeper thought into how and where those sentiments were born. How do we know he's a creep? Did he harass someone? How do we know she's racist? Did she use a racial slur? And who is on the other end of these assaults? Whose responsibility is it to address the harm? Too often, as managers, we fail to follow up—usually to avoid conflict. This inaction leads to worsening toxic work culture.

Continue your Inclusion Revolution by checking in, being present, and listening to the everyday experiences at your company for women, BIPOC, people with disabilities, LGBTQ people, religious minorities, and other marginalized groups. You need this information so that you can create a true culture of belonging. Do you know whether coworkers from less privileged groups feel that they matter and are essential? What are their complaints? What goes unsaid in meetings? Where are the hot spots in employee resignations or patterns of dissatisfaction in your employee surveys? What are the retention and turnover rates when it comes to BIPOC in your company? Are you letting bad behavior slide because it is being perpetuated by a team member you like and respect?

Employees don't leave companies; they leave their managers. They walk away, sometimes flee, from best-in-class companies due to persistently bad experiences with their supervisors. Management, at its core, is about defining and assigning responsibilities, measuring results, spotting inefficiencies, and identifying solutions. Management is also about leadership, and that means building teams, inspiring and motivating them, supporting collaboration, and getting them to do more than they ever thought possible. That means being aware of your biases and preferences and actively seeking out and considering different views and perspectives to inform your decision-making. This also means having the courage to face the truth even when it is uncomfortable, to admit your mistakes, and to challenge the status quo. I'm betting you have hired someone from an underrepresented background before who left your team as a regrettable loss. Ask yourself: Why aren't they sticking around? It's time to tune in to what's going on.

Your responsibility as a manager is to deepen your own understanding, listen to your teams, and challenge, support, and advocate for them. This also means recognizing the courage that it takes for someone of a different race to come to you about something that they believe was racially motivated. Too often, the response to such feedback is disbelief, dismissal, or labeling the person as too sensitive. Instead, deeply listen to your team member's story and pay attention to why you may consider an incident harmless ("I was called someone else's name in the middle of a client meeting") so that you can come to understand the discomfort it caused. And then act in a meaningful way. You have to put down your defenses to show up for your teams.

Good managers surround themselves with people representing diverse perspectives and opinions, who are not afraid to disagree with them. I'm asking you to put away the old playbook of being unemotional, efficient problem-solvers and become compassionate, reflective problem-solvers. You should care about building social bonds with your coworkers. Many are hurting, questioning whether they belong, whether they have rights that will be respected, whether their lives matter, and how to express their feelings and process their questions in a workplace setting. Listen to the pauses and the whispers, watch for the signs of discomfort, and acknowledge that the truth often starts off quiet. Don't dismiss it as gossip or let it slide. When you hear something, ask for more: more information, more detail, more accountability.

Bottom line: Take care of your people. When an issue is raised, act on it. When you see something, say something. Listen to your team, and encourage your team members to listen to each other.

Be an Inclusion Truth Seeker

Ask questions before you provide answers. Listen to the lived experience of others and recognize the good, the bad, and the ugly about your workplace culture. A truth seeker has an open mind and doesn't neglect or overlook information because it goes against what they believe or want to be true. Make it your mission to seek feedback and perspectives on how employees of different races and identities experience work and how you and your organization can do better. That said, be careful that you don't force BIPOC to be problem-solvers when the responsibility for nurturing an inclusive workplace culture is yours.

Expect to get uncomfortable. I have yet to engage in a conversation about racial equity where the simple use of words like "racism," "whiteness," and "privilege" hasn't made people visibly uneasy. For there to be sustainable change, you will have to tolerate and push through discomfort and create opportunities for people to lean into these conversations. And you will have to make it clear that you will not brush past or ignore conflict.

Embarking on a listening journey is a great way to start. I've led many listening sessions. Most have been designed as conversations where leaders have met with members of different employee resource groups to hear their concerns. At Vice Media Group, CEO

Nancy Dubuc and I embarked on a seven-week global listening series following allegations of negative experiences by Black and brown former employees at *Refinery29*. We took the stories of these women very seriously and sought to discover how diversity, equity, and inclusion were experienced across all teams.

To create brave spaces for conversation, we brought in a facilitator, a member of our internal communications team, to guide the discussion. In the welcoming remarks, the facilitator explained that Dubuc and I were there to listen and not respond until the end, when we would offer closing remarks. It was important to have an impartial colleague who the teams trusted to help facilitate the discussion. Alternatively, you can hire a third-party neutral facilitator. The sessions were done on a video chat (this was during the pandemic), were capped at twenty people—small enough to build trust and intimacy but large enough to offer diversity of opinion—and were explicitly framed to examine issues of inclusion, equity, and belonging across our teams. For those most afraid to speak up, we encouraged them to use our anonymous hotline to share their feedback.

At the beginning of each session, we asked participants to reflect on these questions:

- What are the conditions (policies, programs) that may sustain white, male, hetero, cis, and/or able-bodied power and presence within our teams and work?

- In which situations have you felt things to be unfair and unsafe?

The dialogue was further framed in a three-pronged approach, allocating equal time for each section:

1. **Stop**. What are some things we should stop doing that are deterring the growth and presence of coworkers from marginalized groups?

2. **Start**. What are some things we should start doing to better support the growth and presence of coworkers from marginalized groups?

3. **Continue**. What are some things we should continue doing that currently support the growth and presence of coworkers from marginalized groups?

We witnessed a tremendous level of transparency and bravery. Each group lifted up issues and concerns most relevant to their unique experience and geographic location. There were moments of levity, like the time Dubuc—who I had yet to meet in person since I was hired during the lockdown—commented on not knowing how tall I was. When I shared that I was five foot two, her eyes went wide as she blurted, "No way!" She had assumed that my height would match my personality.

The conversations were insightful, raw, and often unsettling. Topics included leadership accountability, management training, career advancement, pay equity, tone policing, and tokenism. In a more subtle way, employees wanted to understand the why. As in, why are certain business and people decisions made? What we heard across the board was an appreciation for being asked to share their experiences. We also heard a desire for real change and action, not just a symbolic gesture of "tell me your story." With each conversation, I witnessed Dubuc progressively stretch herself as she learned more about how race and racism played out across teams, honored the vulnerability of team members, and showed a genuine desire to fix the underlying exclusive systems and processes.

Part diagnostic, part conversation, these sessions helped dissolve interpersonal barriers, dispelled some myths, and served as our source data for the most basic elements of our plan for cultural transformation. Every initiative we designed from that point on—from our second pay-equity study to our learning programs and performance-management processes—was informed by what we learned in those conversations. To keep the learning and engagement going, we launched additional versions of listening sessions with other leaders across the organization.

A note: To create a space for employees to share how they are truly doing, leaders need to be trained in listening skills and model vulnerability themselves by acknowledging what they know and don't know. And they must commit to stay engaged. This sends a powerful signal that it's OK to not be OK with the status quo.

I often hear the stories of employees—disproportionately women and BIPOC—who feel ignored or misunderstood by their managers. By the time I hear about it, they either have one foot out the door or are too beaten down to care. Listening is an essential tool to build an anti-racist workplace. Do you listen with intent to raise understanding about different perspectives (good), or do you focus on solving, convincing, or correcting (bad)? Start your questions with "Help me understand..." not "Wouldn't you agree...?" or "Don't you think...?" And close with "How can I help?"

As a manager, it's important that you make yourself available so that your teams can access you when and if they need you. You need to show a willingness to talk. You also have to show evidence of effort, a willingness to talk openly about thorny or uncomfortable issues, even when they differ from your own experiences, says corporate consultant and educator Reggie Butler. It's what your teams want and need from you. It's the opposite of what we have become accustomed to: a distant and unempathetic managerial standard that has long favored white men. Any variance from an unemotional, know-it-all stance is often dismissed and considered unprofessional. I don't need to intellectualize how I'm feeling. I know how it feels when my power and dignity are stripped away in daily interactions. It's an experience BIPOC employees are all too familiar with.

How can you possibly help your teams overcome these obstacles? They just want to know that you care. Here's a simple approach:

- I have been awed and humbled by what this team has achieved.

- This conversation may surface some tough emotions.

- I want you to know that as your leader I'm not OK with toxic or exclusionary behavior.

- I want to remind you to check in with your team members, and please know that I'm here to lean on at any time.

- Here are some helpful approaches and resources.

As a BIPOC leader, it's both important and difficult to advocate for your emotional needs. It's OK to reply to emails asking for your advice with "I don't have enough time on my plate to offer you thoughtful guidance." In the wake of George Floyd's murder, I received countless emails asking for advice. I put together a list of diversity and anti-racist trainers that I would send with a note: "Thank you for reaching out. These are important conversations that require expertise. I, like many other diversity, equity, and inclusion practitioners of color, am managing a heavy workload while protecting my own well-being. Here is a list of diversity, equity, and inclusion and anti-racist consultants, some of whom I have worked with and others who have been strongly referred. I encourage you to reach out and learn about their offerings and how they may be helpful to you."

Being an ally, listener, and challenger of norms is a continuous process. Part of that process is examining our own biases and educating ourselves about the experiences of people from vulnerable and marginalized identities. Building the muscle of listening, understanding, and reflecting, including the capacity to interpret new information, is an essential skill set. This may mean that, like Nancy Dubuc and I, sometimes you will have to sit in ambiguity, conflict, and discomfort as you take in new information. Those moments can help you gain clarity on what to do next.

Sample Listening Series Discussion Guide

Your role (Leader)

- **Speak**. Set the stage and tone up top. Summarize at end.
- **Listen**. Create a safe and brave space to share. Actively listen to participants.
- **Act**. Commit to an action by the end of the session. You can partner with your HR business partner and chief diversity officer to follow up on the session with action plans.

Conversation starters	We are here because *x*.
	I am interested in hearing firsthand from all of you.
	We know that *y* can be a pretty great place to work, but not everyone has the same experience. I want to hear from you what it's like to work here.
	I'm here to listen and won't have all the answers. Consider this the start of our conversation.
	I want to work with you to improve our overall culture and inclusivity.
Potential discussion themes	What should we start/stop/continue doing to improve our team culture?
	How does the way we work limit or enhance our work?
	How do you feel about your work-life balance?
Wrapping up	Thank them for their time.
	Summarize key themes you have heard.
	Remind them it is just the beginning of an ongoing conversation.
	Don't overpromise. Commit to things you are sure you can deliver.

	Let them know next steps and that they will hear from you shortly.
After the session	Plan on doing some follow-up with participants, through an email, summarizing the key themes that came from the session and your plan of action and next steps. Follow through with anything that was committed to in the discussion. This is critically important.
Tips for inclusive conversations	Be ready to hear a variety of responses that you might not have expected. Repeat what you heard to them (the Oprah interview technique). While you may not understand or agree with all perspectives shared, practice empathetic listening. This is their experience. Don't take that away from them by offering a counterpoint or rushing them to a point. Observe those who have not spoken and create space for them to be heard. Look for opportunities to build trust and actively listen to encourage participant disclosure. Trust can be built by setting expectations, demonstrating vulnerability through personal risks, and being intentional about using inclusive language. Start with awareness of your default behaviors and how you are including or potentially excluding or dismissing others. Questions to mitigate bias as you listen: Do I have an automatic feeling or judgment about this person?

	What may I have discounted and not heard in the right way? How can I consciously intervene to lessen the impact of this bias?

Get Smart with Feedback

Employee feedback is one of the most useful data sources for measuring and improving. A well-crafted, anonymous engagement survey can help you gauge where specific hot spots or problems exist within and across teams. They can further determine how these gaps are impacting the work and experience of your team across different demographics (remember to track that) and where pockets of toxicity or exclusion may hide in the averages.

Survey fatigue can lead to overwhelmed and discontented employees. No matter what you do, there will always be team members who will never feel it's safe enough to come forward and share the truth of their lived experiences of racism at work. But that should not deter you from knowing what is going on. Global research and advisory company Gartner created an inclusion index to help organizations get a holistic view of inclusion across their workforce. Employees are asked to respond to seven statements. The greater degree to which they agree with the statements, the more inclusive the organization:

1. **Fair treatment**. Employees who help the organization achieve its strategic objectives are rewarded and recognized fairly.

2. **Integrating differences**. Employees at my organization respect and value each other's opinions.

3. **Decision-making**. Members of my team fairly consider ideas and suggestions offered by other team members.

4. **Psychological safety**. I feel welcome to express my true feelings at work.

5. **Trust**. Communication we receive from the organization is honest and open.

6. **Belonging**. People in my organization care about me.

7. **Diversity**. Managers at my organization are as diverse as the broader workforce.

The most important element to gauge is if your team members genuinely feel heard, accepted, and empowered to have an impact on decision-making as it relates to their roles. Questions you can also ask: Are your ideas listened to and acted on? Are issues handled, acknowledged, and addressed in a racially and culturally sensitive manner? Do you feel that you can share aspects of yourself without shame or hindrance from career advancement? What was a high point when you felt a sense of belonging with your team? With your company? If you had a magic wand and could grant three wishes so that everyone could feel a sense of belonging in the workplace, what would they be?

Or you could try a multiple-choice approach. What would make you feel like you belong?

- Being recognized for my accomplishments

- Having opportunities to express my opinion freely

- Feeling that my contributions in team meetings are valued

- Feeling comfortable with being myself at work

- Transparent communication about important company developments

- Feeling like my team/company cares about me as a person

- Feedback on my personal growth

- Being assigned work deemed important to the team/company

- Having the company values align with my own personal values

- Being a part of important company meetings

- Seeing executives who look like me

- Seeing coworkers who look like me

And if you feel lost, confused, or stuck on how to approach these issues, ask the open-ended question: What does working here feel like for you?

"I feel like I belong at company *x*" is a true-false statement often found in engagement surveys and is intended to gauge employees' sense of belonging. I'm not convinced that it's the right insight measurement for BIPOC and underrepresented employees. Why would we want to belong in organizations where we have been forced to hide or diminish large parts of ourselves so others can feel comfortable? Where we expend an unbelievable amount of energy and time shrinking ourselves to avoid standing out, swallowing our frustration at the lack of support and advancement, or walking on eggshells to avoid making white people feel uncomfortable?

Ask: What does it mean to be represented in your team and organization? How, if at all, are unconscious biases addressed in your workplace? How comfortable do you feel asking for help, sharing suggestions informally, or challenging the status quo without fear of negative social or professional consequences? These questions can help you surface the root causes of racial disparities in your organization. It can also help you gauge whether leaders and managers are cultivating psychological safety, belonging, and inclusion by modeling and reinforcing the behaviors they expect from the rest of their teams.

While employee engagement surveys are important tools to get a snapshot of an organization's culture, there are pitfalls. Even when you create a safe space for people to speak up, there will be those on your team who have been betrayed and hurt too many times to trust you. I've found myself having to emphasize again and again to employees that surveys are anonymous. I've stressed that the information we gather will never reflect back on them and that we need their honest answers because I can't fix what I don't know. But the fears of repercussions and judgment are real. People won't participate honestly unless you can ensure protection of their anonymity.

When interpreting survey results, it's also important to look at the positive results as much as the lower scores to determine bright spots. We often jump to what is wrong, but something that is working well can be repurposed within other groups or potentially at scale.

You have to be cautious of survey fatigue and of taking too much time to get to an action plan or not acting at all. Issues of bias, harassment, and discrimination at work often go unreported because of fear of retaliation or lack of awareness about how to address grievances or concerns. Employees want to know their opinions will lead to real change in their organizations. If meaningful action is not assured, then no one is going to meaningfully participate.

Many corporate surveys are worded to prime positive responses: What's your favorite thing about working here? What does your boss do best? If you want to receive unfiltered and constructive feedback, you need to offer safe channels where employees can communicate freely without fear of retaliation. Through a combination of internal and external platforms, you can both inform organizational change and build trust. If staff respond that they want pay equity in order to feel valued and invested in the company long-term, you have to demonstrate transparency, both in the responses and in a true and fair internal pay audit. The results have to be shown to the whole company, and corrections must be made immediately as needed, including back pay. Or what if employees feel overstretched and understaffed? What if staff are asking for more hires to help lighten the load and to prevent people from having to work on weekends? What if your team believes that yours is a toxic, racist, sexist workplace where they don't feel they want to remain, much less recruit women and BIPOC for? What if people complain about bad managers and high turnover and ask to know if exit interviews reveal patterns of abuse that have gone unaddressed? If your company is not willing to show that level of transparency, including answering why you can't or won't address something, then don't conduct surveys at all.

Allow for Anonymity and Maintain Multiple Reporting Systems

Confidentiality matters. Most companies also offer anonymous reporting hotlines for employees to speak up when they have legitimate concerns about misconduct. However, these are not stand-alone solutions for establishing an ethical and inclusive culture.

I've found that the most successful approach is to offer multiple channels of communication for raising concerns. If you're trying to get to the underlying issues of why underrepresented employees leave at a higher rate, for example, you may try independent, confidential platforms like tEQuitable. These platforms offer both a sounding board for employees and insights for companies to be and do better. Furthermore, allowing employees to seek and effect solutions before issues of bias, discrimination, or harassment escalate may enable them to regain their confidence. One advantage that tEQuitable has, by design, is that employees immediately receive confidential advice and help figuring out what their next steps should be. They're not asked to relive what happened over the last six months; they're provided with in-the-moment coaching with actionable takeaways.

The cloud communications company Twilio used tEQuitable to give its employees the ability to open up and anonymously share their experiences at work, without fear of retaliation. The data they received highlighted issues hidden under the surface previously considered too disruptive to bring up. These issues were previously hidden well under the surface. Now, management could enact proactive solutions to help curb insidious behaviors before they took hold.

You don't have to only rely on existing feedback channels. A sales leader I worked with created an online form for his team to raise questions or concerns directly to leadership. This was meant to create an additional channel for addressing workplace issues, including microaggressions and racism, for those who did not want to use HR channels. In an email to his team, he wrote, "This form allows you to raise your hand and say, 'I have a question' or 'I want to talk about something'—you can indicate you would like a response over email, or if you would like to arrange a 1:1 meeting with me and/or other members of the leadership team to discuss. There is an option to remain anonymous, and I will do my best to respond to those who choose to do so through group emails or on an all-hands call going forward."

I'm often asked if it's worth it to go to human resources. Are they your friend or foe? There's a common perception that HR is an inefficient and sometimes corrupt agent of the organization, that HR is where claims of misconduct go to die, or worse, that those complaints become cause to penalize you. I'm not going to say this doesn't happen. There are real stories and real data to support those beliefs. Common complaints include: "HR won't help me," "HR will make things worse," or "HR never did anything about it."

As someone who has been inside several of the largest HR teams on the planet, I can tell you that there are well-intentioned, highly capable HR leaders who are relentless in their pursuit of building people-centered organizations grounded in values of inclusion, collaboration, and accountability. Sometimes they are handcuffed by confidentiality that may feel frustrating to you, but that shouldn't stop you from asking them to help defuse or solve complicated workplace situations. That's their job!

And if you are an HR practitioner, here's what I say: This work requires that we remind ourselves of what teams and organizations need us to do, and to pause and think about what type of human-centered leader we need to be for others. Sure, our role requires us to enforce workplace policies and sometimes discipline employees, which is unpleasant though necessary. But long gone are the days of simply policing bad behavior or serving as compliance offers. Our role is to help build more resilient, inclusive, and positive organizational climates in partnership with the teams we support.

Here are some ways to lean on HR.

Partner on difficult conversations

Everyone is so nervous about saying the wrong thing, and HR can act as a skilled mediator. But know that having another person in the room, specifically from HR, can raise anxiety levels. To tame those fears, say, "I have asked our HR partner to join us to help us avoid any misinterpretations and so that you can feel safe in your responses." And then make sure that safety is honored.

Facilitate listening sessions

I've always encouraged my team to serve as facilitators and note-takers during listening sessions. These experiences enable them to build closer ties to teams, glean insights they may not be privy to in their day-to-day work, and learn to guide conversation safely and inclusively. They also help bridge conversations between team members who may feel they are alone in what they are sharing and those who are hearing these stories for the first time.

Reaffirm a sense of fairness

Your HR teams can add fairness and transparency checks to processes across the entire employee journey: attraction, selection, development, promotion, and retention. They can help you identify gaps in those stages, develop rigorous processes for selecting, developing, and promoting members of your team, and develop compensation strategies and materials to ensure everyone on your team understands your pay philosophy and process.

Three Strategies for Better Truth-Seeking Conversations

During these conversations, it's important to really listen, engage, withhold judgment, and not immediately launch into trying to solve things. Yes, you should respond to what you're hearing, but the goal should be to seek to understand what the other person is trying to convey and what is important to them. The listening portion is key, rather than focusing on deciding where their story must go or how it must end. Some strategies:

Acknowledge truths

If there have been reports about gender harassment, discrimination, or abusive conduct, raise them. Don't try to pretend that you're unaware of the issues that have surfaced, even if you can't share specific and confidential details. You can start the conversation with an acknowledgment of what brought you together, admit what you can and can't share, and listen for content and emotion. Don't forget to ask, with care: "How are you doing with all of this?"

Reduce defensiveness

Some people will be intimately familiar with what is happening, while others are just starting on their inclusion journey. Some are

---

tired of (and maybe triggered by) talking about it, and others are eager to join in. Some need rest and healing; others need action. Some may stay silent but actually have a lot to say. Don't discount, dismiss, or blame them. Even if something was not intended to offend, all attention should be on validating and apologizing for the offended person's pain, and your energy should be spent on making it right. Honor whether they want to engage in the conversation or not. You can also offer another opportunity to speak if they don't want to do so in the moment.

Listen, do not debate

Your job here is to listen, *if* your team members or coworkers want to talk to you about their experience. Do not debate them, rush to offer solutions, or extend a different perspective. Be careful to separate intent from effect. You don't want to minimize your colleague's experience by focusing on defending a bad actor's intent. Instead, your act of listening can itself be a step toward their healing. Talking is an important way to work through emotions and understand our experiences. Sometimes they may need to tell the same stories over and over again. Follow their lead. Listen with your heart and mind.

Act On What You Hear

I'm often asked: What do you do with leaders who say they want to deliver on the promise of equality but are unaware about inequities within their teams? My answer is always the same, because the answer *is* always the same. They know. They may not be aware of every example of bad judgment or conduct, or the extent of the social exclusion and condescension across their teams, but they likely have a sense of who the bad players are. And if they don't know, one thing is sure: their inner circle is in the know.

Executive teams, often white and male, carry on behaviors, style, and relationship issues fraught with racial tensions. When the stakes feel high, they prefer to retreat, block, delay, or settle for a lesser goal. Groomed to follow the path of least resistance, they often lean on notions of professionalism and appropriateness as excuses to stifle challenging perspectives or conversations. The result is higher gaps of understanding between senior leadership and the lower ranks. And it's the lower ranks who most suffer the consequences when the system isn't working. That's why white and BIPOC managers at all levels need to seek understanding of their blind spots and their employees' sore spots. If you can't overcome the silences and denials surrounding white fragility, privilege, and abuses of power in your workplace, you can't create conditions for change.

After you listen to the whispers and check in with your team, you must hold yourself accountable for acting on what you've heard, swiftly. That's it. If there are no consequences for behaving in a manner that is not civil, then such behaviors will continue to disrupt the workplace and limit productivity. A company that wants civility to be infused throughout its culture must hold employees at every level accountable for behaving in a civil manner.

As I was moving up the ranks in my career, I longed for leaders who would use their position of authority to challenge toxic behavior. As I grew into my own positions of leadership, I realized that it was up to me to model the behaviors I sought.

Anyone who has ever worked on any of my teams knows that I have very little patience for disrespectful behavior. If I see or hear that someone is being belittled, misunderstood, or mistreated by a peer or manager, I bring the impacted parties together to address the conflict in a constructive way. I do so by naming what I saw or learned—as simple as stating, "I think this is what is happening right now"—giving my team members license to express concerns or experiences, and making it clear that we can be respectful and kind while raising hard issues.

Following through and following up is the final act to creating a culture of belonging. When you do, the person feels that they've been heard and supported and that you have their back. They feel that they're part of a team. Instead, managers often try to avoid conflict and ignore issues. When someone raises an issue that causes discomfort, the response is generally to blame the person for raising the issue rather than reflect on the issue—for example, when an employee tells a manager that a colleague is mistreating Black employees in meetings, and the manager defends the bad actor and criticizes the person who reported the incident. Minimizing the situation, all to avoid the discomfort of correcting a colleague's racist behavior, promotes damaging misconduct. Whistleblowers are often shamed in companies, to the point where millions of workers fear that the professional costs are too high to speak up about harmful behavior.

How you respond to what you're hearing from your employees and from your coworkers is one of the toughest parts of driving change. It requires you to have the courage to speak up and act as an ally, to navigate minefield-laden bureaucratic terrain, and to push for changes that may be outside your power or pay grade. Instead of focusing on being polite and avoiding issues, address those uncomfortable moments before they become intractable problems. I've found it helpful to role-play how I can respond to difficult conversations before they happen. It eases my conflict-adverse anxiety. It's a helpful skill and one we are rarely good at in the moment unless we've worked at building those muscles. I write a script and practice in front of the mirror. I fine-tune that script based on how I may respond to different scenarios. When in doubt, remember that even tiny actions and corrections are a step forward.

What does reliability mean to you? Who is someone you trust or can lean on? What do they do to create that feeling for you? For me, and most leaders I know, trust grows when you follow through on your word. When someone tells you that they're going to do something, and they do it. It's about trusting that you will stand by your word. Distrust grows when people feel that you're not acknowledging or doing anything to address their concerns. When you create a gaping lag time in your response, that void gets filled with panic, anger, frustration, you name it.

The formula is simple: listen, reflect, and do something about what you've learned.

But what if you don't know what to do? If you are not a manager yet, this may look like being open to constructive feedback from coworkers or providing emotional support during difficult times. If you are a manager or leader, this could mean ensuring that your employees know that they will be heard, believed, and safe when raising concerns about inappropriate behavior.

Prioritize timely action with care. When, for example, a racial or otherwise discriminatory incident occurs, recognize the behavior and act on it swiftly. Don't wait until the problematic behavior has been repeated or has occurred over a prolonged period of time. Something as simple and direct as "Why do you think that? Help me understand from your point of view" can be surprisingly effective. Standing up to bias or a racial microaggression without shaming others will help you and your team create change and work better together.

Organizational responses to workplace misconduct range depending on the severity of the incident and behavior. You should have clearly defined grievance and disciplinary procedures, and you must follow them. Engage your HR partner in preparing to discuss specifics of the situation, expectations and standards of behavior in your workplace, and your concerns. In some cases, it may make sense to engage an external investigator.

Sometimes the individuals can come to realize a need for changing racist behaviors or attitudes, including unconscious bias and microaggressions. In those cases, coaching can provide developmental and remedial guidance and encourage sustained behavioral change. In more egregious cases, lax diligence and suppressing complaints simply won't do. It is up to leadership to commit to put accountability mechanisms in place that address racial misconduct, clubby relationships, and the microaggressions that deprive your teams of the respect they deserve at work.

Even if solutions can't be implemented quickly, be up-front with your teams. If it's an issue that will require disciplinary action, like harassment charges, say something to show that you're not sitting in silence: "I've heard you, I reported the incident, and I am working with our HR/leadership team on next steps." While numerous laws have come about to increase transparency and avoid the pervasive silence around workplace discrimination and sexual harassment, it is important that you as a manager maintain confidentiality through-out an investigation process. This is not about protecting wrongdo-ers, but rather about ensuring the integrity of the investigation.

And if the result of an investigation isn't what an employee was hoping for—for example, firing the offender—be honest about the process and what is in your control to change. You can say, "I went through all the channels [enumerate them]. These are the results [share what is permissible]. I appreciate that this is not the outcome you were hoping for, but here's what we plan to do as a leadership team [e.g., training in racially sensitive management, embedding anti-racism principles in management performance reviews]." Being transparent about your processes and interventions is what earns trust and credibility as a leader.

In 2018, Starbucks CEO Howard Schultz handled a racially charged incident in one of the company's Philadelphia chains quickly and decisively. He didn't try to sweep it under the rug or cross his fingers that the Twitterverse would move on to other things (as so many companies hope). He acknowledged what had happened on national TV, owned the mistake, said he was embarrassed and ashamed, issued an authentic apology, and shared a quick solution (shutting down all locations for racial bias training). The effective-ness of his proposed solution is debatable—one-day training rarely delivers long-term effects—but there was a genuine desire to shine a light on an uncomfortable truth. When a leader is transparent and acts quickly to address a racist incident, they send a powerful signal to BIPOC employees that they are safe, valued, and taken seriously.

Don't wait months to address an incident worrying over the perfect thing to say. While every situation is different, and interventions should be customized depending on your team or organizational context, don't be afraid to look into it—even and especially if the offender is a friend, or someone who is senior, or a high performer for the company. If you hear reports that a senior leader, say, routinely bullies junior BIPOC staff, act quickly. Not only is it the right thing to do for your people, but it's also the right thing to do for your organization. Whether you learn that it is consistent abrasive behavior or that it was a one-time event, it is your responsibility to address it directly with the person and HR.

We all have bad days, but as managers and leaders, we set the tone from the top. I was once part of a group email in which a peer—a white male top executive in the company—chastised a junior BIPOC member of my team for presumably botching up a salary negotiation and not knowing how to do her job. After checking in with my team member directly, I learned that she had raised flags about the process but felt forced to act based on direction from the hiring manager on that executive's team, who was more senior than her. She was mortified for being publicly and wrongly flogged by this executive on a group email thread that included peers and other managers. I reassured her that her job was safe and that I would rectify the situation. I then responded to the thread by listing the facts—what had taken place and under whose direction—recognizing that the employee on my team had followed the right protocols and thanking her and her peers for closing the negotiation. I then took my peer aside and let him know that his response was devastating to her. That if he had paused and done his own due diligence instead of attacking a junior employee, we could have safeguarded her dignity. He never apologized; I wish he had. Still, even without the apology, it was important to correct the behavior publicly. If our teams believe that humiliating junior team members is acceptable and will go undisciplined, they will follow suit.

Repair Damage When It Happens

If only fixing workplace conflict were as easy as causing it. Recognizing and addressing instances of conflict and misunderstanding is a great first step to reduce the impact of relationship- and career-damaging moments.

Uncover Truths

Here are statements that shed light on the often-conflicting emotions and experiences at work that we're afraid to say out loud. Try sharing these in an upcoming discussion about your team's culture or diversity, equity, and inclusion initiatives and see how many resonate with your colleagues. Sometimes people need permission—and a mirror—to share their truths and overcome their fears.

What we feel at work

- I'm afraid of being hurtful to others or ignorant of the ways in which I hurt others.

- I'm exhausted by having to constantly explain my lived experience in a way that others can understand.

- I'm over white men getting a trophy for showing up while I need to prove myself over and over again.

- I want to attract, develop, and retain a racially diverse workforce but I don't know where to start.

- I'm tired of being asked to do unpaid additional labor to solve diversity, equity, and inclusion problems, when I should already be walking into an inclusive workplace culture where I can do my best work.

- I worry that we're not addressing the elephant in the room.

- I'm afraid of saying the wrong thing and making a mistake.

- I want to be an ally but am afraid of falling short.

- I'm constantly worrying about being misgendered, mistreated, or judged because of my identity.

What we wonder at work

- How does this really connect to the goals that I have to deliver?

- I look for underrepresented talent. Why can't I find any?

- Why are we talking about people dealing with injustice in the workplace?

- Are our efforts lowering the hiring bar?

- How can I ask my team to support and advance changes when they can't even see the problems to begin with?

- How do I respond to being called out without doing further damage?

- Do leaders really care about diversity, equity, and inclusion?

You've now learned to look for what's not always visible, especially the impact of the unconscious choices you make and behaviors you model. But the most vital step comes next: what you do with this awareness.

Remember when we talked about a growth mindset? Our actions are guided by our inner beliefs, assumptions, and biases about how the world operates. Pay attention to your thinking when listening to the whispers: Are you focused on what they are saying and what they mean, or are you just thinking about what to say next? Are you more concerned with preserving the peace and racial comfort than with grappling with how race matters? Establishing the right mindset won't happen overnight, but the important thing to know is that your internal dialogue influences your perception and behavior.

If you're a manager or leader who identifies as a woman, BIPOC, person with a disability, LGBTQ person, religious minority, or other historically excluded identity, you're not off the hook. Your lived experiences may make you more sensitive to exclusionary experiences, but you still have to do the work. I've been guilty of making gendered assumptions when assigning job responsibilities. I've scaled back inclusivity initiatives when confronted by opposition from my mostly white peers. Each time, I've forced myself to confront and admit my missteps—but not before I had fallen into the traps of my hidden blind spots and white supremacy's manipulations.

"We all have a set of beliefs about our own racial identity—how we interact with other races based on our own individual lived experience—and our belief systems are being challenged right now," says Keesha Jean-Baptiste, head of talent at Hearst. "And when your belief system shifts, you begin to see everything differently. Race is woven into your day-to-day, from where you choose to shop, who you choose to support, and other choices that may have been second nature." White people also have a race. They are not the invisible non-raced norm. Race is not an issue that only Black and brown people have the responsibility of dealing with or solving. Rather, given that racism benefits white people, it has been widely argued that it is white people's responsibility to stop oppressing and to stop blindly allowing oppressive systems.

This is what happens when you keep your rose-colored glasses on: When the Wing hired me as a consultant following a racialized incident that seemed absurd on its face (a fight over a parking spot), I came to learn that this was just the latest in a long string of incidents. Deeper issues of bias, power, and discrimination had routinely been skirted around and silenced. By the time this disagreement happened, there had been years of built-up racial tension, and this event became a headline-making, leadership-destroying upheaval.

Early on, my racism radar buzzed enough to know I couldn't just embark on future-looking diversity and inclusion initiatives for their membership. I first had to attend to the past experiences of staff—staff who, I would soon learn, were hurting from years of neglect and microaggressions. You can't take a step forward until you stand in the present, hold yourself and your company accountable, and get clear on your intentions.

We had to elevate the whispers and engage in conversations about race and how racism showed up in the co-working spaces and behind the scenes. I started our first membership session by saying: "We are here today to give voice to the experiences of people of color, especially Black women, who have been harmed—intentionally and unintentionally—by your practices, behaviors, norms, and expectations. We are here today because there is a gap between the values we espoused and the experience of many in this room."

We first focused on hearing the voices and experiences of those who had been most harmed. We had to uncover for members and the entire staff the ways the status quo was harming BIPOC, especially Black women. And then everyone had to come clean about their roles in supporting that status quo, knowingly or unknowingly. Some did. Some didn't. We used exercises designed to give every person the space and opportunity to speak their minds about the environment within the company and across their teams. This included exercises where the white women in the room were not allowed to speak first. Much too often in cross-racial women's groups, white women take up all the space. We wanted to hold these sessions differently—to create a safe and secure environment that gave everyone a voice by hearing from women of color first, and then opening the mic up to all.

Inevitably, there would always be at least one white woman who I'd have to remind, "It's not your turn. Not all the women of color have spoken yet." The purpose of this type of exercise is to allow those who are from marginalized communities to be able to speak up and be heard without hindrances and obstacles. Inevitably, tensions arise for white participants. I can't tell you how many times I've heard someone erupt with, "You told me I can't defend myself! It's really hard. I wanna respond!"

If someone is harassing a person who is being silenced, the silenced person should be able to defend themselves. These outbursts from silenced white participants are almost never about them being harassed by BIPOC participants. Listening to hard truths is difficult, especially if you've never done it before. But this is not the time to be defensive; this is the time to take it all in. Here's what I want to remind white participants: "This is your mirror. Everything is coming at you, and it's everything that you have been unwilling to face up to this point. Everything that you have been unwilling to acknowledge, decades of unwillingness, being challenged all at once. And your anger is actively deflecting from the truth of the matter—a difficult and uncomfortable truth. The truth."

I was pleasantly taken aback in a few listening sessions at Vice Media Group when, to break the silence, the facilitator would randomly call on a white employee. On several occasions these employees would say, "I'd rather yield my time to a BIPOC colleague who hasn't spoken yet," followed by, "I'm trying to put into practice what I'm learning." If you are a white person and these scenarios are making you uncomfortable, ask yourself: Why does it make me so uncomfortable to allow people of color to have an unconstrained voice? If this is the first time you've engaged in these conversations, challenge your inclination to dismiss or trivialize them because of any discomfort they may cause you. Instead, be open to asking clarifying questions and considering what may have contributed to your reactions.

At the Wing, we also used techniques for staff, in particular, that were adapted from Glenn Singleton's *Courageous Conversations About Race*. These exercises center around storytelling about race: How did race show up for you in the early parts of your life? How do you communicate that? How does it show up for you in the workplace? At every session, we would hear similar comments from white participants: "This really hurts." "This is really upsetting." "I'm tired of talking about this." And during these sessions, we sought to understand the source of anger or frustration. The intent was not to shame participants but rather to move away from deflecting responsibility through emotionally charged outbursts.

It takes a lot of effort and a lot of work to run an organization. The incident that caused the Wing to hire me wouldn't have perhaps exploded if leaders had gotten ahead of issues of pay equity, exclusive workplace culture, and power abuses. Eradicating corrosive practices and promoting anti-racist and culturally inclusive behavior is not like flipping a light switch; it's an ongoing practice. Mistakes will be made. Adjustments will happen. Clarity on who you are and consistency in your behaviors, on both an individual and a company level, can prevent issues such as this one from ever causing harm to your people and your brand.

De-escalating a heated or tense situation at work is hard enough as it is. Adding in racial and gender identity dynamics can make work feel like a daily survival strategy game. You may choose to invest in conflict-management training for your managers that enables them to recognize cognitive bias and how to reach understanding by taking another perspective. You may go the route of a formal training program that is racially inclusive and centers on anti-racism, belonging, and psychological safety, or you can create and join a diversity peer counseling program to help others do what's right when they witness bias and unfairness in the workplace.

Whether you are white or a person of color, you foster belonging and safety by modeling a willingness to listen and creating a space for connection and understanding. I once coached two leaders of a creative team who had recently delivered a presentation to a major potential client. During the pitch, the client's chief marketing officer made several veiled racist comments that went unquestioned but not unnoticed. The creative team members making the pitch were mostly BIPOC. They felt deeply triggered and wanted to call the whole thing off. But the risk of losing this deal during a financial downturn loomed large in everyone's minds.

The creative team leaders reached out to me for guidance on how to move forward. I encouraged them to schedule a follow-up meeting where they could safely and constructively share what they felt they could not raise in the meeting. In preparation for this follow-up discussion, the leaders and I talked about the importance of standing by our values and standing up for our team members, especially those with less privilege. I encouraged them not to shame the client team but rather to describe our team's reactions to the chief marketing officer's comments with empathy, clarity, and a desire to move forward.

The follow-up meeting was a success. The chief marketing officer did not join, unfortunately, but the client team thanked us for being willing to engage in a "courageous conversation" where all were able to see and understand each other's perspectives. Our team leaders felt they had an opportunity to show up with clear and decisive leadership and to reassert our organizational values of diversity, equity, and inclusion. They called it a "transformational moment," where they gained higher levels of integrity, insight, and trust. They didn't win the pitch, but the team leaders gained the respect and trust of their creative peers and a client they hoped to work with in the future. In the end, the chief marketing officer never apologized, but we gained more than an apology. This was not the easy or risk-free route, but it was the right call to set context for understanding, speak up and challenge racist behavior, and model to our teams what courage, professionalism, and grace look like in action.

Your Road Map to Revolution

The culture and norms of a workplace significantly impact employees' sense of inclusion and belonging—as well as job satisfaction and performance. Management is about leadership, and that means inspiring and motivating a team to do more than they ever thought possible. It also means protecting them from harm. Tune in to what's going on, be up-front about your history with racial issues, and act on what you learn. That's how you build trust and belonging.

- **Go on a listening tour**. Investigate and assess what work is like for everyone on your team. Listen carefully and purposefully to all members of your team. Resist the urge to present solutions and wait until everyone is done speaking to offer your closing thoughts and ideas for what comes next.

- **Embrace being open to tough conversations**. As a manager, it's important that you make yourself available so that your teams can access you when and if they need you. You need to show a willingness to listen. Consider using outside facilitators that can help you transform an understanding of personal and structural inequities into commitments and action plans.

- **Offer anonymous ways to share what's going on**. Use surveys to get a holistic view of diversity, equity, and inclusion in your workforce; offer tools that allow people to report wrongdoing; or hire an outside firm to summarize (and even dramatize) the insidious behavior that could be holding people back.

- **Follow through and follow up**. When you hear something, say something and do something. Listen, learn, respond, and act quickly. Even if it's not 100 percent the perfect action, doing something to show that you're taking a situation seriously counts—even if that's just acknowledging that it happened.

- **Lean on your HR team**. Engage your HR partner and determine the best course of action to collect information, seek clarity, and determine responses and actions. Ask them to sit in on or facilitate difficult conversations.

- **Strengthen your emotional intelligence**. This will help you better discern whether a conversation or interaction is going the wrong way. Ask yourself: Have I conducted myself in a way that would lead to a good outcome? Or have I, in some small or large way, conducted myself in a way that has contributed to this situation?

- **Pause and reflect before critiquing the way an issue is raised**. Don't be distracted if someone raises a problem in an angry manner that makes you uncomfortable. You should separate your fear of conflict from the need to listen to the wrongdoing that's being reported. Ask yourself: Do I require people to raise issues in an "acceptable" way? What can I do differently to ensure that all employees feel safe to report racist incidents?

- **Make authentic apologies that demonstrate awareness of the impact of your words or actions on others**. But don't overdo it. Ask yourself: Do I apologize with "You must have heard me wrong" or "Sorry I offended you"? Or, rather, "I just heard what I said. I apologize. I take full ownership of the impact from my comments or actions. And I commit to you that I will do my best to ensure it doesn't happen again"?

8

NO TALENT LEFT BEHIND

L EADERSHIP DOESN'T JUST happen, and promotions don't fall from the sky. Everyone is prone to bias, and we know that the performance evaluations that determine what people get paid and who gets promoted are deeply biased. We further know from research that BIPOC employees, women of color in particular, get promoted less frequently, are rated more harshly in evaluations, and get less support at work to advance in their careers. It is the responsibility of leadership to unbias the performance evaluation process and to provide managers with the tools to understand racial inequity dynamics across the employee life cycle.

The most effective managers use coaching to unlock their employees' potential and improve performance. How do you do that? Assess employee competencies and explore needs and interests. Ask questions that help individuals arrive at their own solutions, recognize and point out strengths more than corrections, and prioritize career path and development needs. The best-performing companies know talent is critical to their success and are twice as likely to invest significant time and resources ensuring the right people are in the right roles and environments where they can thrive. But we continue to fail BIPOC employees by letting their talents and potential waste away.

Take Desiree Booker, a career strategist. She held two communication roles with two different managers, and how each person managed her had a direct impact at how long she stayed at each company. "In one, I had a manager who took the time to nurture and develop me, while the other manager wanted to fire me for every little mistake that I made," Booker says. "The manager who took the time to develop me, he recognized my skills gaps when I was hired, but he saw my potential and was committed to helping me grow. That manager was a senior vice president. It's rare to find that level of investment in talent, especially junior talent, from a senior leader, and his guidance made a tremendous difference in the trajectory of my career."

Without intentional, supportive, and transparent growth and advancement practices, too many BIPOC employees aren't given a fair chance to succeed. A friend recently shared a story about a highly qualified Black woman he hired for his sales team. During the interview process, her talent, experience, and energy were undeniable, and they made her an offer without reservation. A year later, he admitted he thought they had made a mistake, because she wasn't keeping up with her peers. I asked him, "Is she the only woman of color on your team? Is this the first time you're noticing poor performance? Have you asked if anything has been distracting or worrying her that could impact her results?" He said he had checked in with her, and when it seemed that everything was fine, he let it go. Without considering extenuating circumstances, he now believed that she was incapable of doing the job.

"You can't let it go," I told him. "You need to show both concern and empathy for her. Being the only woman of color on a team can be extremely taxing. As a manager of underrepresented talent, you have to dig deeper to build relationships and understand the obstacles she may be facing, especially because they're likely not part of your own repertoire of experiences. What are the barriers to her success that may be invisible to you? Are you providing real-time and ongoing performance and development feedback? What, if anything, is preventing her from reaching her full capacity?"

We all need to know what's expected of us and how success will be measured; otherwise we're left with career-damaging assumptions. Imagine if teachers told their students what contributed to their final grade at the *end* of the school year and said, "Oh, by the way, all those test scores didn't matter. I'm grading you on how much you spoke up in class." When the rules of the game keep changing, only those who have access to and support from the game makers can succeed.

That's what's happening in the workplace. Many managers see performance as either "meets expectations" or not—you're either great at what you do, or you're missing the mark—but the truth is far from that, and there are many factors such as microaggressions, double standards, and bias that can impact the performance of BIPOC, women, LGBTQ people, and other marginalized employees. Research has repeatedly shown that standard talent-management practices like performance reviews and promotional decisions remain stubbornly in favor of men in the workplace, with women of color receiving less support and vaguer performance feedback.

BIPOC employees often get passed over for a promotion, not because of lack of merit, but because their managers have failed to cultivate them. These employees are thwarted by leaders who are ill-equipped to drive high levels of performance, growth, and development with equitable outcomes in mind. Often this is the result of being led, not by an ill-intentioned manager, but rather by one who is uncomfortable giving critical or constructive feedback, especially when there is an element of difference (e.g., race, gender, nationality). The problem is the manager who couches their language, who hedges so much that the employee doesn't actually hear it as feedback. Who fails to see barriers to equity for their team members and their responsibility to eliminate those barriers. More specifically, BIPOC employees' careers suffer from a lack of:

- unbiased feedback from managers;

- performance-management tools;

- individualized development opportunities;

- equal pay;

- internal support and confidants; and

- honest conversations.

Managers are often rewarded for finding the path of least resistance. In the case of the sales manager with the underperforming employee, unexamined assumptions may have led to the wrong conclusion. And this manager's unwillingness to look beneath the racial surface in his organization was a miss. Sales is very quantitative—she wasn't hitting her numbers. That was an undeniable fact. But what else could have impacted her performance? If my friend had probed more with his direct report, he may have discovered the story behind those numbers. Was she being assigned high-growth clients commensurate with those of her peers? Was she having a harder time closing clients because they didn't want to work with a Black person? Was something going on in her personal life that was prohibiting her from being fully present? Was she afraid to ask questions for fear of seeming incapable—a common challenge for Black employees who have long known that they have to work twice as hard to get half as far as their white counterparts?

But he didn't ask these questions, and this high-potential, Black, female rock star left the company. No, not just the company. She left because her manager and peers didn't recognize the systemic hurdles she was facing and did nothing to clear away those obstacles. In these situations, color-blind management—or pretending that racism doesn't exist—pushes out BIPOC staff.

This happens everywhere. Despite all it has said, done, and invested, Google in the fall of 2020 once again was the subject of public outrage over a racialized incident. Google had fired a prominent AI ethics researcher, Timnit Gebru, a Black woman who had criticized the ethical and societal impacts of the technology and the company's lackluster diversity, equity, and inclusion efforts. In an internal email to employees, CEO Sundar Pichai said, "We need to accept responsibility for the fact that a prominent Black, female leader with immense talent left Google unhappily. This loss has had a ripple effect through some of our least represented communities, who saw themselves and some of their experiences reflected in Dr. Gebru's."

I was brought back to the months after I left Google, when a colleague called to say that in a presentation about the high turnover of executives of color in the organization, she named me as a regrettable loss. To her surprise, one white male executive lifted his head up with a questioning look and said, "Daisy is gone? I didn't know she left." I and so many others had left quietly. I can't speak to others' motives, but I chose not to answer the dozens of calls I received from journalists wanting to know why I "really left Google." I knew that if I spoke out, I would only be leaving a mess for the friends and colleagues, mostly BIPOC, who would be tasked with quieting everything down. I knew, at that time, that it would only be a short-lived story that would weigh on the wrong people. Latinx and Black colleagues acknowledged the role I had played in their careers with a beautiful goodbye. That meant everything to me. But at the time, I was not ready to share that I left Google because I had lost faith in leadership's willingness to truly change their workplace culture, norms, and behaviors.

I am proud of Gebru for speaking up and expressing exactly what I and so many have experienced. I am proud of the many Googlers who stood beside her. Google Walkout for Real Change circulated a petition calling on the company to strengthen its commitment to research integrity, stating, "Instead of being embraced by Google as an exceptionally talented and prolific contributor, Dr. Gebru has faced defensiveness, racism, gaslighting, research censorship, and now a retaliatory firing."

No public apologies were made. This wasn't a solo decision, and the world needed to hear from the entire organization. Following an internal investigation, the company announced that it would increase resources for retaining and promoting employees, focus on addressing disputes among workers and managers, and evaluate the performance of vice presidents on diversity and inclusion goals. These bare minimum changes were already in effect or had been advocated for years, albeit poorly supported by leadership. Google, like many other organizations, has lost immensely talented BIPOC professionals and leaders time and again. The difference now was the public outcry and moment of global reckoning.

Here's what you should know: when an employee doesn't see a future at their company and doesn't feel that they belong—for reasons from lack of promotions to everyday exclusions—they will look for opportunities elsewhere. According to a Gallup study, more than 93 percent of millennials of all races left their employers the last time they changed roles; only 7 percent took a new position within the same company. Black employees in general are 30 percent more likely to leave than white employees. Here are the factors Gallup found that lead to flight:

- Lack of opportunities to learn and grow

- Poor quality of manager

- Poor quality of management

- Lack of interest in the type of work

- Lack of opportunities for advancement

- Lack of access to senior leadership

- Racial prejudice and microaggressions

As a manager, it's your job to eliminate these barriers, help people see a clear pathway for their advancement, and assist them in getting there. Because the workplace is not equal for everyone and everyday experiences and opportunities can be drastically different based on who you are, where you came from, and what you look like, it's the combination of providing the right runway for each individual and nurturing talent that will lead to an Inclusion Revolution.

So where to begin? First, look deeper into the factors that lead to racial disparities on your teams and work toward reducing them. You'll have to master the dance between the macro and the micro, the immediate and the long term. The mark of a great leader is understanding people in their infinite complexity, challenging them with a bolder vision of what is possible, and inspiring the team to do their best work. Additionally, great managers help their team when obstacles arise, have difficult conversations in the face of disruptive change, and coach team members through the ups and downs of work life (and life life). It's about creating a culture of transparent performance assessment, fair and equitable treatment, meaningful compensation philosophies, and effective communication. Phew! I know that's a lot, so let's break down how to revolutionize your performance management and be that great boss people will be talking about for years:

Step 1: Know your people
Step 2: Remove bias from performance evaluations
Step 3: Ensure transparency in the goal-setting and promotion process
Step 4: Create individual growth plans
Step 5: Provide better feedback
Step 6: Pay fairly

Step 1: Know Your People

Growing leaders can't start early enough. Who are they? What makes them tick? What are their strengths? What could derail them? The foundation of performance management is understanding the nu-ances of the individuals on your team. It's about the people, people! Advice on how to be a good manager is ubiquitous, but it often fails to specify that women on your team may need help taking credit for their ideas, or that BIPOC may not feel comfortable speaking up in a meeting unless encouraged. Strengths are often obvious; it's figuring out what's holding someone back that has the potential to unleash real magic.

What do you know about the people on your team? I mean, what do you really know about their intellectual curiosity and their state of well-being and mental health? Do you know what charges them up, what drains them, and what's important to them? At your next one-on-one—or, even better, at a lunch, coffee, or tea break—start by asking one of these questions: What is on your mind? What are your favorite things to work on? What would you like to learn if you had more time? If you were not doing this, what would you be doing?

Think of these conversation starters: If you had a free day to spend on anything you like, what would you do? What do you nor-mally do for lunch or when you get a rare break in the day? You'll be surprised by how much this will help your team members feel at ease. What they share can be very telling about what they value, what holds them back, and what they appreciate, fear, or dislike about work—all leading to a stronger sense of trust and belonging.

I often start my leadership meetings with a prompt to enhance our sense of community and to bring joy to our work. Some exam-ples: What is one thing that brought you joy this past week? What is the thing that you just can't get to that is causing you angst? Tell us a short story about who you were at age ten. The creative minded on my team always jump to it. The more introverted labor over their responses. But they all join at the right pace for them, often sharing laughter and a sense of discovery as we learn more about each other. The more I learn about each of my team members, the better I'm able to refine and tailor how I relate to them individually.

That sense of psychological safety has taken time to build. People have a hard time being vulnerable and sharing what they believe is potentially harmful information. This is especially true for BIPOC who do not feel safe enough to express their emotions without fear of retaliation. In many organizations—let's call them bobblehead organizations—everyone bobs their head all day. No one is going to share their innermost fears and dreams unless they're safe to do so. If bobblehead behavior is what's rewarded in your organization, that's what you'll get. You'll miss out on taking worthwhile risks, getting creative, and finding opportunities to grow. The best thing you can do, whether from the very beginning or starting right now, is to genuinely demonstrate interest in your people, to share with them what you're asking them to share with you, and to be consistent with what you promise and how you honor their frankness.

Regular check-ins prevent workers from checking out, says the EY *Belonging Barometer* report, which found that 39 percent of respondents, across gender and age, say that when colleagues check in with them about how they are doing, both personally and professionally, they feel the greatest sense of belonging at work. Across all generations, the check-in took priority over actions such as: public recognition (23 percent), being invited to out-of-office events (20 percent), being asked to join a meeting with senior leaders (14 percent), and being included on emails with senior leaders (9 percent).

There's no fixed equation for how much time you should spend with your team members, but it should be a significant portion of your week, every week. Not surprisingly, employees who spend one-on-one time with their managers are more likely to be engaged. "It's your job to build your people," says Sherice Torres, vice president at Facebook. "When people say to me, 'Oh, this coaching and HR stuff is taking too much of my time,' guess what? That is your job now. To me, the best managers are only spending 20 to 30 percent of their time as an individual contributor or creating deliverables. The vast majority of your time is coaching and building your people and coaching and building your competencies to better coach and build your people."

Beyond rote agenda items and to-dos, check-ins should incorporate a feeling assessment. At Sprinklr, a customer experience management platform, managers focus on happiness questions in their one-on-ones: How happy are you, and what would it take to make you happier? To quantify it, they use a happiness scale. Employees are asked to rate their happiness level on a scale of one to ten, and then to discuss what it would take to make it a ten. Additionally, managers have daily "heartbeat calls," where they check in not just on work but also on how each person is doing personally. They also use an employee engagement tool that they developed to track employee satisfaction with their programs.

You should aim to understand each team member's career aspirations and goals and acknowledge that BIPOC employees may face different hurdles. Employees who discuss performance development goals regularly with their managers are four times as likely to be engaged in their job, according to Gallup. Besides the vital one-on-one time, every employee on your team should do a self-review. Employee self-assessments are a great way to codify mutually agreed-on goals. What do you want to do? How do you want to feel? Where do you want to be? How can we make your work goals more connected to your personal and professional aspirations? How can I help?

Step 2: Remove Bias from Performance Evaluations

Racial bias is often the most damaging factor in your employees' growth and development. Many companies have invested in impressive leadership-development programs for good reason. Identifying and supporting their future leaders is key to their competitive growth and agility in fast-changing markets, and it increases engagement and commitment when employees see clear pathways for growth. But what happens when development plans are laden with racial bias?

Katica Roy, founder and CEO of Pipeline Equity, has found that for every one hundred men promoted or hired to a managerial position, only seventy-nine women are promoted or hired. The gap widens when intersected with race and ethnicity. Only fifty-eight Black women are promoted to manager for every one hundred men. The big picture is that today almost 90 percent of *Fortune* 500 CEOs are still white males (that number was 96.4 percent in 2000). Today, only 1 percent of the *Fortune* 500 CEOs are African Americans, 2.4 percent are East Asians or South Asians, and 3.4 percent are Latinx.

Organizations like Management Leadership for Tomorrow, Code2040, Girls Who Code, the Emma Bowen Foundation, and many others have long provided a playbook for underrepresented talent to ascend through high school, college, and graduate school to the professional ranks. Their theory of change is predicated on surrounding BIPOC talent with support networks of peers and mentors who can provide the professional experience and social capital necessary to launch their careers and accelerate their success. These programs do a wonderful job harnessing talent, but they don't always change the hearts and minds of the people these BIPOC will be interacting with in the institutions where they study, train, and work.

Managers influence their employee's motivations, morale, and career path perhaps most powerfully during the performance review cycle. More than half of a performance rating reflects the rater's own characteristics, not those of the person being rated, according to *Harvard Business Review*. This well-studied phenomenon is called the idiosyncratic rater effect. Katica Roy also shared that only 46 percent of women (versus 51 percent of men) believe promotion criteria are fair and objective. While 42 percent of companies check for bias in reviews and promotions by gender, only 18 percent track outcomes for the compounding bias of race *and* gender.

Be aware of personal or institutional biases on expectations of performance. Because even if you're not keeping track, those who work for you are. Understand that how people approach their work varies based on their influences, experiences, and education or training. Did the person meet the performance expectations, but just in a different way than you anticipated or would have done yourself? It's imperative to monitor performance at the same level and standard, regardless of racial or gender identity, and to monitor your own performance in managing others. For example, ask yourself:

- Who are the people on your team who you regularly offer an extra helping hand?

- Which team members do you grant the benefit of the doubt when mistakes are made?

- Who do you push to meet with on a regular basis?

If you're not answering everyone (or no one), bias may be at play.

To ensure BIPOC talent is not left behind, understand these four common biases that sneak up in performance reviews.

Recency bias

"What have you done for me lately?" It's true, most of us are more likely to remember things that happened recently than things that have happened throughout the entire year or quarter—for example, your performance review cycle.

Do this: Gather information (such as work products, interactions you've had or observed, and outcomes met or exceeded) throughout the review cycle. This could mean using an internal performance-management system, asking an employee to fill out a form for you on a monthly basis, or even having a document where you jot down notes about their progress, challenges, and wins. And if you're the employee who wants to ensure your manager fairly tracks your performance, create your own system. For my one-on-ones with my boss, I share a weekly update that covers the following: a personal check-in, top outcomes for the week, and items for discussion. I use a Google doc so that she and I can revisit throughout the year. During my last performance review, she commented on how useful it was to revisit the weekly reviews. These communications tools can also provide a forum for celebrating success, tracking decisions, unblocking challenges, and offering temperature checks on how people are feeling.

Proximity bias

It's the notion that people place higher value on work that they actually see or are directly aware of. If you work remotely or with a team that is geographically displaced, it's easy to discount work that you aren't actually seeing yourself.

Do this: Managers should have regular check-ins with employees in order to keep up with the current state of their project, day-to-day accomplishments, and obstacles, as well as their well-being.

Confirmation bias

This bias is based on our perception of others. For example, a white male manager may have a preconception that his white male team member is more assertive. This could cause him to more easily recall instances in which the employee made bold statements during a meeting. On the other hand, the manager may perceive his Asian female team members to be less assertive, predisposing him to forget when she suggested an effective solution or was successful in a tough negotiation.

Do this: The most powerful ways to mitigate this bias are frequent manager-employee check-ins (and don't forget to document them through the tools I shared earlier), requesting and considering 360-degree feedback from people the employee works with before reviews, and supplementing these with self-evaluations, where your reports list their own accomplishments and how they met their goals before you consider their performance.

Gender and intersectional bias

Women experience bias not only because of their gender but due to their race, sexual orientation, disability, or other aspects of their identity. In a study by Catalyst, a respondent, who is African American, was once told in a performance review that her hair was "too fun" and that it made people question her maturity. Through analyzing more than twenty-five thousand pieces of peer feedback, Culture Amp has found that individuals tend to focus more on the personality and attitudes of women. On the other hand, men tend to receive feedback that is more based on accomplishments and competence. If you're tempted to use the words "compassionate," "helpful," or "organized" to describe a woman or BIPOC member of your team, reflect a bit more. What kind of leadership skills have they demonstrated? If Jewel mentored new hires whose performance was significantly accelerated, instead of saying she's "incredibly helpful," you could say she "leads by coaching excellence" or "is a determined leader."

Managers should keep in mind that the best leaders inspire leadership in others. Hierarchies and white male supremacy create low expectations for women and BIPOC staff. White men are groomed for leadership from birth. Women and BIPOC are expected to be grateful for being begrudgingly allowed into spaces where white men assume they don't belong and are less often groomed for leadership.

Do this: Ensure that you're providing managers with the tools and training to give structured feedback; they should use formalized criteria to assess their direct reports. Help your managers approach each review in a consistent manner by prompting specific, measurable performance outcomes for each employee. How well and how often did this employee produce quality work? Did their work make the intended impact on larger priorities and projects? Did this employee achieve the goals, projects, and priorities agreed upon this year? If they didn't, why not? This can help them concentrate on assessing all women and nonbinary employees based on their performance, accomplishments, and behaviors rather than racial, ethnic, or personality attributes.

Counteracting bias

In 2012, the National Center for State Courts embarked on a research project to better understand implicit bias among judges and how it impacted court decisions. They found that when the basis for judgment is somewhat vague or subjective—situations without much precedent or that involved new laws—biased judgments were more likely.

The triggers that affected the judges' performance and led to a proclivity toward bias included: stress (a heavy backlog, threats to safety, political pressure, loud construction noise), fatigue (long hours, lack of support), and time pressure (the decision-maker had to form complex judgments quickly and couldn't process all the incoming information). "Decision makers who are rushed, stressed, distracted, or pressured are more likely to apply stereotypes—recalling facts in ways biased by stereotypes and making more stereotypic judgments—than decision makers whose cognitive abilities are not similarly constrained," the report stated.

To counteract this widespread problem—beyond the obvious factors of getting more sleep, trying to slow down, and being more present—there was a call for judges to articulate their reasoning process. Basically, when judges took the time to write down why they were making a decision before announcing it, they were able to assess the validity of the ruling with an eye for implicit bias. Taking that extra step to check your response or decision—writing or typing out your reasoning and then evaluating the decision—can mitigate rash moves driven by bias. Could you imagine writing this: "I passed Tiffany Dufu over for a promotion. I don't deem her to be professional enough because of her wardrobe and accessories." I'm betting you won't be that brutally honest with yourself, but if you want to dismantle long-standing inequities in your workplace, you should be.

Here's a mindful exercise to try in your daily life. Before you make a decision at work—whether it's asking someone to step in as a hand model for a video shoot or deciding who to nominate to speak at a conference—pause to reflect on any assumptions you may have made. Try to evaluate the perception and intention in your decision: Would I have made this same decision if this person were a man, a woman, BIPOC, white, straight, LGBTQ, a mom, a dad, someone who lived in the suburbs, someone from the South?

For instance, people may have assumed Tiffany Dufu wasn't professional enough because of her jewelry, and managers constantly assume a new mother would not want to travel to a conference because she has a young child at home. Inaccurate, biased, and preconceived notions that businesses started by Black founders fail have led to a tremendous lack of funding for Black entrepreneurs (1 percent out of the $150 billion in US venture investment in 2020) and a high rate of loan rejection. In fact, Black entrepreneurs' loan requests are three times less likely to be approved than those of white entrepreneurs, a difference that remains even after accounting for the credit scores and net worth of founders.

Unexamined assumptions do not lead to diverse, equitable, and inclusive workplaces. Assumptions based on stereotypes will only come back to bite you. You need to recognize and outsmart unconscious beliefs that close the door on people's ambitions, innovation, and careers.

Step 3: Ensure Transparency in the Goal-Setting and Promotion Process

Too often, raises, discretionary incentives, and promotions are dependent on who the boss likes, relates to, identifies with, and socializes with. This is bias. I've seen promotions go to the team member who delivered the most recent big win, and not to the one who gets the small, less recognizable wins on a consistent basis. Sometimes, the promotion is given to the person who was the most demanding in a racially or gender accepted way. That is, the white male employee who is more often lauded as ambitious versus BIPOC women who are more prone to being accused of being ungrateful, not a team player, and not willing to wait their turn. That's lazy leadership. To most employees, the promotion process is too obscure. Is it based on timing? Simply asking for it? Budget? Actual merit?

This subjectivity and bias must stop. When it comes to career advancement, there must be well-defined, clear pathways for career progression and benchmarks for promotions, pay raises, and other incentives. Otherwise you can fall into the same "favoring those I like" exclusive habits. No one should feel that they're being passed over for a promotion. They should understand what is necessary to be considered for the next level.

Higher education is notoriously transparent about what it takes to be eligible for a promotion for administrative positions. Purdue University, for example, posts clearly on its website: "Staff promotions take place twice a year. Approved promotions go into effect January 1 and July 1. January 1 promotions must be submitted to the VP of Human Resources by November 1 and July 1 promotions must be submitted by March 31." Most companies aren't this routine, but you can let your team know that promotion reviews happen in x month because that's when budgets are decided, and you have to put forth any promotion proposals by y date.

Then, be clear about what it takes. To assess promotion readiness, Purdue presents this evaluation criteria:

- Skill set (ensuring their skill set matches the requirements of the position)

- Sustained performance (high performance levels in at least the two most recent review cycles)

- Demonstrated steps taken to gain new skills and grow in their career

- Personal motivation and willingness for an increase in level and responsibility

These organizational guidelines are a great start, but to better serve your teams you should sit down with each employee and clearly define specifics under each bullet; otherwise it remains subjective and ripe for interpretation. Which skills are required? What does high performance mean? What does it mean to champion the evolution of our corporate culture? How do you expect someone to demonstrate willingness to learn and grow? How are you measuring motivation? How do you craft the next set of goals and challenges? It takes time, effort, and budget to set your employees up for success with opportunities to grow their skills. This is how you transform workplace culture and business outcomes. Consistent measurement around established performance criteria enables you to equitably disseminate information about what is expected of all employees to get a raise, get promoted, or develop their skills. Then, there are no surprises.

Endeavor, a global entertainment, sports, and fashion company, as part of their talent management practices, is establishing a promotion and career framework whereby they look at each role and establish what is required to be promoted. "This allows for equity, eliminates the unwritten rules of success at companies, and gives individuals greater insight into their career trajectory," says Alicin Reidy Williamson, Endeavor's senior vice president and chief inclusion officer.

To create a fair promotion and performance-management process, you have to (1) establish transparent, measurable, and time-bound goals and (2) assess each individual against these metrics, looking at what they achieve and how they do so. That's it! But, unsurprisingly, it's not that simple. How you assess the individuals is where ambiguity creeps in. It might be tempting to think we can just trust our instincts. But we've learned about where that can lead us with recruitment processes, haven't we? The hard truth is that implicit bias is masterful at creeping in all the time, and it's really difficult to see and therefore stop it in its tracks. The secret weapon: data. Hardwiring anti-bias in performance-management tools and processes helps bypass imperfect and often compromised impressions and enables you to deliver on your aspirations of fairness and meritocracy.

Fortune 500 companies largely have formalized performance-management processes, but many suffer flaws from collecting data that places too much weight on opaque, arbitrary, and biased ratings. Too often, fuzzy reasoning for evaluation is used to excuse ongoing advancement gaps when it comes to race, gender, and other marginalized identities.

Performance-management platforms like Culture Amp and 15Five offer useful guides and tools for delivering structured performance conversations and capturing the data. Try asking: How did you produce quality and impactful results this quarter? How have you demonstrated key characteristics or company values (e.g., teamwork and collaboration or inclusion and belonging)? What, if anything, is hanging you up right now?

Factorial, for example, is software that can help you manage and evaluate employee performance with customized questionnaires and assigned reviewers. Employment Hero uses peer-to-peer recognition and user happiness surveys to help you communicate with your team. These strategies can improve the effectiveness and inclusivity of your performance-management process, as will ensuring that managers' assessments are accurate, consistent, and fair. GE has taken it a step further and seen the benefit of ceasing year-end performance reviews in favor of establishing a continuous dialogue around goals and accountability. They launched an internal app that allows for a constant exchange of feedback through voice memos, quick text notes, and attached documents between all members of a team—not just the traditional boss-subordinate relationship. Think of it like a twenty-four-seven Evernote job tracker. This tremendous amount of data collection helps inform and inspire GE's annual goal-setting conversations, which makes them more meaningful, engaging, robust, and collaborative.

Step 4: Create Individual Growth Plans

Take the time to figure out what all of your team members need to succeed, and what you as a manager can do to clear their path for advancement. Being intentional about understanding the experience of your BIPOC employees will further help you develop strong leaders who find meaning in their work. How you manage the complexity of different experiences, backgrounds, thinking, and communication styles will be the key to creating the trusting, inclusive environment required to unlock the full potential of your team. Good performance management is developing a personalized plan: What will it take for *this person* to advance, grow, and get promoted? And how do we achieve that together?

Thought starters:

- What talent is needed for growth, and how do we best use our talent?

- What are the emotional and tactical skills, training, and support our managers, leaders, and teams need to better support our business and culture strategy?

- How are we developing these skills across our teams?

Then, consider leadership potential versus readiness. Those who are deemed ready are most often granted the promotion, access, and opportunity. Being twice as good is only half the battle. The other half is overcoming the unmerited success of mostly white men whose potential is assumed and not questioned nearly as much as it is for BIPOC employees. To address bias in the velocity at which BIPOC, women, LGBTQ people, and other traditionally underrepresented employees are hired and promoted versus their peers, you need to examine your assumptions about both their potential and readiness to succeed. I have never hired a new team member who had all the competencies desired for their role, but I have made bets based on their past experiences and qualifications that they had the potential to learn, contribute, and grow. I've encouraged hiring managers to consider the unintended consequences of BIPOC and female candidates not being given these same opportunities as their white male counterparts. This is where clarity on how to develop effective career coaching comes in.

Leadership potential is just that: potential. It doesn't automatically or necessarily develop into leadership ability, but potential has a long-term trajectory and can even span an individual's career. In a study about leadership potential versus readiness, Frances Jackson and Emma Hansen note that an employee's potential is judged on their motivations, development orientation, and ability to master complexity, among other attributes needed for strategic and executive roles.

Leadership readiness is focused on the here and now—tomorrow, next week, or maybe even next year as a stretch goal to be reached. Readiness requires propensity to lead, ability to bring out the best in others, authenticity, receptivity to feedback, learning agility, passion for results, adaptability, conceptual thinking, and ability to navigate ambiguity.

To close the gap between leadership potential and leadership readiness, consider the following for your team members:

- **Help employees believe that their growth and advancement is a priority for you**. Some of your employees may already have development goals in mind but don't know how to get started or whether the company will support those plans.

Other employees may not realize you see potential in them or need encouragement to reach for the next step in their career.

- **Offer stretch roles**. Give team members responsibilities just beyond their current capabilities to create an engaged workforce and a culture of mentoring.

- **Facilitate coaching**. At Culture Amp, each employee has access to a professional coach through the Coaching for Everyone program. Coaches help assess where a person is and where they want to be, then guide each person through a strategy to reach their goals.

- **Scan for signals**. You learn a lot by capturing different data points. Ask a diverse number of peers for feedback. What has been their experience with your team members? Do they think they have the energy and determination to achieve their next level of growth? If not, why? Look into how often your team members are invited to key meetings or projects, and what roles they are asked to play. When you have that knowledge, you can help your team members address development opportunities and your organization to become more accountable for the success of all of their employees.

- **Be wary of the prove-it-again bias**. Women of color, especially in male-dominated fields such as science and technology, continually report that they have to provide more evidence of competence than their white male peers. We give more weight to a man's potential than his actual performance. This is especially true when comparing white and BIPOC colleagues. To reduce this bias, detail and share team members' accomplishments and make sure they have equal opportunities to get noticed by people in leadership.

To continually check for biases that creep in when determining someone's trajectory, start with the facts. For each person on your team, identify the top skill or attribute that could get them leadership ready. Pinpoint either something that would have a big impact on this person's career trajectory or something they are motivated to work on and, based on what you learned, offer opportunities for training and coaching. Be proactive in your approach to make that happen; 40 percent of employees who receive poor job training leave their positions within the first year. If you're fortunate enough to have an HR business partner and a learning and development department at your company, reach out and partner with them. A collaborative development-planning approach often leads to higher quality plans and greater growth.

Most established companies already offer training and professional-development classes internally or budget for external courses. Encourage your team to take advantage of these. You should, too! Pixar University offers required trainings as well as optional classes for different disciplines to ensure learning is part of the company culture. Etsy School offers classes like how to navigate a difficult conversation. At Google, courses varied from Coding 101 to enhancing managerial effectiveness.

That's the easy part. More often, it's not just raw skills that someone needs to succeed. There are always invisible promotion requirements. No one is going to say, "Having a senior-level sponsor or advocate will seal the deal for your career path." As a manager, if you know that leadership visibility is important, what are the next steps to secure cross-department support or mentorship? That's where individual coaching can come in to identify advancement opportunities and performance hindrances. Slack, for instance, has a program called Rising Tides, a six-month sponsorship program for a diverse group of emerging leaders who have historically lacked support. Program participants receive career-development training, executive coaching, and one-on-one sponsorship with a Slack executive team member, with a focus on building a supportive community of peers.

I have personally benefited from coaching over the course of my career. Some coaches were assigned for a discrete period as part of a leadership-development program. Some coaches I sought out myself to accelerate my professional growth and development. They have helped me understand my weak spots, internal bullies, beasts, and burdens—imagined or not. I learned that coaching is key to your personal success and that of your team and company.

If you bring a race-conscious lens to common assumptions about leadership and professional development, you can avoid falling into unconscious stereotyping. Once you educate yourself on the unique obstacles your diverse colleagues are facing, you can become better at working to erase persistent barriers to advancement. BIPOC professionals often face a constellation of barriers in their career journeys, from racist hiring practices to unconscious bias in promotions. It's imperative to ask deeper questions and look closer to understand underlying issues. For example, historically, Black women are generally reluctant to ask for help because of the risk of seeming weak, so, as a manager, it's up to you to say, "What are the barriers to your success here, and how can I help you?" Or, more broadly, "No one on this team needs to suffer in silence. My door is always open for any question, and you will never be judged for asking one." As a manager, you should also hone your coaching and mentoring skills with a lens on how to develop colleagues from different backgrounds.

Step 5: Provide Better Feedback

When I think back to that rock star employee on my friend's sales team, it seems unlikely that she received real-time feedback or even suggestions for improvement until it was too late—after her annual sales tanked. She was blindsided.

She's not alone. It won't surprise you that giving feedback is high on a manager's "don't want to do it" list, and so they tend to skip it entirely. Dr. Carla Jeffries of the University of Southern Queensland discovered that people fail to give constructive feedback to protect themselves, not others. It's natural to want to avoid an uncomfortable conversation or hurting another person's feelings, but the ramifications of feedback avoidance are too high. That person sitting in ignorant bliss will never have the chance to understand what they could be doing better until it's way too late, when they get passed over for a promotion or even are the first on the list to be let go. I had to let go of a seasoned Black manager once whose look of surprise still haunts me. When he asked, "What can I do differently?" I said, "I'm afraid there's not much you can do now. Your story here has already been written, and it's too late to change the narrative. My hope is that in your next role, you are given a fair chance to shine and that you ask for and are provided with the feedback and support you deserve, when it matters."

A key ingredient to professional advancement is feedback. Yet feedback is both difficult to give and receive. In 2014, Jack Zenger and Joseph Folkman surveyed workers, and 92 percent of the respondents agreed with the assertion, "Negative (redirecting) feedback, *if delivered appropriately*, is effective at improving performance." Only 8 percent didn't want to hear it. When managers fear that giving feedback to someone who doesn't look like them will be misinterpreted as racist or sexist, it perpetuates an even greater cycle of avoidance. Too often, I see managers fail to be honest with their BIPOC and female team members on what their strengths are and—crucially—where they need to fill gaps or build their skills. It's a huge disservice to the employee, team, and organization.

Performance-management conversations can be a daunting experience for managers and employees, but they're necessary for career growth. Mistakes are par for the course in career growth, but for BIPOC employees whose experience with racial bias in performance or career feedback may have led to demotions or even seeking mental health counseling, it is understandable to be wary. There's always a chance that someone won't take feedback well, but it shouldn't stop you from having the conversation. It's your job. The kindest thing to do is to give someone the right feedback at the right time, even if it unleashes a whole range of emotions. I've seen this bias of kindness too—that is, when you enable people in your organization to wander aimlessly from role to role, often failing miserably in each, because you simply won't come face-to-face with the discomfort of telling them the truth about their performance. I've seen this happen to BIPOC employees, where a white manager can't bear the social risk of being the one to let them go but won't offer constructive feedback. The employee's colleagues complain, often quietly, that they do not pull their weight in team projects, but no one is willing to give them the feedback they deserve—least of all their own manager.

At Vice Media Group, as with many companies, a source of many employee complaints was the inability to give and receive regular constructive feedback. We know from neuroscience that reflecting is a key step in making progress on any skill, as it increases your self-awareness. We also know that managers are not generally effective at providing the feedback we all need to improve performance, much less with a lens on interpersonal bias. To nudge managers and employees to hone their feedback skills, we delivered quarterly self-reflection checks through Culture Amp and promoted them as crucial to nurturing a culture of performance, communication, and transparency. We encouraged managers to discuss responses with their teams and shared resources to help them deliver better feedback conversations.

To give better feedback, we must also be willing to hold ourselves accountable for getting feedback. Ritualize asking for it. What worked well? What could I have done better? What do you think I can improve on, learn, or strengthen?

There's so much mistrust and tension in the workplace. So much concern that criticism may be taken as a form of insensitivity or discrimination. Feedback conversations should not be a gotcha moment or cause for reproach. BIPOC shouldn't have to assume every action is against us, and managers should actively solicit, listen, and be sensitive to the nuances and signals in their organizations. Managers should ask: What felt good and productive in the way that I shared this feedback? Where could I have been better in showing sensitivity to your circumstances? Did I effectively communicate the changes needed for you to improve your impact and performance? Leadership is truly a matter of listening, reflecting, and acting on what you learn. It's never too late to course correct.

Two tips: First, feedback is always best given in the moment. Second, find out how each member of your team likes to receive feedback. I know people who are eager for feedback and others who cower over the slightest criticism. I have eight direct reports, and I know each needs to receive feedback differently based on their lived experience and professional journey. It took me months to get to know them and build the necessary trust so that they could receive my feedback from a place of care, not just authority.

Ask for permission to kick off the conversations ("Is it okay if we talk about your performance/a recent project and share some feedback?"). Or turn the tables and ask, "What do you think is going well? What do you think you could improve on in your relationships with your colleagues? Where do you think this is holding you back?" Always have a follow-up plan. Ask how you can be helpful and decide when to revisit the topic. Keep checking in with the person to continue to garner trust and make sharing feedback even easier next time.

Trust is vital in performance management, and you can lean on that to get beneath the surface. Women, BIPOC, LGBTQ people, and members of other underrepresented groups often carry added pressure to prove their inherent worth. Trust has not always been a two-way street for them. In fact, it's been weaponized against them. This often shows up when a woman or BIPOC is more quickly or more harshly punished for making a mistake, especially compared to white males. They haven't experienced feedback that felt fair, and you have to come to understand where everyone on your team is coming from. As a manager, your job is making sure you understand the factors behind a team member's reluctance to share their weaknesses with you or explain a dip in performance. Ask: Where did you feel you delivered the best results? What made that possible?

Where did you most need support? Where do you think you'll need support moving forward? What does that look like?

Prioritize purpose and meaning when having these conversations. Traditional performance management puts ratings and evaluation at the center, but purpose and meaning are far more powerful in motivating employees than money and ratings, says talent-management advisor Alan Colquitt, the former director of global assessment, workforce research, and organizational effectiveness at Eli Lilly. When Colquitt worked at the company, monthly pulse surveys revealed that there was a significant drop in engagement for 80 percent of employees following the annual performance review process. Worse, that drop stayed down for nearly half the year. So, in 2017 Eli Lilly transformed its performance-management process by eliminating an annual review and ratings system and shifted toward a model of ongoing check-ins on goals with a focus on learning and growth.

Three Ways to Shake Up the Performance Review

A manager's role is to enable and amplify employee contributions that are of value to the organization, and those values and traits necessary for twenty-first-century leadership are shifting. Humility, empathy, inclusivity, accountability, resiliency, transparency— that's what matters in today's economy! Build that in your development plans and performance review metrics.

1. **Gather feedback from multiple sources versus just one manager**. You can increase transparency and diversity of opinions by allowing employees to nominate who should provide feedback as part of their performance review. This can be within their immediate team or cross-functional. Note: We are all biased. Having more people evaluate performance doesn't make opinions less biased, but it does help you balance your own perspective.

2. **Use artificial intelligence tools to detect, mitigate, and remove bias from performance reviews**. AI-enabled solutions such as adverse-impact analysis tools can detect potential discrimination across different groups in promotions and terminations. These insights can, in turn, help organizations take steps to address these discrepancies. Note: despite the great promise of AI, concerns remain that it can perpetuate or even increase biases in talent processes, given that it relies on data collected and developed by humans and is trained by machine learning created by humans. As with all recommendations, it is important to continuously test for bias and make adjustments as necessary.

3. **Emphasize allyship**. Author Kenji Yoshino has been working with one pharmaceutical company that wants to evaluate allyship as part of their performance review. Together, they are trying to determine the metrics of being a good ally in assessing performance outcomes. I have a hunch that their findings will show that allies who provide support, surface issues, or push for changes significantly reduce barriers to advancement and recognition for underrepresented employees.

Tips for Mitigating Bias in Performance Evaluations

Access resources to help you think through and manage your biases before launching into a performance-management conversation. Google gives managers an unbiasing checklist to use during performance management. You can adapt it to your organizational goals, but the key is to ensure you're consistent across all of your performance conversations. Here's how to do that:

1. **Use a rubric**. Rubrics lay out the criteria that you're evaluating so you and your team can stay focused and aligned on

what really matters. An effective rubric defines the criteria against which the employee's performance (goals and results achieved, including supporting core values and behavioral expectations) will be assessed.

2. **Collect evidence and input to inform your assessment (not the other way around).** Avoid confirmation bias by filling out your assessment based on the information you gather about whether the employee did or did not meet expectations. Examples include work products, interactions you've had or observed, and outcomes met. Seek out perspectives from peers and others who interact with your team members to balance your own perspective.

3. **Share specific feedback that will help improve results.** Be specific and use data to share balanced examples of strengths and areas of improvement. Research shows that men tend to receive more detailed, insightful feedback related to technical skills, while women receive less specific feedback that's focused on how they relate to others, such as communication styles and teamwork. The result? Men get a better idea of how to improve their outcomes (as opposed to their likeability), resulting in higher chances for advancement. These differences in feedback are further compounded for BIPOC. When our expectations for the "how" shift based on someone's identity, that's bias creeping in. Make sure that feedback is tied to outcomes and not identity expectations.

Step 6: Pay Fairly

We can't discuss performance management without talking about money. Communication about pay is the most critical element of compensation management, yet it is usually the weakest skill in a manager's tool kit. Although many companies have compensation philosophies and rigid rules in place, there is often a lack of communication to employees about the details from anyone beyond top management and HR. Pay equity analysis, also called pay parity audits, are not yet common across all organizations. Even in companies with clearly defined compensation practices, managers are not often trained on how to talk to employees about how salaries, raises, and bonuses are determined.

Pay perception has a stronger impact on inclusion than what is actually paid. Employees want to know how their pay is determined: if it is fair and at or above market rates, and if their peers are earning the same. There is too much smoke and mirrors around compensation structure, which can lead employees to feel undervalued and underappreciated. Couple this with well-publicized stats about equal pay and employees are left wondering, am I being taken advantage of?

Managers should understand their compensation programs and seek tools, resources, and training. Learn your data: how much your people are being paid and if there are any differences in pay relative to age, race, gender, job description and responsibilities, and a wide range of other criteria. Next, get smart on your salary guidelines (pay ranges or pay grades) and how to communicate them to your teams. If you're a new manager, you may have inherited the salary structure for your team. Ask why people are paid the way they are. You're always going to pay your top performers well, but who is determining who your top performers are? Whose negotiations for higher compensation were more successful—men or women, white people or BIPOC? Who is delivering the most impact on your team?

Also, make sure your team has a clear understanding of your pay principles and constraints. Does your company need to operate with a profit to consider pay increases? It seems obvious, but financial conditions of organizations are not always the same. In 2021, BlackRock gave all employees, from entry-level to director level, an 8 percent salary bump to recognize equal contributions to the company's strong growth. "By investing in you, we are investing in the future of the firm," wrote CEO Larry Fink and COO Rob Kapito in a staff email. The company saw strong profits in 2021 and passed them on to all its employees. The more you can do to demystify the pay process, the more your teams will understand why certain decisions are made and trust final outcomes.

Then, conduct a pay equity audit. The primary driver for pay equity analysis is closing an unfair, biased wage gap and examining the factors behind why someone is paid more or less than another. In the purest of cases, pay inequity is due to market competition and where you are coming from. For instance, a company may pay engineers in Silicon Valley more than ones in other cities because of the local competitive rates driven by Apple and Google.

Unequal pay also arises when women and BIPOC are punished for asking for raises and promotions, in part due to the bias of "you don't really belong here, so you should just be happy to have any job here." When they ask for pay equity, they are often viewed as ungrateful. They can't always use the same strategies and affinity bias boost that white men use. This contributes to the systemic undervaluing of women and BIPOC in raises and promotions. In 2021, compared to each $1 earned by a white, non-Hispanic man, on average:

- Asian American women earned $0.87;

- all women earned $0.82;

- African and Black American women earned $0.62;

- Native American women earned $0.60; and

- Latinas earned $0.55.

At Reddit, Ellen Pao reviewed all the pay bands for every position, then automatically highballed everyone—everyone got the max salary for each position. This eliminated inequality in salary by race and gender. However, some critics said that it deprived staff of chances to sharpen their negotiating skills. (To which I respond, you should offer staff universal training on how to negotiate through companies like WAGER, and then ensure that your managers apply fair practices when granting equitable raises and promotions.) Salesforce has notoriously done the same, as should all companies to ensure that BIPOC and women are paid the same as white men for the same positions.

Be clear with your teams. Say, "We are looking into pay equity in our company, or how you compare against your peers in similar roles. We are aiming to create more fair and equal systems of compensation." You may not always be able to fix every pay gap immediately. Maybe you don't have enough money to exceed market rates. Tell them that. Have the conversation. People want to know that someone has heard what their concerns are and that there is a plan to narrow the gap. That's inclusion, that's fairness, that's leadership.

Your Road Map to Revolution

Managers are curators and stewards of an organization's shared purpose, it's climate and culture. Ensure that your core talent processes, including performance management and promotions, are supporting your diversity, equity, and inclusion goals and your commitment to anti-racism. It's not a pipeline issue; it's a progression issue. What will it take for BIPOC employees to succeed and advance at your company? What does it take to receive a promotion or pay review? Share that info. Be cognizant of the racial dynamics at your organization and understand how this may be affecting a team member's performance or perceptions about their performance.

- **Know your team**. What are their goals? Aspirations? What do they need to learn? What could be holding them back? The better you understand how each team member works, the more you can create an environment in which they can thrive.

- **Look for bias in performance reviews**. As we've discussed throughout the book, bias is unavoidable. Sharpen your awareness to know when you're making assumptions about someone's work, career path, or desire for new opportunities.

- **Define paths to advancement**. When it comes to career advancement, there must be well-defined, clear pathways for career progression and benchmarks for promotions, pay raises, and other incentives. Otherwise, you can fall into the same "favoring those I like" anti-inclusive habits. Everyone should understand what is necessary to be considered for the next level.

- **Create individualized learning plans**. What will it take to get someone ready for the next level? Encourage BIPOC employees to take stretch opportunities. Don't penalize them for their ambition.

- **Don't be afraid to give feedback, especially for BIPOC employees who receive less support at work**. Without candid performance reviews, people don't have a chance to succeed. Confront your fear of feedback; otherwise, you could be holding someone back. Establish trust and deliver your feedback from a place of support and growth.

- **Run pay audits regularly**. Create an action plan to identify and eliminate pay inequity and have up-front and honest conversations about what you are doing to pay your teams equitably.

9

BUILD SUPPORT SCAFFOLDING

S UCCESS IS NOT a solo sport. Everyone needs support along their career path. Without it, you're operating at a deficit. Too often, BIPOC lack support, while their white peers seem to have an unlimited crew of champions and advocates. In the 1970s, Pope Consulting conducted a study at a pharmaceutical company where Black engineers were falling behind in their progress and deliverables compared to the white engineers. Well ahead of the times, the company, rather than push out underperforming engineers, hired a consultant to study the issue. Turns out, it was the closed social networks that prevented Black engineers from getting the mentorship, peer advice, and support they needed to succeed. White managers were uncomfortable mentoring (or befriending) Black staff. Perhaps these managers tended to hire and cultivate staff that reminded them of themselves—again, that's affinity bias. And white peers were uncomfortable extending friendship to Black staff.

This social unease, lack of support, and sense of inequality had a profound effect on performance. When new white engineers had questions, they just asked other white engineers and got on track right away.

Yet Black new hires were afraid of revealing what they didn't know, and so went to the library to study what to do, losing valuable time and dramatically slowing their onboarding process and productivity. "Black employees told us that they were fearful of asking too many questions because it could reinforce a stereotype that they were less intelligent than their white counterparts," Pat Pope, CEO of Pope Consulting, said. "After our study, it was clear that the informal systems of learning and development collapsed, so we told the company that they needed to formalize for their Black employees what the others get informally."

Company leadership responded by creating a curriculum program for all employees and an onboarding program addressing the unique needs of new hires. Within a year, they had permanently closed the achievement gap between Black and white engineers. "It was never an issue of talent. It was an issue of development and structural support," says Pope.

Not having an interpreter of organizational dynamics was damaging the Black engineers' careers.

"Your counterpart will get an opportunity, and you get a chance," says Lucinda Martínez, former executive vice president of brand marketing at HBO and HBO Max. "A real opportunity is an endorsement that also comes with support. It's saying, 'Look, I want you to meet Maria. Maria is amazing. Give her insight into the culture, help her navigate through the unspoken rules. I'm about to give her a stretch role, but she could benefit from your help and support along the way.' A chance is when you throw the person out there and hope that they make it, but no phone calls are made. They are thrown in to fend for themselves. When you get a chance, it comes with no support, and if you make a mistake, you're counted out. That's why many people of color don't make it to the end. And even if you do somehow pull through, the rewards are oftentimes doled out differently. Your counterpart gets a pat on the back; you get a pat on the head. It's nuanced but it's significant."

Your support system can make or break your career, from leading you to a new job to helping you succeed once you've entered the doors. Research from professors Jennifer Merluzzi and Adina Sterling found that Black employees are more likely to be promoted when they are referred by another employee by a factor of 1.2, compared to Black employees without a referral. That internal assurance—that willingness to vouch for someone—was required to deem a BIPOC employee promotable. Interestingly, they found that women received no benefit from being referred. The women at the firm they studied did receive statistically fewer regular promotions than men, but there was no difference in the data if a woman was referred. This could be because those referring women may have less clout than others, a common finding in studies about the mentoring of women.

I'm curious about the organizational clout that these referrers had compared to those referring male candidates. Was it a true referral? Was someone bullishly advocating for the employee or merely sharing a meh recommendation? Were these women part of formal mentorship programs where senior leaders outside their direct management chain could credibly vouch for them? The staggering stats keep coming: The 2019 report *Being Black in Corporate America: An Intersectional Exploration* by Coqual (formerly the Center for Talent Innovation) found that Black women were less likely to have access to the same support and advocacy as white women. The 2021 McKinsey *Women in the Workplace* report found that for every one hundred men who were promoted, only eighty-five women were promoted, only seventy-one Latina women, and only fifty-eight Black women. These numbers have remained stubbornly stuck. This lack of promotion compounds into poor retention rates, and thus your compositional diversity takes a hit again.

So what can you do about it? First, think about the type of career support you have in your own life. I've found that workplace guidance comes in many forms or roles.

1. **Decoder ring**: learned knowledge of office politics, situational awareness

2. **Peer support**: a career community that understands and guides you

3. **Connections**: the people you know who lead you to career opportunities and stretch assignments

4. **Mentorship and sponsorship**: a mentor is someone who provides career advice, guidance, or coaching, while a sponsor is someone who advocates for you

5. **External advisors**: experts and leaders who help influence company culture for the better

Throughout my career, I have a built a nurturing community of peers, mentors, and sponsors, many of whom I met by chance because we ran in different social circles. It took me years to learn how to more proactively and strategically access these networks for professional advancement. As a manager, think about who on your team has relationships that check all these categories. Who has had access to opportunities for professional exposure and growth? Who is provided with coaching, mentorship, sponsorship, and other avenues of support to reach their career goals? From these questions, you can begin to figure out your inclusion blind spots and think about ways to fix them. If you're not sure, ask your team. I often start and end my one-on-ones with, "How can I support you?" By being comfortable identifying what stands in the way of growth, we can unleash our team members' fullest potential.

The struggles of BIPOC and other marginalized employees run the gamut from having their presence, leadership authority, or expertise questioned to figuring out how to show up or speak up without seeming threatening, from determining how much of their own social equity to put on the line to creating clear pathways for others to make racial or gender progress. They face the detrimental effects of negative stereotyping and overt discrimination on a daily basis.

And not seeing yourself represented in the organization or department that you aspire to be in—well, that can be discouraging.

There are two types of actions managers can take. First, you can facilitate these connections and set the tone for your team by participating in or sponsoring diversity-focused events, mentoring someone different from you, communicating regularly with teams on the importance of diversity, equity, and inclusion, and being a vocal supporter of professional development and inclusion of marginalized communities. There have been times I reflexively agreed to speak on a panel or in a company AMA (Ask Me Anything) without thinking about who else on my team or in my network could benefit from the exposure. Being a leader is about shining a light on others.

Second, leverage your leadership to help establish and advocate for programs and policies that can build this scaffolding. This can come in the form of employee resource groups; diversity, equity, and inclusion councils; and mentorship programs. This is allyship: creating connections and opportunities that create a more positive work experience. Here's how you can help build more effective support systems.

Give Out Decoder Rings

As I progressed throughout my career, I was invited to join numerous leadership programs designed for women and BIPOC, yet I was not as often considered for the career-catapulting leadership programs that seemed readily available for white men. When I would eventually join these leadership programs, it was as if I was entering elite social spaces with secret handshakes and codes. I was invited, but I didn't always feel welcome. I appeased the other members' progressive leanings and savior mentalities, but I wasn't enough of a bro when it came to being one of them. I was invited to join but kept at a comfortable distance. Why is that? Is it racism? Is it sexism? Did my presence cause anxiety because they had no clue how to engage with me? Why wasn't I asked to join before? Was it because my performance and potential was not deemed high potential enough, and by who? When I was interviewing for an executive role years ago, the hiring manager said, "Where have you been? I've been searching for this role for nearly a year and you're perfect!" To which I responded, "You haven't looked widely enough." I've often wondered how my career—and that of others, like me, considered high-potential diverse talent—could have been different if I had been routed through those programs and fully welcomed from the start.

It's no secret that every workplace has its own version of office politics, and you will be at a deficit if you don't have access to that nuanced "how to succeed at work" playbook that has been passed down by generations of white people. What we deem as succeeding—surviving really—requires navigational tools, but we're often unaware of their existence or availability to us. As my friend Minda Harts says in her book *The Memo*, "For so long I tried to fight the fact that there are rules to this getting ahead thing. No one sat me down and said, 'Hey girl, this is how you play the game. This is how *they* do it, and this is how *they* win.'" When I joined Time Warner, I called it a decoder ring. It was as if my white colleagues were given a key to all things across the enterprise, and I was blindly making my way without even a compass. You may not even recognize how well you navigate office politics because it comes so naturally to you; it's a subtle systemic challenge to equity in the workplace.

For many white professionals, career advice comes early from their parents and professionals in their networks and continued through the connections made through coveted internships, personal relationships (remember the Friends and Family Program), and exclusive social groups. My mentor Dr. Ella Bell, a thought leader on women in the workplace, framed this for me. She said, "Daisy, it's quite simple. Many of us [referring to BIPOC] didn't grow up with a family for whom dinner table conversations were a time to discuss how to navigate workplace politics. Your colleagues did, and that's why they're far more confident in what to say and when to say it. You're just playing catch-up." Those relationships, that shorthand, facilitates mentorships, sponsorships, and opportunities. For others who may have been the first member of their family to go to a private college (raises hand), or who had parents without experience in the corporate world (raises hand again), they had to find their own way, often facing headwinds invisible to others.

A cautionary word: there is a difference between intention and action, between thoughtful responses and performative acts of "kindness." White men and women have courted me for jobs, created roles for me, hired me, made important introductions, paraded me across organizations, mentored me, and sponsored me but never quite invested in what made me light up. Their support felt superficial—meant to make them feel like a "good" white person, but not in true relationship with me and what I could achieve.

BIPOC managers and leaders have been building our own corporate equity for quite some time and are now in positions to call the shots, change the conditions, and create access and opportunity for those coming behind us. We know what it's like to be the first, and the mix of pride, pressure, and responsibility. We are helping decode for others what took us years to figure out: How to bring our perspectives to the table while not having to carry the weight of being the "only." How to hold a multiplicity of perspectives while acknowledging the shared experience of belonging to our communities. But we still conduct the same calculus very quickly: Is it safe or not to have this conversation? I'm still constantly worrying about raising the race card or speaking about how things impact me because of my Latino heritage. We are not as alone as when we started, but we're still battling systemic racism and all the isms.

Buddy programs, like the ones mentioned in Chapter 5, have proven beneficial for smoothing the onboarding process. I'm a fan of them, but they rely on human capital and time, which are often at a premium. And if there is only one Black "culture buddy," that person won't have time to think, let alone help someone else. You need a scalable option.

How to be more supportive: Revolutionize your employee handbook

I know you're probably thinking: Who reads the employee handbook? Isn't it a collection of mundane legalese about vacation policies, ethics, and other codes of conduct? Yes, that's true, but you also have an opportunity to create a document that offers the keys to success at your organization and helps your team understand the unwritten rules.

When I conducted founder training for Kapor Capital, I was promoting the power of an employee handbook, but founding partner Freada Kapor Klein was dubious. "Employee handbooks are terrible, no one reads them," she said. I agreed but said that they only remain unread and dusty if you don't bring them to life. An employee handbook sets out policies and practices as well as benefits, and it can be an important tool for ensuring inclusion and belonging in the workplace. To me, the handbook is not simply about the legal implications; it's about company nuance and the previously unshared expectations. A company should be transparent about what it expects from the employee (behavior, norms, and work product) and what the employee can expect from it (culture, benefits, promotions and feedback, and process for when others don't meet expectations). From a start-up to a *Fortune* 500, the employee handbook sets expectations, allows you to reinforce your origin story, and shares the company's values and principles. Employees should use it as a guide for information and for handling difficult situations, ranging from when they need to figure out benefits to how to address harassment or discrimination. Without this guide, everything is up for interpretation (or misinterpretation).

When done well, an employee handbook makes the implicit explicit. It lays out expected behaviors, conducts, and best practices; it decodes the cultural nuances of success. Codes of conduct and antidiscrimination and anti-harassment policies are crucial components of any inclusivity initiative, and they must be clear, communicated, and enforced. At Vice Media Group, we prioritized updating our employee handbook by creating a code of conduct and respect in the workplace policies that clearly outlined what it would take to succeed in the organization and the specific behaviors we wanted to encourage and discourage. We intentionally included a section on microaggressions (with instructions on how to address or combat them) and guidance on gender pronouns, and we shared multiple channels for raising concerns. The handbook states what's expected of employees in terms of everyday behaviors of decency and respect. It's not just what you're saying, but how you're saying it.

One of the best examples I've seen comes from the tech and gaming company Valve, which shares everything from company philosophy and onboarding to performance and hiring principles. What stands out is the way they talk about the company and expectations. The opening page reads, "A fearless adventure in knowing what to do when no one's there telling you what to do." It later goes on to say, "This handbook is about the choices you're going to be making and how to think about them. Mainly, it's about how not to freak out now that you're here." It breaks down advancement versus growth, and there's even a chapter on risks ("What if I screw up? But what if we ALL screw up?"). My favorite parts are the fun illustrations that illuminate cultural nuance. For example, there's Figure 3-1: Method to Working Without a Boss.

Step 1. Come up with a bright idea
Step 2. Tell a coworker about it
Step 3. Work on it together
Step 4. Ship it!

In this clever four-part illustration, the company underscores the importance of collaboration. They don't say, "Collaboration is key to our success!" They show how to do it.

If your company has a traditional (read: boring) handbook, reach out to your HR team and suggest helping refresh it. And take it upon yourself to review it with your own team to decode its language. Have a team meeting where you discuss what success looks like at your company. Break it down for them. What are the unspoken rules? What are leadership expectations? How long does advancement take? What could be the reasons why some advance faster than others? How important is it to be seen, to be known? Is yours a culture where partnership is earned versus granted?

Now, I'm fully aware that there are unspoken norms in every workplace that could never be printed in an employee handbook. Like that if you want to get approval on a project you must get John's buy-in, or that visibility is the key to promotion. They're unwritten but they're not unseen. Use your own lived experiences. Say, "Here's what helped me when I was trying to get approval for a new head count." Or, "Here's how I learned to navigate this place." Know that it's not going to be the same for everyone. A white guy may advise me to walk into the CEO's office with the bravado of, well, a white man and demand we push forward with a long-delayed project, but that might not work for this woman who has to battle the lingering perceptions of the fiery Latina. Address that. Think of how you can dissolve stereotypes and find ways for your team members to embrace their power with organizational awareness, confidence, and authenticity. The more you can share these shortcuts and prime them for office life (and politics), the more set up they will be to succeed.

Foster Peer Relationships

Tiffany Dufu, founder of the Cru, a peer mentorship platform, credits her own group of "badass peer mentors" for blazing her path forward. She says they embrace her vulnerability and allow her to share her greatest triumphs and worst fears without judgment. And they hold her accountable. They check in on her goals, help devise plans, and give her the encouragement and cheerleading she may need. "I do all of this for them as well," she says. "It's like we're all climbing a mountain together, tethered to one another to ensure that all of us reach the summit." I'm proud to be a member of Dufu's Cru. These close, trusting relationships have helped catalyze my potential. She has created a place where social capital is offered and exchanged.

Relationships like these are the cornerstone of belonging, and when you can bring people together at work in an environment of psychological safety, these personal interactions develop favorable social bonds. Researchers David Wilder and John E. Thompson found that people seemed to form favorable views toward people they spent time with, even if they were people they previously disliked or had stereotyped unfavorably, reports Culture Amp.

Imagine you're surrounded by people who you do like and who aren't showing bias. Gallup has consistently found that having a best friend at work leads to better engagement, happiness, and performance. It's not surprising when you consider that we spend more time with our coworkers than with our families on any given day. Remember the impact on me when I realized I didn't have a best friend at Disney? The people around you have a strong influence on you and your potential success, but it can be difficult for women and BIPOC to make connections at work when they constantly receive social signals that set them apart. Social belonging is a fundamental human need, and yet 40 percent of people say that they feel isolated at work.

How to be more supportive: *Champion employee resource groups*

At every company in which I've worked, I've seen employee resource groups range in structure and style from committees filled with junior employees who use them as a place to connect and navigate the ways of work, to incredibly influential groups that shape company culture, products, and diversity, equity, and inclusion practices. At their essence, employee resource groups have been created to respond to the lack of representation and community for women, BIPOC, LGBTQ people, and other underrepresented groups. They are typically employee-led groups formed around common backgrounds, such as gender, race, ethnicity, and sexual orientation. When run well, they offer employees community, camaraderie, and connections to the organization. In fact, these groups may be the fastest, most scalable option to attract, retain, and invest in the advancement of underrepresented employees, but they need structure and support. Employee resource groups have a voice, but they don't always have a strong voice.

Affinity groups, another term for employee resource groups, can often devolve into social groups or book clubs rather than action-orientated reform organizations. In some ways, they can have the unintended effect of encouraging people to self-segregate. There are plenty of pitfalls, but to run these groups effectively you need to diversify the hierarchy. When junior BIPOC make up the majority of an affinity group, they generally do not have the power and positional privilege to speak up and reform white male leadership. You need engagement from top and mid-level leaders who can help garner support for new programs and ideas.

An employee resource group should welcome everyone of all levels, but it would be ideal to invite company stakeholders to the table who are willing to help shape vision, policy, and an operational road map. Ideally, that would include an executive sponsor, two to three mid-level managers, an HR representative, and a rich cross-section of all races and identities. Employee resource groups should remain safe spaces for employees, so consider extending the invitation to top leadership for one key meeting or event. Think back to the story of CEO Brian O'Kelley in Chapter 2. It was an invitation to a female-focused employee resource group that provided the insight that the women of his workplace were feeling seriously excluded.

Here's how you can help an employee resource group achieve their goals.

Volunteer to be an executive sponsor

Senior leaders can help to both accelerate progress and remove blockers. You need to be willing to spend your political and financial capital. The leader doesn't have to identify within that group but does need to advocate for the group at the most senior levels of the company and open doors to connections and resources.

Reward employee resource group leaders

Not every organization is in a place where they can pay all group members, but companies should be mindful of providing meaningful rewards, such as high marks on performance reviews or the ability to connect with senior leadership. Authors Minda Harts, Sarah Lacy, and Eve Rodsky persuasively lay out the case for paying employee resource group leaders (who are disproportionately women and BIPOC). "ERGs are very real networks that require skilled internal champions," they write in *Fast Company*. "Yet many researchers still argue it's a net drain on women's careers, even potentially hurting their ability to get promoted because it takes time away from the job they're getting evaluated on." Some companies can follow the lead of Twitter, which announced a new compensation program for its employee resource group leaders. "This work is essential to Twitter's success—it is not a 'side hustle' or 'volunteer activity,'" said Dalana Brand, Twitter's vice president of people experience and head of inclusion and diversity. Challenge your peers to reward and compensate their employee resource group leaders when financially possible. Companies that want to take the first step to be more than a performative ally need to value and reward people for the time it takes to execute the work of employee resource groups.

Listen in and act

I'm often asked, "Hey, if I am white, can I attend an employee resource group meeting? I want to be an ally, but I also don't want to encroach on their safe space." The answer is yes, if you're invited. Successful employee resource groups recognize that they need outside support to take action. Just in the last year alone, affinity groups have had a 60 percent decrease in how many Black people are leading them, says Aubrey Blanche, global head of equitable design and impact at Culture Amp.

That alleviates the least privileged people from taking on the most work. If you're a white man, spend an equal amount of unpaid time thinking about how to change systemic unfairness and bias—attend conferences about diversity and inclusion—and take action. Then talk to other white peers in the company about what you have learned, and what you plan to do differently going forward.

Widen Your Network and Expand Others'

Networking is a necessary tool for climbing the corporate ladder. As a manager, you should encourage and facilitate opportunities for your team members to forge important professional connections while also assessing your own relationships. It's worth analyzing your circle: Who's in there? Who is sitting just outside your boundary? Who you surround yourself with, whose input you seek, and whose input you frequently validate is how you build a sense of community for some and not for others. This is where bias tends to be reinforced. It also creates a whisper network of opportunity. Every move you make has a ripple effect whether you realize it or not. It's the go-to on your team when you have to assign a last-minute task, or the person you most often text when you're curious about something. There's a difference between those who you reflexively welcome and those you keep at a distance. These instinctual behaviors are what create reciprocal relationships, opportunities, and a feeling of belonging.

Take a moment to think about and write down answers to the following questions:

- Who do you have breakfast or lunch with on most days?

- Who is your first call when you need help with a project?

- Whose ideas do you question more often or have less patience for?

- Who do you prioritize when building out a project team?

The answers may not jump out at you right away, but if you take stock of your daily routines, you may start to see some patterns emerge. The good news is that you have the power to change your networking practices. In her book *The Person You Mean to Be: How Good People Fight Bias*, Dolly Chugh explains the metaphor of headwinds and tailwinds, as coined by Shai Davidai and Thomas Gilovich, to explain the invisibility of systemic differences. Similarly, we can use headwinds and tailwinds as a metaphor to explain our perception of the advantages and disadvantages we face. Headwinds are the challenges, big or small, visible or invisible, that make life harder for some but not all people. Tailwinds are the forces that propel you forward that are easily unnoticed or forgotten. Because headwinds and tailwinds are often invisible, they can lead us to minimize people who are facing headwinds and ignore the advantages conferred by tailwinds.

During Women's History Month, Jennifer DaSilva, president of creative agency Berlin Cameron, publicly announced her personal goal of connecting four women every weekday throughout the month. She set aside one night a week after her kids went to bed to make connections. She became so passionate about it that she started an event series to open dialogues and foster more vulnerable connections. Eventually, she challenged her social followers to take on the same goal—to connect four women a week—and help support one another. She has personally connected thousands of women and inspired others to join in.

We won't truly expand our networks and communities until we begin to have honest and informed conversations about the intersections of race and gender and decide to do something about it. I love the spirit of DaSilva's Connect4Women initiative. Taking ownership of relationship building, opening doors, and supporting others on their career paths is an integral part of creating a more diverse workforce. But here's where the real opportunity lies: Who are you connecting with? Do they all look the same? How many connections are you making that are cross-cultural, cross-racial, and cross-identity? Those are the questions I asked DaSilva when she asked me to join—and I'm so glad I did. She has recalled that conversation as an opportunity to truly reflect on her intentions and outcomes.

Here's an exercise for you: List two or three people on your team and outside of the workplace who you would go to if you had an issue to discuss. Next, categorize them by their demographics: race, gender, religion, abilities, sexual orientation, gender identity, age, and so on. What does that look like? Chances are that the list looks very much like you and probably thinks like you. Look at your social media profiles: Who are you connected to on LinkedIn? If your followers are 98 percent white and male, that's your story, and that can change by broadening your network.

But please don't start blindly connecting with all the BIPOC suggested through LinkedIn. Expanding your networks takes time, thought, and care. Reach out with a note that speaks to what you value about their experience or profile. Ask to be connected through a mutual friend and allow the other person to decline. Seek out difference while recognizing that the emotional vigilance of those you wish to connect with may be rightfully high. Or focus on people in your company. Seek out the perspective of someone different from you, even if that just means grabbing a coffee or tea with someone you wouldn't ordinarily talk to.

Your peers and colleagues are no different. If you were to ask those same who-do-you-lunch-with questions of your CEO or board members, what do you think they would say? Who holds power across the organization? How is that power distributed or abused? Whose behavior is consistently excused? What harms are downplayed? Whose voice or what perspective is missing from decision-making? You can build a diverse network that challenges and pushes you forward by digging deeper into this simple exercise.

How to be more supportive: *Create valuable connections*

Start internally. Expanding your professional relationships is not simply the result of fabricated social interactions. How you initiate conversations about race with employees or bring up dialogue about the experiences of different cultures in your workplace can also help enhance your connections. Start a one-on-one or team conversation about matters that impact these employees' communities. Try encouraging dialogue, not debate. Model to others what being an empathetic listener looks like by doing just that: creating a space for sharing and listening. Remember, you learn by listening, not talking. Begin by honestly acknowledging your intentions: "The truth is that I haven't known how to start this conversation. I want us to get better at working together. I have made mistakes, haven't known enough, and likely haven't done enough before, but I want to change that. And I want to start by building a better relationship with you." However you start the conversation, it's about opening the door.

You can also engage in ongoing check-ins. Natural points to check in with your team are performance-management or goal-setting conversations. The key is to understand their fears, concerns, and challenges, as well as their hopes, desires, and dreams. You can begin by saying, "Last time we spoke, you said gaining alignment from your peers on a cross-functional project was a challenge for you. How is that going? How confident do you feel with where the company is going? How are you/your team progressing toward your goals? What's hanging you up right now? Where do you want to grow? What could I be doing better to support you/your team?" Look for entry points along the way to continue to have this dialogue. This makes it easier to build relationships and bring people along with you. It's not just this conversation but every conversation.

Put Mentorship and Sponsorship into Practice

Having a personal team of advisors is not just having access to a life jacket; it's getting a ticket on the speed boat. This is particularly true for women, BIPOC, LGBTQ people, and members of underrepresented communities in the workplace who face systemic obstacles along every step of their careers. Sponsorship and mentorship are slightly different relationships. Mentorship is about upskilling; sponsorship is about putting your professional equity at stake to help someone succeed. With mentorship, you're advising someone; with sponsorship, you're sharing your access and privilege, for some, even hard-earned political influence and power. Professor Herminia Ibarra argues that for these kinds of relationships to flourish, both executives and their organizations must be clear about what steps they might take in order to ensure employees have the full sponsorship support they need. She says, "While a mentor is someone who has knowledge and will share it with you, a sponsor is a person who has power and will use it for you."

It's what has been documented as the missing piece for the true advancement of women and BIPOC into leadership. "In general, women are over-mentored and under-sponsored, and female founders are over-mentored and underfunded," says Katica Roy, founder and CEO of Pipeline Equity, a company that leverages artificial intelligence to identify and drive economic gains through gender equity. While there is equal merit in both relationships, mentors stand beside you, while a sponsor stands in front of you, clearing the path ahead. Sometimes they can be one and the same.

It's most beneficial when you can have both. My mentors and sponsors have offered me different degrees of support. Those I have worked directly with have offered insider knowledge about how to advance in an organization, advocated for a promotion before I thought I was ready, and made introductions to influential people in their network who have opened up doors to opportunities I may have never been considered for. They have also checked me when I've grown impatient, made me face my development gaps, and shared mistakes of their own to help me avoid making the same ones. And I, in turn, have honored the relationship by sharing insights and resources not on their radar, prioritizing their asks, and honoring their contributions to my career. The most effective mentor relationships happen naturally, but when only 37 percent of professionals say they have a mentor, managers have to step in to bring their teams along.

How to be more supportive: Start mentoring

Coaches speak to you, mentors speak with you, and sponsors speak for you. Make a pledge to mentor someone who needs it most, someone who doesn't look like you or had the same experiences and upbringing as you. "I stopped mentoring men," says Brian O'Kelley, now cofounder and CEO of Waybridge. "And once I did, the women I mentored gained more opportunities and access to special projects because of my capital at the company." That's what good mentoring does. It's a guiding hand, a gentle nudge, and that voice of assurance that says, "Don't give up!"

Mentor relationships can be mutually beneficial. Don't look at mentorship as an opportunity to simply pass on your knowledge. Think of it as a chance to gain insight into a different perspective, understand new trends, and hone your intergenerational and cross-cultural communication and leadership style. Ask your mentee your own business and career questions, too, for a fresh point of view. "Every once in a while I come across a woman who will tell me that she doesn't have time to mentor," says the Cru founder Tiffany Dufu. "She'll actually complain about all of the requests she gets from young women in her organization. While I do understand the overwhelm of a full inbox, it's important to recognize that mentees are a critical part of our success ecosystem. They help me more than they probably realize. My mentees keep me grounded and relevant, and they've helped me to advance my leadership in countless ways. From childcare to fashion emergencies, to editorial advice and research, there's just no way I'd be where I am without their support."

How to be more supportive: Stick your neck out for your team

A sponsorship relationship is founded on a deeper sense of trust in each other, sometimes built over years, and a real confidence in the person's potential. As in the case of access to critical roles in an organization, the playing field for sponsorship relationships remains uneven. People's tendency to gravitate toward those with a similar social identity, such as gender and race, increases the likelihood that powerful white men will sponsor and advocate for other white men when leadership opportunities arise.

Here's a secret: you are a sponsor! "A lot of times we talk about these coveted sponsorship relationships, but actually your first sponsor is going to be your manager or a leader within your reporting line," says Cindy Pace, vice president, global chief diversity and inclusion officer at MetLife. That's your role as a manager, to be there for your team. Lean into sponsorship to promote underrepresented groups. Leaders have a responsibility to represent and advocate for high-potential employees. Introduce them to someone in your network who can make further connections for them. Be a coach, a cheerleader, and a sage all wrapped in one. Internal mobility is often an untapped opportunity. If you're doing your job well, your rate of internal transfers and promotions will increase, incentivizing personal development and growth.

Internal research at Deutsche Bank revealed that female managing directors who left the firm to work for competitors were not doing so to improve their work-life balance. Rather, they'd been offered bigger jobs externally that they weren't considered for internally. Deutsche Bank responded by creating a sponsorship program aimed at assigning more women to critical posts. It paired employees with executive committee members to increase the female talent pool's exposure to the committee and ensure that the women had influential advocates for promotion. Now, one-third of the participants are in larger roles than they were a year ago, and another third are deemed ready by senior management and HR to take on broader responsibilities.

How to be more supportive: *Launch a mentorship program focused on specific career advancement opportunities*

Seventy-one percent of *Fortune* 500 companies have mentoring programs, but these relationships rarely evolve into stronger advocate relationships, the space where sponsorship thrives. In fact, most of the time—based on poor matches, unengaged participants, and a lack of goals—these relationships fizzle. When there is a specific strategy and shared mission, participants are more apt to have a successful relationship. Unilever, for example, decided to create programs to help advance women into management in hot-spot areas. Its supply chain female mentoring program matched more than forty-five senior leaders at the vice-president level and above to mentor and coach more than ninety women directors in departments where women historically have found it difficult to succeed. The company recognized a leak in their pipeline and set up a mentorship program to fix it. Having a tactical goal—to figure out why women weren't succeeding in these departments—gave mentors a mission they could rally behind, creating a more effective and impactful program.

Likewise, in 2020 MetLife launched EXCELERATE (a play on "accelerating excellence"), a talent-sponsorship program aimed at addressing equity gaps in leadership roles. This program has a few things going for it. One, it's sponsored by the CEO and executive group, so you know it's a company priority. Two, it provides real support for advancement in the form of executive sponsorship, coaching, and virtual learning, as well as visibility, access, and engagement with C-suite executive leaders. The initial pilot program was focused on a US cohort that included Black and Latino talent, with 67 percent of the cohort made up of women of color. And it's working. The majority of the participants have taken expanded leadership roles and responsibilities. Moving forward, the program will expand globally to include all underrepresented groups.

How to be more supportive: Build mentorship programs that can evolve into sponsorships

You cannot force relationships, nor can you demand that someone spend their personal capital on someone they may not be enthusiastic about. An automatic mentor-sponsor program would allow BIPOC staff access to senior leaders who have the influence and access to help pave the way for advancement. Mentors of color who wanted to invest in me were incredibly impactful as I rose in the ranks, yet there are often few senior staff of color at companies and even less with enough bandwidth to meet the needs of all junior BIPOC. White male leaders must be part of the solution. Or you can pay BIPOC mentors for these extra duties. And if you do that, the BIPOC person should be allotted additional space—like more personal days, flex time, and time to achieve annual performance goals—since all that additional support takes time away from the work they are evaluated on for their own career advancement.

The best program I've seen to date was the Sage program at Google. Sages (mentors) and sagees (mentees) were paired up based on personal and professional interests. I participated as a sage, and my sagee, Adrianna Samaniego, selected me largely because of our shared Latinx heritage. In our monthly meetings, many of which we had over a meal, I played several supporting roles. I offered advice about tough choices I had faced myself, helped her strategize how to be more effective in her role, and made connections that helped her gain admittance into the MBA program of her choice.

What made this program unique is that everyone had to attend a mandatory one-day workshop, in which sages, mostly white managers, participated in cultural sensitivity training designed to help them gain confidence in navigating cultural and racial differences. My white peers, fellow sages, left the program far better equipped not only to mentor across difference but also to manage more inclusively. Samaniego and I have remained close as our relationship has evolved from that of a mentor providing career advice to that of a sponsor making critical introductions for career opportunities. Through various career transitions and cross-country moves, we remain each other's advocates.

Seek Diverse Internal and External Support

At Vice Media Group, we created two diversity, equity, and inclusion advisory bodies—an external board and an internal council—to help us improve and influence culture, structures, behaviors, and representation across the company. They were tasked with monitoring goals and objectives, bringing in novel ideas and knowledge, and ensuring alignment with our business and people strategy. We sought advice from diverse sources to reduce the risk of strategic inertia, only confirming our own views. These groups further engendered a collective sense of purpose, structure, and commitment necessary for sustainable change.

In companies like Comcast and Sodexo, having an external diversity board is a requirement, ensuring that strategies and practices are not stuck in an internal silo. They also play a key role in holding leaders accountable. An active council or board can do much more than simply track quarterly progress. They can be game changers by doing exactly what exceptional leaders do: challenging executives with a bolder vision of what is possible and leveraging their wisdom and influence to help achieve outstanding results. When they get intimate with employees—that is, offer office hours or speak at internal events—they can better understand where people are stumbling and where progress is achievable.

There's always value in external voices that question what you're doing and that don't have the unspoken pressures to maintain the company culture within the current status quo. Workplace culture is often difficult to see on the inside; it's the water you're swimming in, and so it can be hard for insiders to change it or even see the need for change. External voices can be great sources of knowledge and credibility, constantly reflecting on what you need and helping build the right support structures. Emily Best, of crowdfunding platform for diverse storytelling Seed&Spark, values the candor of her advisory board. "They have to be people who would call you on your BS, especially if you're a white manager like me," she says. "You don't want to build an advisory board who is just there to make you feel good about yourself. You want them to challenge you."

Internal advisory boards can also use pressure to get things done. When the meditation app Headspace announced the creation of an internal diversity council, more than sixty people immediately volunteered. That led to event planning that integrated diversity, equity, and inclusion from the initial design, plus a budget for a dedicated group of employees to run the council. Alicin Reidy Williamson of Endeavor created an internal diversity and inclusion group of leaders from various departments across the company. "To gain insight and buy-in, I asked leaders to think about what success looked like in key areas such as retention, partnerships, recruiting, etc., within their specific areas of expertise and through a diversity, equity, and inclusion lens. That is how we were able to cross-collaborate across a commitment to diversity and inclusion that reflected the needs of the company," she says.

Years ago, I helped launch a women's initiative at Disney. As I looked across the advisory group tasked with developing the new programming, a group of mostly white women, it was clear to me that the lens through which we were looking at women's advancement left out the experiences of women of color, women like me. I had experienced firsthand the exclusion and hurt that comes from not being welcomed into mostly white social networks. But this was my opportunity to change that. In one of our first planning meetings for Women's History Month, I took a bet that paid off.

With a healthy mix of corporate charm and courage, I proposed leading a bespoke event on behalf of my division that would focus on the workplace experiences of women of color. At this point in my career, I had gained confidence and earned credibility as a corporate leader. But even then I knew that I needed to frame my recommendation as a limited-risk proposition. How much attention could this event garner? How many women of color could I possibly bring together? Well, it was one of the most attended events that month. We hosted a panel with top female executives of color in the entertainment industry, and the event was open to all employees. It was a no-holds-barred talk about the barriers they had faced moving up in their careers. It was by women of color for women of color. We could finally hold space for each other and see each other in our journey.

In the evening, we held an invitation-only dinner for our female executives of color with the panelists. I still have the photo from that dinner, and the friendships and connections have lasted.

To this day, the women of color in the company, including those who are no longer there, recall that experience as the first time many of them felt seen and valued. I'll never forget the white male manager who called me up to say, "Daisy, I don't know what you just did, but Roberta just came back from your event cheerfully talking about how wonderful it was. She has a pep in her step that I've never seen before. Please do more!" Had I not created a support system where BIPOC women felt not only welcomed but strengthened, who knows how long they would have stayed at Disney. Had I not acted on what I knew women of color needed to experience in the workplace, we would not have been able to move beyond the pervasive blind spot of women's programs only catering to white women, instead of removing barriers and clearing the path for all women.

Your Road Map to Revolution

To evolve as an equitable and anti-racist manager, you must prioritize the support of those most disproportionately harmed by racism and white supremacy. As I've shared in prior chapters, many talent systems and organizational cultures have built-in biases that privilege certain groups over others. These biases undermine the progress of BIPOC talent. Not all feedback and support is created equal. Design solutions that reduce obstacles for racially diverse team members and help everyone advance in their careers.

- **Decode office politics and reveal what often goes unsaid**. Remove barriers for performance. Revamp your employee handbook and make it fun and informative. Hone your coaching skills and be candid with employees about what leads to advancement at your company.

- **Give employee resource groups the support and recognition they deserve**. While not a magic bullet, employee resource groups provide critical connections and career development opportunities. If invited, sit in on meetings to listen to what employees really need. Offer to help take action on policies mentioned and lend a hand when needed. Consider rewarding or compensating group leaders for their service.

- **Widen your reach**. Demonstrate an authentic commitment to propelling the careers of BIPOC talent by extending personal invitations to professional events and networks. And ensure they're made to feel welcome when they join. Change it up by seeking new friends and connections who are unlike you with different life experiences.

- **Start mentoring**. It's that simple. Foster mentorship programs focused on specific entry points, whether that's advancing BIPOC and other marginalized groups into executive leadership roles or developing talent in new departments.

- **Integrate external perspectives**. Create a board of internal and external diversity, equity, and inclusion advisors. Pay them and welcome them to help influence policy, process, and culture change.

10

GET TO THE HEART OF ACCOUNTABILITY

I **LOATHE THE TERM** "cancel culture," the practice of publicly sham-ing a person or institution for behavior deemed unacceptable. The term has been weaponized to derail conversations about account-ability and consequences, which is what we should be focusing on. Professor Loretta Ross, among others, has long been asking, "What if instead of calling people out, we call them in?" She explains that being called out for accidentally misgendering a classmate, as hap-pened to her, or for admitting admiration for a cultural icon who is now seen in a different light alienates people and makes them afraid of speaking up. We can't truly be in trusting relationships at work if our team members feel that they need to withhold infor-mation or are deathly afraid of making any misstep out of fear of retribution.

Instead, she advocates for "calling in" with grace and patience in a private message. Simply take a breath before commenting, screen-shotting, or demanding that someone "do better." When we call someone in for words or actions that are hurtful, we acknowledge that we all make mistakes. We help someone discover that their behavior is harmful and how to change it. The courageous conversations, compassion, and context she calls for are deeply needed in our society and in our workplaces.

I'm not referring to those who have gotten away with horrible and often criminal behavior for so long that any semblance of consequences is seen as unfair, when in fact it's basic justice. Politicians and law enforcement officials who fail to live up to their oaths, executives who are serial sexual harassers, and business leaders who discriminate against and abuse those under them—those people need to be called out. And there should be clear consequences for the wrongdoers and the allies who have protected them.

The non-explosive cases of workplace misconduct that result in slaps on the hand also fail to change culture. The company may issue a blanket apology or non-apology, while the bad actor is exempt from remediation or self-reflection. Where is the accountability beyond some public show of mea culpa? What would it take for the person who caused harm to recognize the extent of their misconduct, identify strategies to address their behaviors or attitudes, and effect change?

We're all accountable for what happens on our watch. There is no neutral. Accountability matters. But instead of canceling first, try calling in.

1. **Lead with curiosity instead of anger**. Ask yourself: Am I calling out a person or systemic behavior? What am I hoping to achieve?

2. **Focus on the specific behavior and how it affected you or others**. Don't let small infractions escalate. Sometimes we don't know what we don't know.

3. **Approach the conversation or message with respect and kindness while explaining the impact of their actions or language**. If in person, which is preferable,

ask: What was your intention when you said *x*? How might the other person view this situation? What effect would you like to have?

4. **Think about what may make you feel defensive if you're the person who caused harm**. Are you prioritizing your own feelings? What is holding you back from admitting responsibility? Should you be doing more listening? Reflect on the difference between impact and intent. Remind yourself that words carry weight.

"Accountability" is sometimes used interchangeably with "responsibility," which means being dependable. Being accountable is how dependability is demonstrated. It is about examining how accountable we are to ourselves and others. We should be clear about what we value and how we act, what's expected, and what happens as a result of the actions that we take. It is about committing to behave in a specific and intentional way to bring about full inclusion and equity. Everyone comes to this work with different levels of comfort, knowledge, and ability to translate good intentions into action. No one person can single-handedly eliminate racial bias and discrimination. It requires an ongoing commitment, persistence, and a willingness to pursue change where you are. I know you have it in you.

Most of us are naturally adept at deflecting responsibility, especially when things feel awkward or controversial. When that happens, the common reaction is to revert back to our seven-year-old selves by quickly explaining our way out of whatever jam we're in. Too often, the first thought is, "It's not my fault," rather than accepting responsibility for our role. It's far easier to blame poor performance on others, like the team member who didn't share the information with you on time, instead of acknowledging your role in having asked for it at the last minute. Academics have long reported multiple forms of white defensiveness—including white denial, white diversion, and white fragility—to describe deflection responses by white people in discussions about systemic discrimination, racism, and white privilege.

Whatever our racial background, we all fall into these traps. You do it. I do it too. We behave differently when no one is looking. We all want to avoid trouble and blame. The truth is that in every situation, there are factors outside and within our control. You can choose to not protect bad behavior, rather than being subject to constraints imposed by power and politics. That's what great leaders do. Not using your power and privilege to enable equity and inclusion is also a decision. No one gets a pass. Revolutions are ripe with threatening distractions—that's just the nature of things—but you can make choices that make the most significant difference.

You must commit to building radically inclusive and equity-minded workplaces, bringing others along with you, and holding them and yourself accountable. That's the only way we will make progress. When we launched our second annual diversity, equity, and inclusion report at Vice Media Group—the first in my eight-month tenure in the company—I intentionally listed one focus area for the following year: holding managers and leaders accountable and investing in their development to sustain their impact. From creating psychological safety in their teams to having fair and consistent performance-management conversations, I wanted it to be clear that we needed to infuse accountability at the organizational and individual level. Nancy Dubuc, our CEO, also declared that diversity, equity, and inclusion were a priority and a leadership challenge for our entire industry. That is accountability. And it starts with you.

Policies and best practices don't create change by themselves; they need people like you to own them, uphold them, measure their effectiveness, and hold people who defy them accountable. It means acting in the spirit of your espoused values on a daily basis. It means being willing to change your behaviors, norms, and workplace environment to embrace the needs of diverse talent, ideas, customers, viewers, and markets. It means holding yourself responsible for actions you take as an individual (personal), those you take with others as a team (organizational), and those that dismantle business norms that passively maintain unearned advantages for white team members (systemic). It means being a change agent.

Now, I'm guessing you may be feeling the weight of the world on your shoulders right now. I get it. Nearly every *Fortune* 500 company has a chief diversity officer, chief people officer, or another title bestowed on a person (usually a woman of color like myself) who has been charged with getting this work right and who has probably failed. It's not for lack of effort, skill, or competency. We cannot do this alone. We are set up to fail from the very beginning with fledgling budgets, unclear and at times inconsistent priorities, and lack of senior- and middle-management support. We are meant to somehow fix things without making white senior staff uncomfortable, without making changes to the workplace's norms and practices, and without taking too much time from the business functions of the employee body. It's as if diversity, equity, and inclusion work is somehow extra credit and not foundational to building the best teams that can do their best work.

We fail because an Inclusion Revolution is not won by a single person. We need everyone to do the work and be willing to course correct along the way. Here's how to build your accountability muscles.

Engage the Champions, Uncommitted, and Detractors

We don't have a shared understanding of what diversity, equity, and inclusion in the workplace means. There isn't enough acknowledgment that this work depends on your organization's unique context. For some, it's a nice-to-have, for others it's a defensive activity, and for still others it's a necessity for workplace survival.

I frequently meet managers who are worried about recruitment but not about including people once they're in the door—managers who want to give BIPOC team members an opportunity to learn and grow but then discount them the second they make a mistake, even before they're given a chance to succeed. Too often, employees assume that the solutions will come from CEOs and senior leaders and ignore the people who can deliver the most direct change: those in the middle. Middle managers often figure this work is on the CEO or diversity and inclusion manager to fix. Or they may simply be afraid of losing their clout, stability, and control. How dare you tell me that I don't know how to manage my team, or that I have to give up what I have worked so hard for? Some middle managers have also seen this diversity work wax and wane over the years. They figure the company will move on to other things. That is shortsighted.

The average white male manager often thinks, "I'm a white man, and I feel like I can't do anything right. I'm on the wrong side of diversity." This is not a zero-sum game. We move in a world where racism is stubbornly unrelenting, where we assume the competence of white people over Black people. I have heard from white men who say they feel excluded from organizational diversity and inclusion efforts and perceive that they are being held back from advancement in favor of candidates who come from diverse backgrounds. These are harmful perceptions. One set of people getting fair opportunities does not mean another set of people lose theirs. We all benefit when white men also champion a new way of working.

Continuing to believe in a broken, uncivil workplace system that humiliates and discourages whole swaths of people makes fools of us all. Buying into unchallenged truisms and centuries-old systems of racial injustices and misogyny makes us mediocre participants in workplace theater. Instead of forcing different people into existing systems, try building new relationships and new systems. Learn from the lived experience of your colleagues: "This is what it feels like," "This is what is needed," and "This is what success looks like." Build trust by sharing what you know (there's value in your lived experience too), your power, and your privilege. Shared power and privilege will lead to the elusive business and social outcomes we've sought for decades.

Start by creating a clear vision that helps others understand what's at stake. Explain how to embody this vision in every decision they make. How do you do that? Much the same way you do with any business initiative. You plan and execute an internal campaign to introduce and explain what you intend to do, and what it means for everyone. You then reinforce new behavioral and operational expectations by weaving these into the fabric of your organizational practices—from how you conduct meetings to how you prepare for sales pitches. Here's an operational plan you can try.

- **Consider perspectives of champions, advocates, skeptics, and dissenters alike**. How will this impact each person? Understand what your teams care most about, what motivates them, what engages and energizes them, and what may be missing.

- **Prepare for resistance, but don't overinvest your limited time and resources**. Map out potential objections, listen to feedback, and prepare responses to potential roadblocks. Identify the most influential employees—those who shape the attitudes of those around them—and have them communicate your plan with compassion and understanding. They can be your most effective champions.

- **Ask yourself**:
  - What could you create if you faced no constraints (other than legal ones)?
  - Why do some actively engage with and support this vision?
  - Why haven't others bought into the vision and action plans? When some say, "This is too much change," they generally mean "I don't want to change" or "I'm afraid of what this change means for me."
  - What reasons and examples are most likely to surface?
  - What are their biggest fears or perceived losses?

○ Who and what can get in the way? What are the risks you're willing to take to reduce inertia and show what's possible?

- **Cocreate team goals and priorities**:
  ○ We will focus on _____ priorities, including _____, _____, and _____.
  ○ We will execute by _____ and _____.
  ○ We will measure with _____ and _____.
  ○ We will communicate through_____and_____.
  ○ We will reward through _____ and _____ and will hold those who do not meet our expectations to _____ and _____.
  ○ These are the stakeholders: _____, _____, _____. (You can consider a RACI model, or a responsibility assignment matrix, which describes the participation by various roles in completing tasks or deliverables for a project or business process. It stands for responsible, accountable, consulted, and informed.)

When resistance appears, and it will, use what you gather to help you understand all that could go wrong. This forces you to think outside the box and build better solutions. Creating an atmosphere of us versus them is not the goal; it's the farthest thing from this work. Rather, this is an opportunity to put into practice the lessons I've shared about building bridges and connections.

Engaging everyone in the process is the key to creating shared purpose and incentives. Take a note from the travel company Expedia, who hosted an Inclusion and Diversity Analytics Hackathon in 2020. A hackathon is an event popular at tech companies where programmers and participants "hack together" a new idea, often in a crazy short amount of time like twenty-four hours. It's a moment for pure outside-the-box innovation, and a winner is crowned for the best idea or product.

Expedia's goal for this hackathon was to create new products to improve their inclusion and diversity analytics. While developing products in a fun, charged-up environment can be rewarding, the company's commitment to bringing the winning ideas to life made participants feel even more inspired and motivated to participate. This wasn't just for fun; there were tangible results. Expedia's senior-level executives acted as judges, and the company held itself accountable for turning the award winners into real-life products. Lean into the ingenuity that can be found across your teams, especially those closest to the work—the BIPOC junior ranks least on your radar—to reimagine and transform your organization.

Goals Are at the Heart of Accountability

Researchers tried to answer the question "Can raising awareness reduce bias?" by looking at racial bias among referees in NBA games in a 2014 study at the Brookings Institution. They found that "personal fouls are more likely to be called against basketball players when they are officiated by an opposite-race refereeing crew than when officiated by an own-race refereeing crew." Once this study was widely shared and covered by major outlets, they tracked the effect of the media coverage on future behavior. What did they uncover? The bias disappeared, suggesting that raising awareness and publicly holding people accountable can effect change.

Like a good marketing strategy, you may need to craft a single powerful message or tagline that you repeat consistently to remind your teams at all levels what you're trying to achieve, why, and what role they play in that change. This is not about blindly repeating slogans but rather helping everyone find their voice and role. Define it for your organization. You or your managers can direct people's energy by clearly and vividly articulating what is in it for them when you manage this change successfully.

That power can come in the form of shared goals and public commitments. Expedia gives every employee at least one personal inclusion goal, Procter & Gamble continually sets and resets specific targets for their leaders, and APCO Worldwide rolled out an inclusivity contract for their employees that defined targets for leadership. Several media companies have committed to expanding representation of BIPOC talent, including launching inclusion riders and diversity protocols to bolster representation in front of and behind the camera. A step beyond requiring "best efforts," Disney's inclusion standards require that 50 percent or more of regular or recurring actors come from underrepresented groups. That level of customization and clarity for diversity, equity, and inclusion efforts, while early in practice, has the potential to motivate and sustain individual and collective accountability across this industry.

Company-wide diversity goals have been highly publicized, like Hilton promising that 50 percent of new hire candidates will be from diverse backgrounds and Adidas committing $120 million to causes related to ending racial injustice between 2020 and 2025.

In 2003, a law in Norway mandated that both women and men must be represented at a minimum level of 40 percent of board seats for publicly listed limited liability companies. This law both accomplished its representational goal and narrowed the gender pay gap among board directors. Since then, other places have followed suit, including California, which signed a law in 2018 that required publicly held companies with executive offices in the state to have at least one female director on their boards by 2019. When the bill was signed, 180 of the 650 public companies in California had zero women on their boards. Progress was made: now, there are just fifteen, or 2.3 percent of company boards, who are not following suit. But the bill didn't stop there. It also stipulated that by the end of 2021, one seat wasn't enough for boards with six or more directors; they would have to fill two seats or face financial penalty. We can't create accountability if what we're asking people to be accountable for is not achievable or realistic. These goals provided clear and ambitious expectations for what was expected, and they were achievable.

These actions matter. They turn the tide of transparency and accountability. Nasdaq now requires listed companies to disclose their diversity figures as well as have at least one woman and one minority represented on their board. When Apple announced, "Beginning in 2021, an environmental, social, and governance modifier based on Apple Values and other key community initiatives will be incorporated into our annual cash incentive program," the business community took note. Apple lists values that include environmental practices (such as using recycled materials in products), diversity and inclusion among its workforce, and the privacy and security of its devices. Now, the compensation committee of its board of directors will use the modifier to increase or decrease bonus payouts by up to 10 percent. That means that executive performance payouts will depend on leadership's ability to meet their diversity and inclusion goals.

Mercer estimates that 15 to 20 percent of S&P 500 companies include diversity, equity, and inclusion metrics in their executive incentive plans. While many organizations are focused on building a more diverse pipeline (rightfully so), we also need to hold everyone in the organization, specifically those at the top, accountable for performance. The progress has been slow even though we've seen the push for years. I'm counting on Apple and Nasdaq's moves and support from larger institutions, investors, and shareholders to accelerate progress and drive greater scrutiny on performance and outcomes.

You can start by setting concrete, intersectional goals and targets. That means taking into account the various points of intersection that could influence the employee experience: race, gender, gender identity, age, sexual orientation, and tenure within the organization. As newer generations move into the workplace, it will be increasingly important to be aware of and responsive to the evolving nature of peoples' identities. Goals involve accountability because people invest more effort when they expect that they will have to explain their actions and outcomes. Ensure that everyone can weigh in and feel that they can lend a hand to drive progress. How? By making sure that everyone knows what you're trying to achieve, why, and by when. People like scorecards for a reason—they provide immediate feedback about what's working and what isn't.

In crafting individual goals, tap into your team's passion or talents. For someone who loves to write, add a goal of writing a certain number of blog posts about your culture that highlight diverse perspectives. Or, for the organizer on your team, you could establish a goal around internal events with a target number of participants. Or, for all, a goal could be ensuring all members of the team have an opportunity to ask questions and share opinions, which can be measured by post-meeting feedback. Be clear on what achieving these goals looks like. For example, Lawrence Berkeley National Laboratory, a US Department of Energy lab managed by the University of California, shared these sample goals:

- **Goal**: Participate in trainings that would specifically enhance my cultural competency.
  - Goal met by: Attended LGBTQ awareness training during Pride month to increase my awareness.

- **Goal**: Participate in professional activities that would increase my experience in interacting with people from cultural backgrounds other than my own.
  - Goal met by: Joined African American employee resource group to support and promote their annual activities and initiatives.

- **Goal**: Make sure that web pages, documents, forms, etc. are Americans with Disabilities Act (ADA) compliant and accessible to all users.
  - Goal met by: Partnered with IT department to review division website and electronic documents to ensure ADA compliance.

Develop these together, asking individuals for suggestions, to make this a collaborative and generative process.

Be Accountable to Yourself

For me, accountability means recognizing that the buck stops here. It means humbly acknowledging my stumbles and blind spots, as I've shared throughout this book. And it means ensuring I'm taking the same concrete actions I ask others to take on the road to dismantling inequity in the workplace. It's never easy. It can feel debilitating at times, like a weight on your shoulders that just won't give. But that's when I need to remind myself that the weight I carry is many times lighter because of the privileges that I hold. Some of which I've earned through sweat and tears, and some—like identifying as a heterosexual, cisgender woman—I've done nothing to earn but have benefited from my entire life.

A study released by the Hispanic Association on Corporate Responsibility called *Empow(h)er: Understanding Workplace Barriers for Latinas* aimed to shed light on what Latinas should do to advance in their careers. I have been a longtime supporter of HACR and its president Cid Wilson, but I had to roll my eyes. Not because I don't believe we need to take ownership of our careers; that's never been in question for me. I am the daughter of immigrants, and everything has always been my responsibility: getting into college, securing scholarships and work-study gigs to pay for it, waitressing at every break because I couldn't afford nonpaying internships, securing jobs after graduating to pay off school loans, and navigating workplaces for which I had little cultural knowledge and even less navigational know-how. All of that.

Yet, here I am, again, being told that as a Latina *I* have to be fixed, not the corporate cultures, systems, and leadership. The first step is flipping this imbalance. I believe you know this and that you're ready to go on this journey. But when in doubt, ask yourself: Who and what needs to change?

"What am I internalizing about the things I've heard before that I haven't been willing to accept about my company, or my role as a leader?" says Keesha Jean-Baptiste of Hearst. "What is it that I have discounted and not heard in the right way? Those questions are hard to ask of oneself and certainly for any leader that's not comfortable with being vulnerable, but we're cycling through the same problem because there is a lack of leadership accountability and acknowledgment that the problem is sometimes you."

When I asked Jamia Wilson, vice president and executive editor at Penguin Random House, to identify what's different for women of color in corporate culture from the nonprofit world, she quickly responded, "The constant hypervigilance and expectation that as a woman of color I need to fix everything immediately." It would be helpful for white leaders, especially those who have unearned privilege and power, to understand the distinct barriers and burdens that BIPOC employees face at work. "You have to be on the chessboard figuring out the short-term moves to protect your queen and those long-term moves that will happen at the end of the game," she says. And as BIPOC leaders, it's important to identify our own values and triggers. Leadership is examining what power we hold and how it can be shared.

Be Accountable to Your Consumers, Users, and Audience Too

Part of the reason companies with diverse teams see larger profits comes down to a bubble analogy. When your product designers, salespeople, content creators, and marketers all look and act the same, you are making decisions based on largely monolithic perspectives that can lead to blind spots. By overlooking and outright neglecting a huge market of people, you miss opportunities because you don't know they exist. Let's start with the more obvious, research-backed truth that diversity of thought, experience, and background drives value. There's overwhelming evidence that if you don't have diversity—that is, a balance of thought, experience, and backgrounds—on your team, you're going to miss something.

Take the reported issues for people of color in Google's facial recognition software. Or look at the fact that female-size crash dummies weren't used by the National Highway Traffic Safety Administration until 2003, even though studies showed that "women, having smaller bones and lower bone density, are at greater risk than men of suffering injury or death in crashes." In these instances, the lack of diversity on the product and engineering side created major, even deadly, challenges for a huge proportion of their customers. These are damaging blind spots.

Balanced teams are better at problem identification, creativity, and innovation. They create and design services, products, promotional materials, and content with everyone in mind and bring an inclusive perspective to all aspects of design, research, reach, and engagement. Every organization has a consumer, whether you're creating tangible goods or are a health-care nonprofit. The everyday decisions you make to serve that consumer—from the imagery you use to the vendors you partner with—create the foundation of your value and ability to embrace change.

Tapping into the diverse perspectives and experiences of your employees can be the difference between reaching previously untapped markets and becoming obsolete. Candice Morgan, the head of inclusion and diversity at Pinterest, spoke to a young pinner who shared that she felt the brand didn't present content that was relevant to her. When she searched for hairstyles or spring makeup looks, the ensuing results were filled with white women with wavy blonde hair dressed for Coachella. Page two, page three—all the same. To get the beauty and fashion advice she sought, she told Morgan, she had to customize her search with words like "Black" or "natural hair" or "makeup for dark skin tones." Why would she keep using Pinterest if the site made it so hard to find images that represented her?

This struck a chord with Morgan, who was implementing the same search hacks. In turn, she pitched the company on an engineering, product, and design project to develop more inclusive searches, specifically for beauty and hair. Now, when you search for a beauty-related idea on Pinterest, a skin tone range will pop up so you can personalize your results. This partnership between tech and diversity helped create a better sense of belonging for Pinterest's multicultural community.

Similarly, Banana Republic's True Hues collection—a line of nude undergarments and accessories in eight shades, from pale pink to a dark espresso brown, designed to celebrate a range of skin tones—delivered great results for the company. Customers and employees alike warmly welcomed what they had sought after for years: a product that truly complemented their skin tones, not a falsely constructed definition of "nude." Social media metrics went through the roof, and sales in the first month alone increased in double digits. This work doesn't happen in silos; it requires being willing to listen to the voices of your employees and empowering them to test and iterate solutions.

Focus on the work behind the scenes too. Start with your sphere of control. For example, supplier diversity programs—which vendors you use for supplies and services—are an external way to commit to diversity, equity, and inclusion practices. Women- and minority-owned businesses often can't compete with pricing and discounts from larger corporations. You can help level the playing field by changing the often-arbitrary rules that determine who your company does business with.

Capital One, for example, has a robust supplier diversity program, which increases access and opportunity for minority-, woman-, veteran-, disability-, and LGBTQ-owned businesses. This includes a supplier diversity mentoring program aimed at closing equity gaps for small business owners. They also have sourcing mandates for their associates to search for new suppliers.

Even smaller companies can audit their vendors to create change. I know a junior employee who was responsible for ordering the office supplies for her publishing company, and when she looked deeper into the company that manufactured the bubble wrap they used to package their books, she discovered that the company made large donations to an allegedly racist politician. So what did she do? She shared this information with her bosses and presented a new vendor who aligned with their values. They fired the bad egg and hired the good. This seemingly small act made a positive impact on her company and the new vendor.

Measure Effectiveness

This is not a one-and-done process. Like a garden, you have to continue to water it, pull out the weeds, and prune what's not growing. Celebrate the wins and acknowledge the missed opportunities or missteps. It's intimidating to get in front of a room of people and tell them where you've failed. I know; I've done it. This is human work; it's not meant to be flawless or perfect. It requires constant trial and error and iteration. It's never too late to start over. One foot in front of the other.

You have to critically examine your workforce data across intersectional lines, take the temperature of the organization, watch out for signals and trends, and analyze performance. Engagement surveys, listening series, and focus groups may not solve everything instantly, but they can help you gather useful data. Revisit Chapter 7 for survey samples. Your goal should be to constantly scan for trends, both positive and negative, as to what's working and what's not. Specifically:

- Which areas are receiving a lot of attention?

- What are some specific gripes or praises?

- What's missing altogether that you expected to see?

- Are we measuring the right things?

Surveys can also uncover information that your team is lacking. If you're receiving feedback that employees outside of the United States do not feel connected to the diversity, equity, and inclusion strategy you have outlined, make a point to talk to them about it and learn about what you don't know. Where can you shift your messaging and resources to allow for bespoke solutions across the globe?

Use the data to guide you and track your progress versus your plan. Data can keep you in check; use it to define areas of opportunity that can be targeted for goals and subgoals. For example, when you look at the promotion rates for women and BIPOC, external hiring rates, and involuntary exit rates, what can that tell you about where you have holes to mend? What are the contributing factors across the employee life cycle? Think broadly, too: share and break down company-wide goals at the division, unit, department, or team level.

Then, turn the mirror on yourself. You can draw on action statements to imagine the reality you want to create. They are also a great way to measure your own progress and check in on your personal accountability. Hint: these work whether you are white or BIPOC.

If you're a non-manager:

- I critically question and reject negative stereotypes of my colleagues.

- I amplify what my coworkers say during meetings and give them credit for their ideas.

- I bring new perspectives and ideas that are of value to my team.

- I do not let microaggressions limit my career or that of anyone else. Instead, I raise instances of indirect, subtle, or intentional discrimination with the channels (manager, HR, confidential hotline, etc.) available to me.

If you're a people manager:

- I proactively cultivate diverse networks within my organization and social circles, considering new voices, perspectives, and ideas.

- I am accountable for my actions and decisions, even when I am enforcing policy handed from above.

- I willingly seek to reduce bias about experience, knowledge, and credibility when hiring, developing, or promoting people on my team.

If you're an executive leader:

- I use my leadership, power, and privilege to reduce inequity across the organization.

- I speak authentically, vulnerably, and with empathy. A veneer of perfection and lack of emotion has no place in my leadership style.

- I seek out people on the margins of the organization, find and create ways to include them in company initiatives, celebrate their wins (big or small), and bring their names up in meetings where they might not have been otherwise mentioned.

- I refuse to frame our journey to become a more diverse, equitable, and inclusive organization as a battle between whiteness and Blackness, us versus them.

- I make open and public commitments to developing a diverse leadership bench.

- I am specific on the dimensions of diversity that I seek—race, gender identity or expression, sexual orientation, age, nationality, ability—and why.

Idea to Steal: Try a "To Be" List Instead of a To-Do List

Michael Fisher, CEO of the Cincinnati Children's Hospital Medical Center, uses a "to be" list. In an interview with McKinsey, Fisher explains: "I never purposefully gave thought to whether there's a way to be really *intentional* about how I want to show up every day. So I've added a 'to be' list to my repertoire. Today, for example, I want to be generous and genuine. I hope I'm that way every day. But today, I want to make sure it stays top of mind. On a different day this week—and look, you can see it here in my calendar—I knew that part of my job was to be collaborative and catalytic. So I pick out two qualities, two kinds of 'to be,' every morning as part of my normal routine." By holding himself accountable to how he's showing up, he engenders more trust with his team.

Now imagine if your "to be" list included, "This will amplify the voice or contribution of an underrepresented member of my team, and I will pay attention to the intersectional identities of these employees." Or, "Today, I will reflect on my privilege and share an example of a privilege that I have taken for granted and that has afforded me unearned access or power." Or, "This week, I will share an invisible inequity in our workforce each day so we can call attention to the problem and devise solutions as a team." Take a moment with me to imagine that. You can do that, right?

Accelerate What's Right by Leading the Way

The tone is set at the top and trickles down. An inclusive leader has done the personal work of understanding what they want to achieve and why. They've examined their fears, assumptions, and privileges. An inclusive leader is one who articulates a clear case for organizational change, sets concrete goals with key benchmarks, and models welcoming and respectful behavior. An inclusive leader requires structured, well-resourced, and clearly articulated diversity, equity, and inclusion strategies and action plans, as they do with any other business priority. An inclusive leader leads.

Make civility the norm. When it's not, it's a sign that the organization's culture is not characterized by respectful communication and collaboration. Sometimes it can be as easy as encouraging your managers and leaders to practice respectful inquiry, the act of leaders asking employees questions and listening intently to their answers. Beyond being respectful and courteous—an obvious good practice, no?—it involves relinquishing control (a pervasive tool of white supremacy) and demonstrates trust in others.

Incivility can be a bug—it's contagious—but it doesn't have to be a feature. Look internally to see if there are behavioral norms or operational practices that need to change. For example, if your employee satisfaction surveys or exit interviews indicate that workers don't feel respected or heard by management, deliver mandatory training and coaching for managers, now.

If respect and civility have not been the norm, let employees know that things are going to change. Don't continue to tolerate workplace communication or behaviors that are not respectful and empathetic. Handle it as you would any kind of business change: by defining behavioral expectations, communicating them widely, providing support resources, and modeling the right behaviors.

To spread accountability:

- In meetings, talk about diversity, equity, and inclusion to ensure your teams know that you have a personal commitment and investment in this work.

- When designing the measures most important to monitor for your strategy or performance-management practices, encourage your team to integrate measurable diversity, equity, and inclusion goals. You should partner with your HR or other relevant teams and let ethics guide you, but you don't have to wait for others to tell you what to measure. You know what's important for your team.

- Spend time reflecting on and taking in feedback about your leadership behaviors.

- Survey your organization to ensure that you're preserving and/or advancing efforts that employees care about.

- Take action when you witness discriminatory, exclusive, harassing, or unfair behavior.

In 2020, *Bon Appétit* magazine was one of many companies that saw its leadership fall. After a social media post about how the brand stands with its Black employees, those employees spoke up. Assistant food editor Sohla El-Waylly shared on Instagram that she had been used in *Bon Appétit's* popular videos "as a display of diversity," but, unlike her white video costars, she didn't get paid. More stories came to light about a toxic test-kitchen culture, and a racist photo emerged of longtime editor Adam Rapoport to seal the deal. Rapoport and his boss, Matt Duckor, likely left the magazine's publisher, Condé Nast, due to the public outcry.

Gone are the days when it was acceptable for women to endure sexually inappropriate overtures from bosses and peers, when LGBTQ employees quietly acquiesced to compartmentalizing their personal and professional lives, and when BIPOC employees were expected to endure indignities, exclusions, and professional dead ends. While the outcome was deserved, the effect of being canceled can lead to an ineffectual culture of fear at the top. And that fear—of repercussions, of making a mistake, of speaking out, of being caught—can diminish efforts to do what's right. This fear is one of the reasons why toxic leadership has existed without penalty until now. There are important steps all mid-level managers and leaders can take to ensure diversity, equity, and inclusion becomes a shared responsibility.

1. **Define goals**. If there is not a clearly articulated diversity, equity, and inclusion vision, set of goals, or action plan in place, ask for one. If there is, talk about it with your own team and share why diversity, equity, inclusion, belonging, and psychological safety are important to you and the business. Share this regularly through various channels and platforms (email, Slack, shared documents) to learn, connect, and inspire action.

2. **Help others embrace change**. Different people are at various stages on their diversity equity and inclusion journey. Even the smallest changes may be met with fear, resistance, or denial. Open up space for dialogue and engagement with your colleagues and teams so that they may weigh in with challenging questions, concerns, and solutions.

3. **Speak up, even if you know there will be fallout**. Companies must create a culture that encourages individuals to speak up in the moment and condemns bad behavior. The rise in corporate activism in the past decade means that people now look to business leaders not only to run their companies but also to take a stand on personal, political, or moral issues—those that impact them at a larger societal level and those within their workplace. Starbucks's public commitment to hire ten thousand refugees globally by 2022, Apple's CEO op-ed calling out "religious freedom laws" as discriminatory, and PayPal and many other companies' refusal to set up shop in North Carolina after the state enacted its "bathroom bill" (requiring people to use bathrooms or locker rooms in schools and other public

facilities that match the gender on their birth certificate rather than their gender identity) are just a few examples.

4. **Ask for and set adequate budgets**. If something is important to your business, you invest in it. Aubrey Blanche, global head of equitable design and impact at Culture Amp, calls budgets "moral contracts." Minimal budgets and cheap and free solutions have not remedied the problem. There is no universal structure for determining a budget for your diversity, equity, and inclusion strategy: it must be custom designed to fit your company's goals. This strategy warrants its own resourcing, expertise, and full-time leadership. When building your budget, account for the costs of headcount, external vendors (targeted training, development, and well-being), outreach and recruitment, and employee engagement (employee resource groups, programming, and social impact partnerships).

5. **Model courageous conversations**. Create a regular dialogue on a variety of diversity, equity, and inclusion topics such as stereotypes and judgments at work, building a climate of authenticity where there is acceptance and respect for expressing emotions, practicing allyship, and making invisible inequities visible. Don't shy away from controversial issues but don't force intimacy. Host AMAs or "lightning talks," giving employees the room to share their own experiences and solutions. Keep in mind that many BIPOC employees have purposely emotionally detached from their organizations for their own sanity and safety. We spend an incredible amount of energy trying to avoid offending our white peers because we know that can be, and has been, dangerous for us. If leaders don't do the hard work of following through on commitments made in these conversations, you won't hear the truths you

need to hear. There are ways to make these commitments more measurable and concrete, such as a certain number of meetings in a quarter or a particular number of attendees. The more you do, the more others will take notice and follow suit.

White people are unpracticed and uncomfortable talking about racism, privilege, and oppression. It's how they're socialized: avoid all topics related to race because you'll look bad if you admit that you notice it in other people. Color blindness is not real and it's not a wise management strategy. Coworkers are stuck not quite knowing what to say or how to step in to help, often fearing they could lose their jobs or standing in the organization. I have been approached in private more times than I can count to apologize for others' bad behavior or intervene on behalf of a leader who wants their peers to stop insulting others. But when I've asked them to join me in publicly advocating for racial equality or confronting discrimination, those same caring coworkers back away, not willing to risk their relationships or expend their work capital.

You'd be surprised by the things I hear as a chief people officer. Or maybe not. The same executives who are quick to judge, criticize, or condemn others for not including them in a meeting or update report have the hardest time confronting their peers. They jump between silently policing behavior that they feel hurts them—"I wish he would just shut up. He's terrible"—and not standing up for those who are actually being harmed. I once had three executives—two white women and one white man—complain about each other. When I asked them to share their experience directly with their peers, they responded, "I'm afraid of the consequences. If I speak up, they'll treat me worse. It's not worth it." It never dawned on them that they had less to risk and more to gain in service of the organization than those more to junior to them, who were suffering from far worse behaviors.

That has to change.

The specific conversations that come next are what frighten you the most. I get it. I also know you can find your courage. Over the course of my career, I've often seen people enter these conversations with trepidation. Here's the thing: we're all going to mess up, often. Let's lean on each other to learn what we don't know, push forward when we want to give up, and create a system for course correction along the way. Companies like Culture Amp and Skillcrush have published their commitments to becoming anti-racist organizations along with detailed plans and months later shared what they were learning on the journey.

There were gains. Culture Amp's stretch metric to improve the representation of Black campers (the nickname for their team members) showed improvements, as did employee-belonging sentiment. While Skillcrush did not have any hiring activity to report, their founder and CEO Adda Birnir's transparency and vulnerability in admitting they had a long way to go, while continuing to tie progress to well-defined actions, showed promise. "Anti-racism is a muscle and it's a muscle we hadn't been exercising, so, exercising it is, unsurprisingly, uncomfortable and we're forced to face how weak our anti-racism muscle feels," Birnir wrote. Risk of inaction is larger and makes the outcome of a diverse, equitable, and inclusive culture more uncertain.

Check In: What If You Are the Problem?

Our experiences at work are profoundly shaped by our power and privilege. More often than not, high-power and high-privilege leaders see bad behavior and don't perceive it to be a big problem, while lower-level workers experience it and perceive it as extremely damaging and stressful. Failing to build perspective through constant introspection and reflection about your own behaviors, management practices, and beliefs can mean that you're unable to see when you are, in fact, the problem.

I hear from many BIPOC that they feel frustrated that their manager is not connecting with them, not communicating with them, not giving them clear directions and goals, or obstructing them from advancing in their career. You may think you're talking to your BIPOC team members—you may meet regularly for business check-ins—but you're not helping them unravel the inner pathways that they need to navigate in order to advance further in their careers. Ask yourself: What have I done as a manager to help BIPOC succeed? How present have I been? Am I overfocused on correcting instead of coaching? If you realize that you might be part of the problem, here is some advice:

1. **Practice inclusive empathy**. Don't get defensive, but rather try to cut to the heart of what your employees or coworkers are feeling and experiencing. Build a deeper understanding of what they need work to do for them in addition to what you need them to do for you. Be willing to dig into how your own behaviors may be limiting their ability to trust and engage with you.

2. **Champion vulnerability that is rooted in curiosity**. Let them know what's tripped you up in your own career and how you have overcome your own lapses. Ask for their views of what could be better and what they want you to understand about their work environment or circumstances. Be willing to admit that what works for you, as a white man or woman, may not work for a woman of color. And be willing to admit that as a BIPOC leader, the strategies that worked for you may not work for another BIPOC employee. Try to devise solutions together. Remember, your vulnerability doesn't diminish your capacity to lead; it enhances it.

3. **Raise your team members' accountability by communicating community norms**. "As a team, these behaviors are acceptable, and these are not." This signals to everyone what your team accepts and promotes and what you don't. It makes it harder to sweep problems under the rug.

Your Road Map to Revolution

We're all accountable for what happens on our watch. As the old saying goes: What gets measured gets managed. What gets managed, gets done. Accountability can mean a lot of things to a lot of people. To me, it's about consistently showing up for my colleagues and teams. Make a commitment to yourself, your team, your coworkers, and your company to champion a new way of working where inclusion and belonging are the norm. There has never been a moment like now, when people are willing to put the work in, to learn from past mistakes, and to do better. The future is bright, there is evidence of change, and there is still a lot of work to do for us to eradicate racial inequity across our workplaces.

- **Don't fall into the cancel-culture trap**. No matter the wrong, there are ways to call people in that recognize the individual instead of viewing them simply as representations of systems from which they benefit. Lead with curiosity instead of anger. Be willing to change how you behave. Don't protect those who cause harm. Instead of dodging responsibility, bring others along.

- **Create connections through vision and mission**. Communicate the why for you, the teams that you are part of, and your larger organization. Seek out the most influential employees—those who shape the attitudes of those around them. Invite and inspire everyone to find their voice and role.

- **Define short- and long-term goals**. Create individual inclusivity goals with measurable outcomes. Scan for new opportunities to create a more inclusive workforce, from a vendor supply program to innovative product development.

- **Show a commitment to courageous conversations**. How you act, talk, and walk in the workplace carries weight. Think about the difference between impact and intent. Remember that the personal is professional and the professional is personal.

- **Continue to measure your success**. Diversity, equity, and inclusion is not a one-and-done process. Track your progress. Celebrate the wins. When progress stalls, demand that your leaders lead. Throughout, revise your goals and resources to meet changing needs.

- **Build a movement**. As you near the end of our journey, ask yourself this:
  - ○ Is my organization giving everyone what they need to thrive?
  - ○ What role do I want to play in my organization to achieve my diversity, equity, and inclusion ambitions?
  - ○ What beliefs or long-held assumptions (blind spots) do I need to explicitly reset?
  - ○ What will I commit to do on an ongoing basis to further understand how white supremacy and anti-Blackness are built into systems that enable my privilege?
  - ○ What can I do to call out and correct anti-Black behaviors, systems, and culture in my workplace?

11

PERSIST

I NEVER ANTICIPATED AN easy road on the journey to create more diverse, inclusive, and equal workplaces. I knew early in my career that succeeding at work would be more difficult for me than for white people, and the world told me so. I knew that the going would be tough at times, as with all things worth fighting for, but that I could make a difference and add to the growing body of work that strives to make workplaces more diverse, equitable, inclusive, and, ultimately, just. Over the course of two decades as a professional and leader in some of the most admired global corporations, finding hope in progress has sometimes been difficult.

It's easy to throw your hands up. I can't tell you how many times I have felt defeated, enraged, and demoralized by my bosses, by my colleagues, by the lack of progress, by broken promises and diluted goals, and by the constant news cycle. We all want to be where we are supported and encouraged to grow. Instead, many of us are tolerated yet not accepted; we are put on display for optics, yet disempowered and silenced. Despite all the good intentions and work of

295

the past three decades, progress has been slow, even after the events of 2020 necessitated an accelerated timeline for change. I was often triggered when I saw corporations, nonprofits, start-ups, and venture firms expressing their support for the Black Lives Matter movement, knowing how deeply systemic racism persisted within their walls. It's hard not to lean into cynicism when you've seen that movie play over and over again, when you see companies and new diversity leaders becoming prey to coded "make it happen" directives that lack understanding and nuance out of urgency to tick a box. This is often the directive, as long as the work doesn't require discomfort or political risk, doesn't cost too much, and doesn't take time away from white executives' "real jobs" of profit generation. When will we learn? I hope the time is now.

"Change is inevitable. Growth is optional," says Zander Grashow, coauthor of *The Practice of Adaptive Leadership* and founder of Good Wolf Group. It's important to remember that we are still building, iterating, and trying to see what is working to transform the workplace. This is not about burning down the house but living in construction. Change is not going to happen overnight; it's not going to happen the second you close this book. But if you take all that you've learned and continue to put one foot in front of the other, it will come. This is how we learn to see beyond our own perspective and through the lens of others. How we expand collaboration beyond our closest circles. How we tap into collective genius to be more creative, innovative, and successful.

Call in a friend. This is not a solo performance. We expect many things from leaders in organizations. We look to them for solutions when times are challenging, and we expect them to do what is right. We hope they have a moral compass that points due north and that they are good strategists and engaged people managers. But even the most ethical decision-maker and ally grapples with uncertainty. When I struggle to find the resolve to have courageous conversations or build common ground, I reach out to my community for wisdom and guidance.

I once texted my friend J. Bob Alotta, vice president of global programs, Mozilla Foundation, with an SOS asking for advice. We had just released our diversity, equity, and inclusion report and in our internal announcement, when referencing gains in gender representation, we referred to "men and women-identifying" employees. We were quickly called in by our LGBTQ community group leaders about our un-inclusive misstep. "Why not also say male-identifying?" "The language is problematic because some employees may identify as female, and others may identify as women." "As a nonbinary employee, I feel unseen." They were right. While we did present charts with a nonbinary category, we did not refer to it in the employee note and we used language that missed our intentions. When data collection and reporting practices are at odds with a person's identity, the feeling of control and being seen and experienced as valid is lost. I wasn't sure how to respond without causing more harm.

After listening to me, Alotta said, "I wonder about actually not trying to 'fix' this but live in the beautiful tension of it." Her advice bolstered me to create a space for dialogue, learning, and humility. I responded proactively by sharing the feedback with our communications and leadership teams and drafting a response to the LGBTQ community group. I acknowledged my responsibility in our failure, articulated the sticky points about our data collection efforts, and committed to remaining aware of and responsive to the evolving nature of people's identities. Through my prompt response and action, I regained their trust, and we learned to do better in the future.

I have been tempted throughout my career to mute who I am, to protect my tenuous place in the corporate pecking order. To hold back my curiosity and ambition because it made others uncomfortable. To scale down my empathy and passion because they were considered deterrents to making sound decisions. To not speak candidly about the assumptions, presumptions, everyday slights, and systemic inequities I faced.

Revealing my Dominican and Puerto Rican heritage has made me both an insider and an outsider in corporate and social spaces.

Sometimes low expectations have been set for me before I could even reveal my credentials or know-how, and other times doors have opened because I invoked a comfortable enough image with my "india" (non-Black) features. I did let go of parts of myself in moments and stages of my career, but I found my footing and confidence along the way with the help of many friends and wise leaders—though not without incurring quite a few scars.

Holding back who I am would have made me less of a worthy candidate for the promotions I earned. It would have made me less authentic to leaders, peers, and those who reported to me. Most important, it would have made me less effective in breaking down the barriers that continually hold women and BIPOC back from professional opportunity and advancement—roadblocks that make workplaces unwelcoming, unequal, and unsafe. I've persisted, iterated, and career switched to make my mission possible, and so can you.

This moment in history has proven that the status quo doesn't work. It doesn't work for institutions, and it doesn't work for individuals. BIPOC mentees have often shared stories of being told that to be successful they needed to sound and look more "white." Every time I hear a version of this statement, my heart sinks and my often wide and welcoming smile disappears. It's much easier to be who you are if everyone around you looks like you. It's much easier to celebrate someone's comments when they sound like your own. It's much, much harder to be the only, the first, the token. The path to professional success should not mean having to contort to someone else's image of who they think you should be. We can stop protecting whiteness. We must if we're going to build workplaces that work for everyone.

I'm no longer willing to contort myself into a caricature of white professional standards. I will not play poker face with my dreams and aspirations. No one should. But I still find that I am at times providing too much comfort for those who hold social and institutional power. Old power structures will be destabilized, and old rules will lose potency. This is what history teaches us. Will we listen?

My call, my ask, my message to you is this: instead of filling the void with short-lived promises, address the root causes of racial inequity. Managers and leaders, and those with aspirations to rise through the ranks, need to look in the mirror and listen to feedback from BIPOC and other marginalized employees without punishing them for their honesty. Companies must be willing to change their cultures and structures to welcome and advance all talent, especially those who have been underrepresented and restricted from achieving their fullest potential. This requires white executives to be honest about their failures and for BIPOC employees to feel safe enough to ask for what they need: individual and institutional support. White people need to admit that they have benefited from systems that hoard institutional privilege, systemic support, and social capital, and that workplace norms that have been invisible to white people are what blocks BIPOC employees from success. Workplace culture and systemic change is the real job, because without skilled teams who are invested in their work and retained because their contributions are valued, companies will continue to lose talented people again and again.

Organizations must nurture BIPOC talent, and employees must feel that they have the permission, confidence, and information to call out racist aggression when they see it. That is what it means to be an ally, a champion, an advocate. This skill is cultivated through action. Speaking up about toxic behavior and workplace bullying reduces the feeling of isolation that drives highly qualified, ambitious BIPOC away from spaces where they deserve to be. But that's not enough. The revolutionary approach I call on aligns words with actions, empathy with transparent processes, and accountability with material changes in people's behavior.

Forward-thinking people in positions of leadership have leveraged their power to take long-term social stands. Just look at Nike's 2018 decision to double down on Colin Kaepernick with the ad slogan "Believe in something. Even if it means sacrificing everything." The controversial choice paid off: Nike claimed $163 million in earned media, a 31 percent boost in sales, and a $6 billion increase in brand value.

There are organizations making necessary changes. I have mentioned several throughout this book. The Hollywood community, for one, has signaled active progress through a host of initiatives that will hopefully show real results:

- The Academy of Motion Picture Arts and Sciences rolled out representation and inclusion standards for the Oscars.

- ViacomCBS established the First Time Directors program, aimed at increasing BIPOC and female representation in films. CBS committed a minimum 25 percent of the network's annual development budget to projects from BIPOC creators and established a target for its writers' rooms to be staffed with a minimum of 50 percent BIPOC by the 2022–2023 broadcast season.

- Warner Media launched a production diversity policy and a diversity and inclusion report covering workforce, content, and community initiatives.

- WME and Endeavor announced more than thirty actions designed to support Black voices and storytellers, along with a plan to diversify its own ranks.

Pixar's *Soul*, a computer-animated fantasy comedy-drama, follows a middle school teacher named Joe Gardner who seeks to reunite his soul and his body after they are accidentally separated just before his big break as a jazz musician. In a movie industry known for its lack of diverse representation on and off screen, this was the first time Pixar told a Black man's story in an animated film. Joe Gardner's role could have easily been another example of the trope where Black leads in animated movies are transformed into animals or other creatures. Who remembers Chris Rock's 2012 Oscar speech referencing his work voicing a zebra in *Madagascar* and Eddie Murphy's role as Donkey in the *Shrek* series? Rock said, "I love animation because in the world of animation, you can be anything you wanna be. If you're a fat woman, you can play a skinny princess. If you're a short, wimpy guy, you can play a tall gladiator. If you're a white man, you can play an Arabian prince. And if you're a Black man, you can play a donkey or a zebra. You can't play white? My God!"

For *Soul*, the directors created a brain trust, which included the company's Black animators and storytellers. They further worked with a cinematographer to ensure they captured Black skin accurately on screen and for the first time in their history held an advance screening for an entirely Black audience to ensure the film avoided harmful Black stereotypes. Kemp Powers, the film's codirector and the first African American to codirect a Disney animated feature, said, "I feel that Pixar is one of the few places that's been very genuine in recognizing the shortcomings and making a tremendous effort to start to rectify it."

Sadly, not everyone has shown as much soul. Despite films like *Black Panther* and *A Wrinkle in Time* serving as proof that megahits are possible when Black creative leaders are empowered to hire Black crews and to rethink everything from lighting to hair and makeup, these films remain outliers.

Why do so many organizations fail to create an equitable and inclusive environment for all employees? The answer is twofold: we underestimate the challenge of making belonging, equity, and inclusion stick, and we have failed to explain to everyone involved what's available on the other side.

Making Belonging, Equity, and Inclusion Stick

First, to achieve real inclusion, we cannot overlook the extra effort our brains have to make to include others and the level of discomfort associated with going against some of our most basic instincts. This discomfort holds true both for the underrepresented employees and for those in the majority. As I've shared before, underrepresented groups face the brunt of these feelings of exclusion, which, according to research by Naomi Eisenberger at University of California, Los Angeles, "may be just as emotionally distressing as experiences of physical pain." Yes, the world is at an inflection point. But we must take the time to understand people's fears, motivations, and willingness to change. This is where the grappling begins.

Second, we cannot fix decades of structural inequity by tinkering at the margins. There's often a lack of incentives for involving everyone in driving change together. But here's what we must also admit to ourselves, the big, white elephant in the room: if institutions and organizations are serious about correcting wrongs and addressing structural failures, then the people in positions of power must be willing to get out of their own way and out of the way of those who can replace current leaders and decision-makers. It's one thing to say that emerging leadership must be given the mentorship, sponsorship, resources, and timeline necessary to succeed. It's another to willingly give up your seat for them to do so.

A natural resistance to diversity, equity, and inclusion efforts stems from people's fear of losing what they have—that is, power, clout, and status, and all of their unearned inclusion. Achieving greater parity requires those decision-making authorities to recognize that, yes, you will have to give up something. How much are you willing to give up for equity as a white manager? How much are you willing to risk for equity as a BIPOC manager?

What's Available on the Other Side

We're living in a period of history where systems are crumbling under their own weight. The problems we face in workplaces— discrimination, inequality—have been woven into organizational fabric by design. This time of unprecedented change and increased demand represents an opportunity to break new ground, champion new voices, tell new stories, and challenge the status quo. White supremacy is a thing, but it's not the only thing. From sexism and racism to ableism and ageism, the fight for workplace inclusion is a battle on many fronts. Matters can be complicated further by internal disagreements over what to focus on. Many of us often dwell in the paralyzing place where our fears reside. We numb ourselves into inaction because we don't know where to begin. Just start!

Diversity, equity, and inclusion is a continuum, an ongoing journey of unlearning the deeply rooted dogmas that guide the way individuals, organizations, and systems operate. You have to be in it for the long haul. Transforming systems takes time, resources, and patience. The greatest point of resistance is often the greatest learning opportunity. I believe we can, in our own spaces, be active agitators and revolutionaries. There's a win for you, me, and us.

Here's what I envision: radically inclusive and equity-minded workplaces where leaders and team members are empathetically anti-racist; where creativity and innovation come from everywhere; where all aspects of our identities are represented equitably at all levels across organizations and institutions; where safe, fair, and dignified work is the norm; where wellness is built into organizational design; and where we are willing to test, iterate, and pivot so that everyone can be successful.

I want BIPOC to share in wealth creation, and I want to live in a world where more women, people of color, and historically underrepresented groups are leading key parts of our economy and civil society. I'm not the only one. The future of work is now, and our workplaces must consist of an integrated focus on diversity, inclusive cultures, equitable benefits, and fair policies. Those organizations that do not advance diversity, equity, and inclusion risk their bottom line, brand, and chance for success. The question is not whether we will achieve gender, LGBTQ, and racial equality someday, but whether we are courageous enough to reimagine and rebuild the organizational culture of the future today. I challenge you to dig into your courage reserves and exercise real bravery now. I challenge you to persist.

Persist When You Make a Mistake (or Are Afraid To)

Many of us want to change conditions in our workplaces so that everyone can thrive, yet sometimes we are terrified of messing up, saying the wrong thing, or not being able to do enough.

I was two weeks into my role as chief people officer at Vice Media Group when George Floyd was murdered, and our nation underwent a social-justice reckoning that was long overdue. I couldn't ignore what was happening around me. I didn't yet know many of our over two thousand global employees personally, but I knew that many were experiencing pain and frustration. I was. Despite working fourteen-hour days, I had never felt more convinced that this was exactly where I was supposed to be: in the middle of the maelstrom, helping others figure out what to do next. On May 29, 2020, here's what I wrote:

> While this is not the context I was imagining introducing myself to all of you, this week has hit me especially hard, and I felt it was urgent to send a note of solidarity to my new colleagues across the world. In addition to being a proud Latina, I have also dedicated my career to leading large-scale organizational change and fostering diverse, equitable, and inclusive cultures in companies big and small. While this is just week three for me at Vice Media Group, I am personally and professionally committed to supporting our diverse teams across the world—and a big part of that is having the difficult conversations.
>
> Many of us across Vice Media Group are experiencing compounded trauma. . . . Many of you may be asking what you can do and how you can better support Black people on your teams, our communities, and others personally feeling the impact of COVID-19 and multiple crises. We would like to inform you that . . . as a company we are also currently developing an

educational digital event series focused on unpacking diversity, inclusion, discrimination, and oppression, please look for more info on this in the coming month.

Sent. As I calmly waited, the replies came in. "Thank you for acknowledging our reality." "Thank you for sharing these resources." The emails didn't stop. I wasn't looking for a pat on the back; instead, it became clear that everyone is terrified to talk about race at work, and few leaders are willing to put themselves in the uncomfortable place of trying to find the words. Sometimes you will get it right (especially if you have a team of allies to review your message); sometimes you won't. The key is to show grace, make an effort, and try again. What matters is that you are willing to open the dialogue and learn from your mistakes.

If you're overwhelmed by a real fear of messing up, saying the wrong thing, or not being able to do enough, I get it. The key is to fail fast and recover quickly. When you make missteps, and you will, how you react is more important than what you did. How you recover says more about who you are. And know that you can't expect to be forgiven right away, because saying sorry doesn't eliminate accumulated pain. But when you persist with kind, authentic, genuine care, broken relationships can be mended.

There have been moments when I, too, haven't gotten the transformative work of diversity, equity, and inclusion right. When I was the global head of diversity and inclusion at Moody's Investors Service in 2008, we piloted multicultural and women's groups as part of our efforts to support underrepresented employees. In 2009, as we prepared to launch our official employee resource groups, one of the founding members of the multicultural group, who self-identified as gay, courageously confronted me with one question: How can you speak about creating safe spaces for everyone and not launch an LGBT (the "Q" would come later) group concurrently? The honest answer? Fear. Fear that I couldn't garner the same level of support and advocacy for a community that continued to face social exclusion, harassment, and homophobia within our hallways. Fear of endangering the personal or professional safety of these employees by exposing them publicly to the company. Fear that it could risk the other employee resource group launches if we faced opposition. Fear of failure.

In the same way that I have asked my white male friends and colleagues to step outside their own privileged experience to consider the inequities and uncivil behavior endured by women and BIPOC, I was being held accountable to do the same for colleagues missing from the conversation. I made a misstep. I did not look inward to address my own assumptions and fears, and I neglected to consider that in order to drive lasting change, I needed to exert pressure on the status quo for all marginalized employees.

I have learned. I've confronted my own privilege as an able-bodied, cisgender, heterosexual, brown-skinned Latina, and I've grown increasingly committed to intersectionality as a means to build transformational, sustainable change—and to get it right. I'm proud to share that not only did we launch the multicultural, women, and LGBT employee resource groups all at once, but our CEO personally sanctioned the LGBT&A (allies) group—an introduction of the term "allies" before it was in vogue. We held a safe space for LGBTQ employees. The CEO listened to their stories. And he gave his full endorsement for managers and individual contributors to create an inclusive and safe workplace where all employees could live their lives openly, without fear of personal or professional recrimination.

We righted a wrong by listening, learning, and acting. I am asking you to do the same.

Persist When You Face Resistance

I've heard recently from several new diversity, equity, and inclusion leaders that they're struggling with the resistance they're facing in their organizations. Despite all the public commitments and pledges

from CEOs, founders, and nonprofit leaders, resistance to dismantling inequity in the workplace is real, pervasive, and insidious.
We have been given a front-row seat to the systemic racism that
allowed for a lack of direct charges against Breonna Taylor's killers,
a Supreme Court nomination that could reduce the likelihood that
everyone receives equal treatment under the law, and a former president who incited a riot at the Capitol.

Here's what I tell them: The root cause of resistance is fear. Fear
of losing power, clout, status, or a place in the pecking order. Fear
of messing up or of not doing enough. Fear of losing the exceptions
from punishment that some have long enjoyed. Fear that opening up
for collaboration means ceding territory and control. You will always
face resistance, but you must persist. You need to build muscles
you've never flexed before: an expansive capacity for empathy, anti-
racism, influencing skills, and fortitude to persist. This resistance
will show up in individual, group, and organizational forms. It's the
reason why we haven't realized equity in workplaces. But through
persistence and constant iteration, we will find the way.

Change moves at the speed of trust. Resistance to diversity, equity, and inclusion is not uncommon, and it shows up in many ways.

- **Presumed shared, implicit norms where leaders question the work of diversity, equity, and inclusion**. "We
  shouldn't be taking employees away from their jobs to do diversity work."

- **Pushback on solutions**. "Can you present a more cost-
  effective solution?"

- **Fear-based resistance**. "I don't want to lose my job for this."

- **Lack of readiness**. "That's not how we have done things
  here." "_____ is not appropriate for our workplace or employees."

- **Evasiveness** (perhaps the most common form of resistance). "It's not scalable." "It's not the right time." "We don't need to focus on systemic change or culture now." Also known as, "This makes me uncomfortable."

Shrinking from this work is not an option. The cover has been blown and expectations have shifted. Many of us have unwittingly faced moments where we had to turn the lens on ourselves. We have been forced to reckon with the legacy of racism and complicity, including our own, that has resulted in disparate impacts across our companies. We have come face-to-face with the realization that racism is hardwired into our organizational structures and infrastructure, behavioral tendencies, leadership, and board dynamics.

Key to this work will be sustaining conversations and structural improvements beyond moments when discomfort arises, diversions occur, or competing priorities present themselves. There is no end to this work, this conversation; it's not a topic to be tucked away and brought out during periods of discontent or for curious examination. For too long, we've erred on the side of making people, mostly white people, comfortable with change. Discomfort is a daily condition for BIPOC and other marginalized employees in your organization. Why should anyone, especially those who have long tolerated these injustices, expect to be exempt? This work is no longer about placating grievances but about creating real conditions for lasting and sustainable progress. Otherwise, you risk people reverting to comfortable norms that reinforce the very inequalities we're seeking to change.

Persist When You Feel Fatigued

I'm sure at times reading this book you may have felt overwhelmed. I have a detailed knowledge of that sense of hopelessness and frustration when there is so much work you don't know where to begin. Or maybe you're suffering from initiative fatigue and getting stuck in the PR moment. Creating expectations that you won't meet leads to employees—not to mention yourself—feeling dissatisfied, confused, and disconnected.

Diversity fatigue is real. The topic of diversity, equity, and inclusion is everywhere, and people are tired of talking about it. Also, caring hurts. I've often felt frustrated when my emotional and physical labor did not seem to lead to meaningful outcomes. It's a fight that takes resources and energy, and it's hard to stay interested, much less committed, when you're barely seeing progress. The result? Passivity and tuning out.

There is so much caring yet a shortage of effective action. Diversity, equity, and inclusion, specifically a focus on racial inequity, has become trendy. Historically, the field itself has been thought of as performative—either touchy-feely diversity training programs or corporate grandstanding—but now it's gaining a lot more credibility with dedicated academic and certification programs and becoming more widespread as a professional practice. The flip side to more people wanting to get involved, and more people calling out the wrongs of the past and present, is that when progress is frustratingly slow, more people get discouraged.

The fact is that long before the compound traumas of COVID-19 and social unrest, diversity, equity, and inclusion efforts had stalled across most industries. Let's just talk about tech, which is one of the industries that has been most vocal about its efforts. Atlassian's 2018 *State of Diversity and Inclusion in U.S. Tech* report found that diversity and inclusion efforts had greatly slowed down. There was an almost 50 percent decrease in individual participation in diversity initiatives year over year. Meanwhile, adoption of company-wide initiatives in the United States had stayed flat, while Silicon Valley companies registered fewer formal diversity and inclusion programs than the previous year. And less than 30 percent of underrepresented groups reported having a sense of belonging, representation, and high levels of retention at their respective companies. Those findings remain stubbornly the same in tech and other industries.

Don't give in to feeling overwhelmed

Just like you can't get caught up in performative, false heroics, don't let the complexity of these problems hold you under a spell. Pay attention to your mindset, examine your motivations, and deepen your understanding of racism. We don't know what we don't know. You have to be willing to be comfortable in discomfort. Cultivate a growth mindset as a continuous learner, eager for new resources and information to help you be a better ally, advocate, and accomplice in the fight for equity. Set your preconceptions aside to allow more space to hear and learn from the perspectives of others. Approach conversations from a place of curiosity and create space for the weightiness of the issues your team members face every day. Preserving and honoring our humanity is always the right thing to do. Whether you are a white or BIPOC manager, we can all find the will to challenge racism, transphobia, ageism, misogyny, and other forms of oppression.

Scientifically, this is hard. It raises the fight-or-flight response. And this happens on a continuum. We feel threatened psychologically. We worry about the threat response in others. Even thinking about challenging the behavior and actions of others can result in a huge response neurologically. Everything gets heightened. I get it. I've felt it. Your heart beats a mile a minute. You consider a million scenarios in your head, and when you finally decide on what to say and how, the meeting or moment is over. Did you know breathing is the only automatic function over which we have voluntary control? Breathing techniques can help regulate your brain functions, reduce your anxiety and fear, and increase your ability to reason.

Try this:

1. In a seated position exhale all of your air.

2. Inhale for a count of five.

3. Hold your breath for a count of five.

4. Exhale for a count of five.

5. Hold your breath for a count of five.

6. Keep the pattern going and repeat this cycle three times.

I have to remind myself to do this, and when I do, it makes all the difference. It dims the voices in my head and helps me see what is happening around me with a clearer view. And the best part is that you can do it while nobody notices! Try it.

We take for granted the historical context around how racism has shaped things over time—education, housing, jobs, health care, and equal treatment in the criminal justice system. The deep racial and ethnic inequities that exist in your workplace are a direct result of persistent structural racism: the historical and contemporary policies, practices, and norms that create and maintain white supremacy. It's a tightly interwoven system of social, cultural, and institutional practices whose sole purpose is to keep racism in place.

So, yes, this work is hard, but picking up this book is one step to understanding and fighting for this Inclusion Revolution. I'm reminded of Amanda Gorman's poetry at the 2021 US presidential inauguration, where she delivered clear-eyed hope of what's possible for our nation: "There is always light. If only we're brave enough to see it. If only we're brave enough to be it."

Persist by Fighting for "Us," All of Us

I'm often asked, especially by young women of color, how I maintain my authenticity in the workplace. The ability to bring your whole self to work is a complex subject mired in social, political, and economic tensions. It requires a deep sense of self, political and situational awareness, and a heavy dose of courage. While I have long driven diversity, equity, and inclusion strategies aimed at transforming corporate cultures, remaining true to my character has been both a work in progress and a defining trait. I can be me—kind, bold, lighthearted, brave, and steadfast—because others have fought for me, lovingly and fiercely.

I was reminded of this when we celebrated my father's sixtieth birthday on a family trip to the Bahamas. It was a perfect way to cheer a man deeply rooted in his Caribbean heritage and who places the highest value on family togetherness.

During his birthday dinner, we all teased my father when he announced he wanted to say a few words about everyone at the table. As is common when my impassioned papi speaks, we were all in tears, most of all him. When it came to me, he began with a story he has selectively shared over the years. He recalled the day he first saw me, when, as a fifteen-year-old still discovering who he was, he was struck with a clear and distinct realization. He felt an instant, selfless love for his baby daughter. That fierce feeling was quickly followed by a deep sense of protection, which to him simply meant he would fight for me, always. And fight for me he has.

The first time my streetwise father fought for me, he was eighteen years old. Fearing what would become of me if I was raised by my teenage mother in a Midtown Manhattan community riddled with crime and poverty, he asked his parents to raise me in their home in the Dominican Republic. And so, on his next visit, he took me with him, never to return. Although it was not a fully hatched plan, he expected to encounter some level of resistance. There was none. My mother relinquished me—perhaps uncertain about her parenting abilities, perhaps recognizing I could lead a better life elsewhere. In that moment, she sacrificed her needs for mine, and my father changed my life.

Years later, in my junior year of high school, my father was advised that I needed to complete my PSATs in the United States to improve my chances of entering an American university. He quickly bought a small house in New Jersey that he could ill afford where I moved with my grandparents, who devotedly came along to help with the transition. This was all so I could achieve what my father had fought for since my infancy: my happiness and success through education, access, and opportunity.

Knowing that I have people in my corner willing to fight for me—whether it be my father, grandparents, and aunts, or the friends, bosses, and mentors who have heartily advocated for me over the years—has allowed me to show up fully and authentically and to champion the same for others.

I've been firmly anchored in who I am, often despite what others expected of me, because I've been fought for when I most needed it. Light has been shone on me so that I can open doors and lighten the load for others.

Just like my father fought for me, I fight so that my daughter grows up to be self-assured, strong, and unafraid to advocate for herself and others. My and my daughter's circumstances are far easier than those of my father, and I have him to thank for that. Her voice, courage, and kindness are my way of honoring him and lighting the path forward so that the journey toward dismantling inequity is a little less lonely, easier to navigate, and more joyful.

We are in a global moment of reckoning and awareness, and I know that many white leaders and managers are wrestling with what to do and how to respond. While you can't undo the harms of nearly a half millennium of degradation and dehumanization of Black people in the United States and globally, there is a path forward for you to be a force for good. This will take patience, vulnerability, empathy, and courage, and it will require you to devote a large percentage of your time to the people aspect of your job. It matters. You must be willing to sacrifice your own comfort. At the end of the day, this work is about you. It starts and ends with you. You must be intentional about inclusion and belonging. Part of building stronger connections is knowing each other and understanding that our lived experiences have been vastly different.

"What's the difference between a moment, a movement, and transformation? If you're just in it to capitalize on the moment, you will fail fast. If you're trying to create a cultural movement, that's what gets us to lasting change," says Keesha Jean-Baptiste.

I know it can be hard to accept that with privilege comes unearned inclusion and harm, especially when that runs counter to your personal values. I have heard white leaders say: "People of color just think that they can throw everything at us, and that we can solve everything for them. I can't solve the world's societal problems!"

No, maybe you can't. But what you *can* do is stop perpetuating the world's societal problems through your own actions. What you *can* do is understand that, as part of the majority, you've been living your entire life in a space where you think that you're not contributing to the problem, when, really, you are. And that's the problem. I've found that there's a wall inherently up when we begin taking on the work of changing culture. It's a wall that says, "I don't care." It's a wall that says, "This has nothing to do with me. I'm not like that at all." It's a wall that says, "I don't have time for this. I can barely keep my head afloat."

That's what keeps the middle manager stuck, along with questions about how they will be rewarded for their efforts, measurability, lack of authority to make a difference, and a sense that they're at the mercy of whatever policies are created.

This isn't an attack on your character but rather an opportunity to unlock what holds you back from being the colleague, partner, or leader you want to be. This is a key step on the road to allyship. You have the power to change. And the responsibility is yours.

For my BIPOC peers and colleagues who for far too long have shouldered the burdens placed on you, this book is also for you. I, like you, have a stake in this revolution. I know many of you are exhausted from years of compartmentalizing the personal turmoil in society and at work. Many of us also sit at the intersection of bias and privilege. We feel shame, doubt, and guilt about the privileges we hold. And we also feel resentment, anger, and pain from bearing bias. We, too, must determine our what and our why for doing this work before deciding what solutions to apply. That requires us to examine how much bandwidth we have and sometimes pause and disengage for our own mental health. That's OK too.

Intractable as it may seem, the problem of racism and inequity in the workplace is a problem that can be solved with the right information, incentives, investment, and courage. I firmly believe that we can find a meaningful path for career success in workplaces that were not built for us but that are seeking to transform so that we can all thrive. We, too, have a role to play in making workplaces work for everyone, and we have a choice about what that role will be. For some of us, it may mean building bigger bridges across communities of color and other marginalized communities. I believe we can build extraordinary friendships between white and BIPOC colleagues, design concrete and accessible solutions, and create real and lasting change together.

People can change. Institutions can change. Doing so requires everyone to hold each other accountable, to aim for reconciliation, to fight for each other, and to change the power dynamics between those who are harmed and those who cause or benefit from harm to others.

The future is bright, change is attainable, and there is so much we can continue to do to enhance workplace culture. This is a moment in time to reimagine and redefine the future. By enabling others to exceed their potential, we collectively rise. I see a difference now; I see a different collective future.

To **persist** in this complex and emotionally heavy work, you need to be clear on what you're trying to achieve (**reflect**), be willing to make tough calls (**visualize**), and embrace real moments of courage (**act**), like we have shown throughout this book. This is what we are up against.

Nevertheless, I persist.

And I want you to persist too.

Don't give up on your fellow humans. Persist through it all because on the other side is a more equitable future for all. It starts and ends with you.

I hope that reading this book has shaken you up a bit and strengthened your resolve to hold yourself and your organization accountable for systemic patterns of inequity. That you will have not one but a series of clarifying moments on your journey to create an equitable, inclusive, and engaged workplace. These moments may include a deeper understanding of the personal practices or habits that may be unconsciously thwarting those efforts and an understanding of how to get onto the right path toward the world we all want to live and work in.

Hope rests on the belief that things can be different and that we have the agency to make that change. My hope isn't foolish or naive. It's evidence based. I've presented that throughout this book. We can be better, and we have the tools.

I engage in this work because I believe change is possible. I am trying to make work safe, equitable, and inclusive—for all people—because it is possible, worthy, and important. I believe you are too. Let's strengthen our muscles together. We have a once-in-a-generation opportunity to dismantle racial inequities in the workplace. I am counting on you to help realize this as a shared vision. It's up to all of us to drive this change forward. Let's get the Inclusion Revolution started.

FURTHER RESOURCES FOR THE INCLUSION REVOLUTION

For further resources, including the latest in performance-management software and my current recommended reading list, go to www .daisyauger-dominguez.com.

ACKNOWLEDGMENTS

This book honors the revolutionary spirit of my late grand-uncle Rafael Tomás Fernández Domínguez, who played a key role in leading the Dominican Republic civil war of 1965 and was recognized as a hero by the government in 1999 for his dedication and respect to democratic ideals.

When I sat down to write these acknowledgments, one word kept running through my mind: ubuntu. Ubuntu is an African concept in which your sense of self is shaped by your relationships with other people. In South Africa, they call Ubuntu: *I am, because of you*. Thank you, Michael Gross, for introducing me to this concept and always reminding our Coro class of 1998—Lisa Cowan, Zander Grashow, Amy Sweet, Ken Young, Jason Gill, Valerie Santos, Kiran Makam, Yoojin Lee, Saran White, and Alix Saint-Amand—of our shared humanity.

I am, because of so many amazing humans in my life. It would take writing another book to name all those who have shared their love, wisdom, compassion, and kindness. These are a few who have been especially pivotal on my journey.

Writing a book while working full time can be arduous and isolating, but I had Kathleen Harris in my corner every step of the way. Kathleen, you helped me get out of my head, push past my corporate speak, and shape my vision and stories. I am forever grateful for your heart, talent, wit, and friendship.

Acknowledgments

I owe a debt of gratitude for my formative learning in social justice, race, intersectionality, and equity to Teresa Amott, John Ernest "Ernie" Keen, Linden Lewis, and the late Walter Stafford.

To Rossana Rosado, Luis Miranda, the late Lisa Quiroz, Fred Terrell, Ella Bell, Roz Hudnell, Freada Kapor Klein, Anita Hill, and Lorraine Cortés-Vásquez, whose sage wisdom and generosity have paved the way for me and countless others.

To the many diversity, equity, and inclusion leaders and practitioners who inspire and teach me every day to be better, do better.

To my sheroes, Yrthya Dinzey-Flores, Tiffany Dufu, Cindy Pace, Diana Cruz Solash, and Helene Yan, who lovingly push me onward and upward.

I was lucky to meet my terrific agent, Johanna Castillo, before the world was forced into lockdown. Your belief in me, my story, and Latinx voices meant everything. That coffee meeting changed my life!

To Emi Ikkanda and the brilliant team at Hachette Book Group and Seal Press for championing my work and voice, and breathing life into the story I wanted to tell.

To everyone who agreed to be interviewed for this book: Bob Alotta, Emily Best, Aubrey Blanche, Tiffany Dufu, Keesha Jean-Baptiste, Freada Kapor Klein, Lisa Kenny, Lucinda Martínez, Brian O'Kelley, Cindy Pace, Vanessa Roanhorse, Katica Roy, Bird Runningwater, Reshma Saujani, Deepti Sharma, Meghan Stabler, Sherice Torres, Alicin Reidy Williamson, Cid Wilson, Jamia Wilson, Kenji Yoshino, and many others whose wisdom I drew on.

To the bosses who showed me it was possible to lead with heart and courage: Nicole Johnson, Chee Mee Hu, Steve Milovich, and Nancy Dubuc.

To Jennifer Justice, who always demands that I get more and makes it happen.

To Rha Goddess, who emboldened my sense of what's possible.

To Phil Clark and Dori Alexander for always being willing to give me golden editorial feedback.

Acknowledgments

To Bart Oosterveld and Adam Whiteman, my first white male allies and lifelong friends.

To my Vice Media Group work family, who create human-centered work that pushes the world forward.

To my sister friends, Dominique Jones, Erica González, Elizabeth de Leon, and Katy Romero, and mi hermano del alma, Angel Tirado-Morales, who always have my back.

To my childhood friends who first showed me what it means to straddle multiple cultures and identities: Rie Arvesen, Anneke Schapelhouman, and the late Chi Wai (David) So.

To my Bucknell peeps and first social justice warriors, Chhavi Seth, Rich Shiu, and Natalia Espinal.

To Brandy Baucom, who helped this "island foreigner" navigate the "tough" waters of New Milford H.S.

To my Planned Parenthood Federation of America, Brooklyn Children's Museum, Robert S. Clark Foundation, and Facing History and Ourselves board partners who are doing the work every day.

To my adopted Auger family, Ric and Joan Auger, Matt and Ursula Auger, Karyn and Josh Banke, and my niece and nephews, Ellie and Aidan Auger, Jordan and Luke Banke.

I was raised in a non-traditional family structure, and it made all the difference in my life. To my dearest grandparents Ramon Arcadio Fernández Domínguez and Elena Miniño (Mami y Papi), my forever smiling late great-grandmother Juana Evangelista Rodríguez Veloz (Mamá Chichí), and my adored father (also Papi), Ramón Domínguez (Cachito). To my extra blessing of a stepmother, Haydee Domínguez; my fierce tias-madres, Maritza Siegel and María Elena Domínguez; my brilliant brothers, Sonny Ray and Legend Domínguez; my beloved primos-hermanos, Petal Carr, Laksmi and Visnu González, Natalia Báez, Brisa Siegel, and Melissa Machado; my gifted aunt Josefina Miniño, late uncle Papa Molina and primos José Antonio y Evangelina Molina; my doting uncles Michael Siegel and Víctor Báez; and the new

321

generation who fill us with hope, Luis Arturo González, Valentina De Leon, and Lia González.

To my husband, Christopher Auger-Domínguez, the single best person I know. Thank you for holding me, spoiling me, pushing me, teaching me, nurturing me, and anchoring me. Te amo.

And to Emma Auger-Domínguez, with whom I have been madly, deeply, and intensely in love since the day you were born. It is a joyful and humbling honor to be your mother. I love you more.

NOTES

Chapter 1

This chapter sets up the premise that it's vital to interrogate your intentions and ask yourself: Why do I want to do this work? It begins with a question from TV host Dr. Marc Lamont Hill on an episode of *Black News Tonight* in May 2021. He asked conservative activist Christopher Rufo, "Name something you like about being white." I have found the reflective exercises in the book *Leadership on the Line* by Ronald A. Heifetz and Marty Linsky to be most helpful. They coined the phrase "getting off the dance floor and going to the balcony." It is an essential first step to diversity, equity, and inclusion efforts to look at the big picture and create goals and actions with a lasting effect. To help define your why, I looked to research from Deloitte and Culture Amp on how belonging improves retention. Whitney Johnson helped quantify this in "The Value of Belonging at Work," published in the *Harvard Business Review*. I also cite psychologist Abraham Maslow's work in this discussion about the importance of creating a culture of belonging. In Maslow's hierarchy of needs, belonging and the need to connect is right there after food, water, and self-esteem. Research from Boston Consulting Group confirms that managers have the most effect on the performance and well-being of their teams. But bias is everywhere, and there persists an us-versus-them subcurrent in the workplace due to decades of social programming, as cited by Mary E. Casey and Shannon Murphy Robinson in their book *Neuroscience of Inclusion: New Skills for New Times*. I also talk about the need for reparations, citing Ta-Nehisi Coates's work and using that as a guide in creating a road map for change. Finally, I make the case for belonging, citing studies from Catalyst on the emotional tax levied on Black employees at work and *Social Psychology of Inclusion and Exclusion*. From these works and others by John A. Powell, there's no question that increasing inclusion and belonging at work leads to a stronger, more productive, and more profitable company.

Chapter 2

To begin this chapter, it is essential to understand why the workplace looks so white and why it can't be fixed by an immediate hiring spree. I lean on Peggy McIntosh's work on white privilege and the invisible backpack. Michael Sandel, professor of political philosophy at Harvard University, coined the phrase "tyranny of merit," which urges individuals to look at their "meritocratic hubris" and stop believing that their success is their own doing. That led me to ideas from Dolly Chugh and David Hekman on how to use your privilege to create a more equitable workforce. In determining how to set effective hiring goals, I looked to the extensive work Ellen Pao has done for Project Include, as well as case studies from Twitter and Nike. Hiring goals always raise the question of what's legal. To answer this, I relied on my extensive experience working with in-house counsel as well as documentation from Jackson Lewis on "Court Rulings Stress National Importance of Diversity Goals but Set Limits on Methods." To support these ideas, I researched critical mass theory, using Rosabeth Moss Kanter's articulation of critical mass theory as a threshold to guide organizational transformations. Finally, I cite academic researchers Siri Chilazi and Iris Bohnet's work on behavior change and the "will" and the "way." They say you need the motivation and the skills to get the work done. The motivation can come in part through goals incentivization. Case studies from Accenture, Johnson & Johnson, Nike, and Mercer, as well as reports from UN Women, Women 20, and the World Economic Forum, have discussed the power of setting big goals tied with individual accountability. CNBC reported on the success of reaching goals when you tell someone about them. Finally, I used public reports from the Academy of Motion Picture Arts and Sciences, as well as supporting stories from the *New York Times*, to share the progress made by the Oscars organization to improve its lack of diversity.

Chapter 3

This chapter focuses on the implicit bias laden in the recruiting process. To fully understand its effect, I was informed by studies from Marianne Bertrand and Sendhil Mullainathan that support the fact that white names are more employable than non-white ones. Joan Williams and Sky Mihaylo also cite name bias in their research published in the *Harvard Business Review*. This is further echoed by Devah Pager, Bruce Western, and Naomi Sugie in their paper "Sequencing Disadvantage: Barriers to Employment Facing Young Black and White Men with Criminal Records," and by Sonia Kang and her colleagues, who "whitened résumés" to test the implications on the recruiting process. Not surprisingly, when BIPOC whitewashed their résumés, they were granted more access to opportunity. Why does this persist? Recruiters only spend seconds reviewing résumés, according to an eye-tracking study from Ladders, and need to make gut calls—"gut" meaning biased. Applicant tracking systems can help; *Forbes* reports the majority of *Fortune* 500 companies use them. But these, too, can fall into bias traps. Stopping the use of résumés is a smart solution. Research from Dave Heller titled "Work Experience Poor Predictor of Future Job Performance" confirmed this. Another way to combat bias is stopping the Friends and Family Program. Survey data from LinkedIn spotlighted the fact that the majority of jobs are filled via networking, while data from Public Religion Research Institute found that 75 percent of white Americans have "entirely white social networks." Job descriptions can help attract more diverse candidates. Christina Cauterucci covered the correlation between gendered words in job descriptions and a lack of female applicants in *Slate*.

Chapter 4

The truth is, bad hires happen. A study from CareerBuilder revealed that a bad hire can cost a company anywhere from $25,000 to $50,000. Paradigm research found that 98 percent of organizations have candidate pools more racially and ethnically diverse than their existing workforces. According to Paradigm staff, this was based on research between 2016 and 2017 across approximately twenty companies. This chapter begins with the idea that bias is everywhere. Preeminent scholars on implicit bias Iris Bohnet, author of *What Works*, and law professor Kenji Yoshino, author of *Covering*, confirm this, as do Phoebe K. Chua and Melissa Mazmanian, who write that current hiring practices at large tech companies lead to class bias. Their paper, titled "Are You One of Us?," suggests that when BIPOC do land an interview, they may not be evaluated fairly and are held to higher double standards. It's an uphill battle: research from Howard Giles and Tamara Rakić proves that we are extremely sensitive to those with accents. Additionally, research from Justin Friesen found that whites struggle to tell real from fake smiles on Black faces, which can lead to misinterpretations and misunderstandings. To offer solutions, I sought studies to confirm that broadening your candidate pool will lead to a more diverse workforce. Research from Stefanie Johnson published in the *Harvard Business Review* found that when there's only one woman in your candidate pool, there's statistically no chance she'll be hired. In discussing how to interview for "culture add," I sought studies from Lean In's 2020 report *The State of Black Women in Corporate America* and the United Nations.

Chapter 5

I start with Catalyst's report on psychological safety, which notes that only 56 percent of Black employees were vocal about important or difficult issues in the workplace, compared with 74 percent of white employees. To establish belonging from the start, take a close look at your onboarding process. Karie Willyerd's *Harvard Business Review* article "Social Tools Can Improve Employee Onboarding" stresses that the first six months of an employee's tenure can determine their likelihood to stay, citing a study done by the Aberdeen Group. The company Buffer provides a great case study for how to do onboarding right, with the assignment of buddies to new team members. But it takes more than one person to create a welcoming environment. Research from Lucille Nahemow and colleagues discusses how similarities at work can lead to friendships and stronger bonds; this can be exclusionary at its core. Case studies from Culture Amp provided ideas for how to break these bonds and create new ones, as does the book, *The Proust Questionnaire*, which provides a series of icebreakers favored by Marcel Proust. Empathy is the fuel workplaces need to succeed. Dr. Brené Brown has done much writing on this, citing the four attributes of empathy from nursing scholar Theresa Wiseman. Case studies from Ford, BetterUp, and Friends with Holograms show how day-in-the-life experiences can help create a more empathetic workforce and a culture of belonging, which leads to more diversity. The reason that is so important is supported by research from David Rock and Heidi Grant, as well as Matthew Corritore and colleagues in their analyses for *Harvard Business Review*. Finally, I dig into the power of your words on others. Research from Jennifer Sandoval and Derald Wing Sue discusses the harm of microaggressions and micro-invalidations on an individual.

Chapter 6

The chapter begins with a study on psychological safety, a term first coined by Amy Edmondson in her work "Psychological Safety and Learning Behavior in Work Teams," published in 1999. More recently, author Charles Duhigg investigated the building blocks of a "perfect team," specifically at Google, and published his results in an article for the *New York Times*. That confirmed my belief that psychological safety was the defining factor. Adam Grant's book

Notes

Think Again was also a great source into what psychological safety is and isn't. Aaron De Smet's work for McKinsey highlighted the critical role of leadership development in terms of psychological safety. This led me to Timothy R. Clark's book *The 4 Stages of Psychological Safety: Defining the Path to Inclusion and Innovation*. Stories from the Obama White House were great proof points for my research, like when the women became unofficial allies in meetings and when Obama had to shut down toxic-masculinity behaviors that were intimidating to other employees. In thinking about psychological safety and who is allowed to make a mistake, I found a tweet from author Celeste Ng that said, "Privilege is about who is allowed to make mistakes." This led to thoughts on using privilege for good and allyship, which can be complicated. Research from Lean In shows that most BIPOC do not believe they have allies at work, even when others consider themselves to be allies. Here's what allies can do: mitigate microaggressions and eradicate the need to cover at work. Research from Deloitte shows that the proliferation of covering is a key sign of a non-inclusive culture. I read about Sam Polk writing about Wall Street's "culture of brutal conformity" to misogyny and the bro culture that forced the disrespect and exclusion of women. In *Uncovering Talent: A New Model of Inclusion*, published by Deloitte, Dr. Christie Smith and Kenji Yoshino take a deep dive into the widespread occurrence of covering at work and the impacts on inclusion.

Chapter 7

In discussing the use and effectiveness of anonymous surveys, I looked at Gartner's recent work on an inclusion index, which was featured in Lauren Romansky's article in the *Harvard Business Review*. I read case studies on tEQuitable's website to learn more use cases of their reporting software, including the one I mentioned from Twilio. Most of this chapter relies on my personal, firsthand experience through years of observation, practice, and learning.

Chapter 8

Research has repeatedly shown that standard talent-management practices like performance reviews and promotional decisions remain stubbornly in favor of men in the workplace, with women of color receiving less support and vaguer performance feedback. I read a study from David G. Smith and colleagues on the "The Power of Language," as well as Zuhairah Washington and Laura Morgan Roberts's analysis for *Harvard Business Review*, "Women of Color Get Less Support at Work." While writing this book, news erupted of the firing of a Google employee, prominent AI ethics researcher Timnit Gebru. Much was written about this, and I looked at Shelly Banjo's article in *Bloomberg*, which printed the internal memo/mea culpa from Google's CEO, as well as a Medium post from the Google Walkout organization. Several sources and studies were helpful in deducing the reasons people leave companies, especially BIPOC employees, from Brandon Rigoni and Amy Adkins's work for Gallup and Coqual's report on *Being Black in Corporate America*. The EY *Belonging Barometer* provided key data, including the benefit of regular check-ins. Also, the influence of managers' performance review and feedback on their employees' motivation and morale was supported by research by Marcus Buckingham and Katica Roy. Roy also shared that only 46 percent of women (versus 51 percent of men) believe promotion criteria are fair and objective. Lean In's *Women in the Workplace* study shared data on the prevalence of bias in reviews and promotions by gender. Through analyzing more than twenty-five thousand pieces of peer feedback, Culture Amp has found that individuals tend to focus more on the personality and attitudes of women. To understand more about bias and awareness, I read a study by the National Center for State Courts, which highlighted implicit bias among judges. Bias has real implications, as shown by data from Gené Teare's article for Crunchbase that highlighted the lack of funding to Black founders. In researching feedback and professional development, Frances Jackson and Emma Hansen's study on "Leadership Potential Versus Readiness" in *Human Resources* was invaluable. I also relied on Dr. Carla Jeffries's work on feedback and why your employees want to hear the negative feedback, and research from Shelley J. Correll on how vague feedback is holding women back. A case study from Eli Lilly helped provide proof of the need to cease the annual review. I tapped into my own resources to share the unbiasing checklist Google uses during performance reviews. The chapter ends with information on pay equity. I used information from Ellen Pao's *Reset*, as well as data from Equal Pay Today.

Chapter 9

I spoke with the leaders at Pope Consulting to hear firsthand their account of the company's groundbreaking research in the 1970s on what was holding Black engineers back from advancement. This led me to research from professors Jennifer Merluzzi and Adina Sterling that found that Black employees are more likely to be promoted when they are referred by another employee by a factor of 1.2, compared to Black employees without a referral. The 2019 report *Being Black in Corporate America* by Coqual and McKinsey's *Women in the Workplace*

2019 provided invaluable data on promotion rates based on demographics. In researching employee handbooks, I recall conversations with Freada Kapor Klein, as well as assets provided by the Valve company website. Culture Amp was a great resource for research on support systems and the impact of who you choose to spend time with, including research from David Wilder and John E. Thompson. I read *HR Dive*'s report on Twitter paying resource groups to understand who was putting this idea into practice. In developing insight into why and how to expand your network, I read Dolly Chugh's *The Person You Mean to Be: How Good People Fight Bias*, as well as research from Shai Davidai and Thomas Gilovich, who use headwinds and tailwinds as a metaphor to explain our perception of the advantages and disadvantages that we face. Internal research from Deutsche Bank came from an article in *Harvard Business Review* by Herminia Ibarra: "Why Men Still Get More Promotions than Women." Cindy Pace provided case studies on mentorship at MetLife, and Catalyst explored what was happening at Unilever.

Chapter 10

In reflecting on cancel culture and its implications, I read Jessica Bennett's article in the *New York Times* "What If Instead of Calling People Out, We Called Them In?," which featured the work of Professor Loretta Ross. My perspective on the dangers of cancel culture aligned with that of Professor Ross, and I found her insights on alternative methods of "calling people in" to be most helpful. On holding your team accountable, I speak to the power of cross-company initiatives and goals. Do they even matter? Research from Devin Pope confirms that awareness does lead to action, and accountability to that awareness even more so. Case studies on Expedia, Adidas, and Hilton are highlighted, as well as the 2014 economics study at the Brookings Institution, which researched the effect of bias training on NBA referees. I shared goal samples as published by Berkeley Lab. In studying the impact of goals, I looked to California Partners Project, which published data about the new laws regarding public company boards in the state, as well as a press release detailing the positive impact of Norwegian law on corporate boards. Additionally, public reports on Nasdaq, Mercer, and Apple shed light on those companies' commitments. In exploring individual accountability, I cite the Hispanic Association on Corporate Responsibility's *Empow(h)er: Understanding Workplace Barriers for Latinas*, as well as Culture Amp's self-published plans and goals and McKinsey interview. ABC News provided a strong report on how women were not factored into the automotive industry's crash tests, while case studies of Pinterest and Banana Republic provided insight into designing with an inclusive lens.

Chapter 11

In this final chapter, I highlight those who are doing great work and profiting from it, like David Robb's report on the Anita Hill op-ed about the Hollywood Commission's progress and policy, as well as Angelica LaVito's reporting for CNBC on how Nike's investment in Colin Kaepernick has paid off. And I remind readers of what it looks like when it's not working, sharing research by Naomi Eisenberger at UCLA on how underrepresented groups face the brunt of feelings of exclusion. Yes, progress has been made, but it has also been stalled, as evident in reports like Atlassian's 2018 *State of Diversity and Inclusion in U.S. Tech* report.

BIBLIOGRAPHY

Adler, Lou. "New Survey Reveals 85% of All Jobs Are Filled Via Networking." LinkedIn, February 29, 2016. www.linkedin.com/pulse/new-survey-reveals -85-all-jobs-filled-via-networking-lou-adler/.

Apple. "Apple to Acquire Beats Music & Beats Electronics." News release, May 28, 2014. www.apple.com/newsroom/2014/05/28Apple-to-Acquire-Beats -Music-Beats-Electronics/#:~:text=CUPERTINO%2C%20California%E2%80 %94May%2028%2C,founders%20Jimmy%20Iovine%20and%20Dr.

Atlassian. *Atlassian Sustainability Report.* Sydney, Australia: Atlassian, 2020. www.atlassian.com/diversity/survey/2018.

Banjo, Shelly, Dina Bass, and Mark Bergen. "Google CEO Apologizes for Handling of Departure of AI Expert." *Bloomberg*, December 9, 2020. www .bloomberg.com/news/articles/2020-12-09/google-ceo-apologizes-for-han dling-of-departure-of-ai-researcher.

BBC. "50:50 The Equality Project." N.d. www.bbc.co.uk/5050.

Bennett, Jessica. "What If Instead of Calling People Out, We Called Them In?" *New York Times*, November 19, 2020. www.nytimes.com/2020/11/19 /style/loretta-ross-smith-college-cancel-culture.html.

Bertrand, Marianne, and Sendhil Mullainathan. "Are Emily and Greg More Employable than Lakisha and Jamal? A Field Experiment on Labor Market Discrimination." *American Economic Review* 94, no. 4 (September 2004): 991–1013.

Bhalla, Vikram, Deborah Lovich, Jean-Michel Caye, Christopher Daniel, and Liza Stutts. "How Frontline Leaders Can Deliver Breakout Performance." Boston Consulting Group, November 21, 2016. www.bcg.com/publications /2016/people-organization-how-frontline-leaders-can-deliver-breakout-per formance.

Bibliography

Birnir, Adda. "A Long-Term Plan for Anti-Racism at Skillcrush." Skillcrush. Last updated March 16, 2021. skillcrush.com/blog/anti-racism-long-term/.

Blanche, Aubrey. "Update on Culture Amp's Anti-Racism Plan and Goals." Culture Amp. Accessed March 23, 2021. www.cultureamp.com/blog/update-on -culture-amps-anti-racism-plan-and-goals/.

Bohnet, Iris. *What Works: Gender Equality by Design*. Cambridge, MA: Harvard University Press, 2018.

Bohnet, Iris, and Siri Chilazi. *Goals and Targets for Diversity, Equity, and Inclusion: The Gender Proportionality Aspiration*. Cambridge, MA: Harvard Kennedy School, 2020. https://wappp.hks.harvard.edu/files/wappp/files/dei_goals _in_us_tech_executive_summary_bohnet_chilazi.pdf.

Bourke, Juliet. "Six Signature Traits of Inclusive Leadership." Deloitte, April 14, 2016. www2.deloitte.com/us/en/insights/topics/talent/six-signature-traits-of-in clusive-leadership.html.

Brand, Dalana. "Inclusion & Diversity Report September 2019." Twitter, September 18, 2019. https://blog.twitter.com/en_us/topics/company/2019/inclusion -and-diversity-report-september-2019.

Brook, Timothy, Jerome Bourgon, and Gregory Blue. *Death by a Thousand Cuts*. Cambridge, MA: Harvard University Press, 2008.

Buckingham, Marcus, and Ashley Goodall. "The Feedback Fallacy." *Harvard Business Review*, March–April 2019. hbr.org/2019/03/the-feedback-fallacy.

California Partners Project. *Claim Your Seat: Women of Color on California's Public Company Boards*. San Francisco, CA: California Partners Project. www.calpartnersproject.org/wocclaimyourseat.

CareerBuilder. "Nearly Seven in Ten Businesses Affected by a Bad Hire in the Past Year, According to CareerBuilder Survey." PR Newswire, December 13, 2012. press.careerbuilder.com/2012-12-13-Nearly-Seven-in-Ten-Busi nesses-Affected-by-a-Bad-Hire-in-the-Past-Year-According-to-CareerBuilder -Survey.

Carr, Evan W., Andrew Reece, Gabriella Rosen Kellerman, and Alexi Robichaux. "The Value of Belonging at Work." *Harvard Business Review*, December 16, 2019. hbr.org/2019/12/the-value-of-belonging-at-work.

Carter, William C., and Henri-Jean Servat, eds. *The Proust Questionnaire*. New York: Assouline, 2005.

Casey, Mary E., and Shannon Murphy Robinson. *Neuroscience of Inclusion: New Skills for New Times*. Denver, CO: Outskirts Press, 2017.

Catalyst. "Unilever: Changing the Game, Unlocking the Future (Case Study)." March 12, 2020. www.catalyst.org/research/unilever-case-study/.

Bibliography

Cauterucci, Christina. "Use Gendered Words in Job Descriptions? Expect Way Fewer Applicants." *Slate*, September 22, 2016. slate.com/human-interest /2016/09/way-fewer-people-apply-when-job-descriptions-contain-gendered -words.html.

Childs, Sarah, and Lena Krook Mona. "Critical Mass Theory and Women's Political Representation." *Political Studies* 56, no. 3 (2008): 725–736. https://doi .org/10.1111/j.1467-9248.2007.00712.x.

Chua, Phoebe, and Melissa Mazmanian. "Are You One of Us? Current Hiring Practices Suggest the Potential for Class Biases in Large Tech Companies." *Proceedings of the ACM on Human-Computer Interaction* 3, no. 143 (October 2020): 1–20. https://doi.org/10.1145/3415214.

Chugh, Dolly. *The Person You Mean to Be: How Good People Fight Bias.* New York: Harper Business, 2018.

Chugh, Dolly. "Use Your Everyday Privilege to Help Others." *Harvard Business Review*, September 18, 2018. hbr.org/2018/09/use-your-everyday-privilege-to -help-others.

Clark, Timothy R. *The 4 Stages of Psychological Safety: Defining the Path to Inclusion and Innovation.* San Francisco, CA: Berrett-Koehler Publishers, 2020.

Coates, Ta-Nehisi. "The Case for Reparations." *Atlantic*, June 2014. www.theat lantic.com/magazine/archive/2014/06/the-case-for-reparations/361631/.

Cooper, Terri. "Inclusion Survey: Uncovering Talent." Deloitte. Accessed October 29, 2020. www2.deloitte.com/us/en/pages/about-deloitte/articles/covering -in-the-workplace.html.

Coqual. *Being Black in Corporate America: An Intersectional Exploration.* New York: Coqual, 2019. coqual.org/reports/being-black-in-corporate-america-an -intersectional-exploration/.

Correll, Shelley, and Caroline Simard. "Research: Vague Feedback Is Holding Women Back." *Harvard Business Review*, April 29, 2016. https://hbr.org /2016/04/research-vague-feedback-is-holding-women-back.

Corritore, Matthew, Amir Goldberg, and Sameer B. Srivastava. "The New Analytics of Culture." *Harvard Business Review*, January–February 2020. https:// hbr.org/2020/01/the-new-analytics-of-culture.

Cox, Daniel, Juhem Navarro-Rivera, and Robert P. Jones. "Race, Religion, and Political Affiliation of Americans' Core Social Networks." Public Religion Research Institute, August 3, 2016. www.prri.org/research/poll-race-religion -politics-americans-social-networks/.

Culture Amp. *Impact of Engagement Whitepaper.* Melbourne, Australia: Culture Amp, n.d.

Bibliography

Davidai, Shai, and Gilovich, Thomas. "The Headwinds/Tailwinds Asymmetry: An Availability Bias in Assessments of Barriers and Blessings." *Journal of Personality and Social Psychology* 111, no. 6 (December 2016): 835–851. https://doi.apa.org/doiLanding?doi=10.1037%2Fpspa0000066.

Davis, Clayton. "Oscars Announce New Inclusion Requirements for Best Picture Eligibility." *Variety*, September 8, 2020. variety.com/2020/film/news/oscars -inclusion-standards-best-picture-diversity-1234762727/.

De Smet, Aaron, Kim Rubenstein, Gunnar Schrah, Mike Vierow, and Amy Edmondson. "Psychological Safety and the Critical Role of Leadership Development." McKinsey & Company, February 11, 2021. www.mckinsey.com/busi ness-functions/organization/our-insights/psychological-safety-and-the-criti cal-role-of-leadership-development.

Dewar, Carolyn, Scott Keller, Kevin Sneader, and Kurt Strovink. "The CEO Moment: Leadership for a New Era." *McKinsey Quarterly*, July 21, 2020. www.mckinsey.com/featured-insights/leadership/the-ceo-moment-leader ship-for-a-new-era.

D'Innocenzio, Anne. "Adidas HR Head Resigns as Company Addresses Diversity Issues." AP, July 1, 2020. https://apnews.com/article/f10bfe20abf1e 27334c75705d60d82ba.

Donaldson, Ben. "Selecting the Next UN Secretary-General." *E-International Relations*, September 19, 2020. www.e-ir.info/2020/09/19/opinion-selecting-the -next-un-secretary-general/.

Dorniak-Wall, Kristina. "Performance Management Post-COVID-19: Things to Consider." Culture Amp. Accessed July 2, 2020. explore.cultureamp.com/c /performance-manageme-1?x=cE1SdN.

Duhigg, Charles. "What Google Learned from Its Quest to Build the Perfect Team." *New York Times*, February 25, 2016. www.nytimes.com/2016/02/28/magazine /what-google-learned-from-its-quest-to-build-the-perfect-team.html.

Edmondson, Amy. "Psychological Safety and Learning Behavior in Work Teams." *Administrative Science Quarterly* 44, no. 2 (June 1999): 350–383. www.jstor .org/stable/2666999.

Eilperin, Juliet. "White House Women Want to Be in the Room Where It Happens." *Washington Post*, September 13, 2016. www.washingtonpost.com/news/power post/wp/2016/09/13/white-house-women-are-now-in-the-room-where-it-hap pens/.

Eisenberger, Naomi I. "The Neural Bases of Social Pain: Evidence for Shared Representations with Physical Pain." *Psychosomatic Medicine* 74, no. 2 (2012): 126–135. https://doi.org/10.1097/PSY.0b013e3182464dd1.

Bibliography

Equal Pay Today. "2021 Equal Pay Days." N.d. www.equalpaytoday.org/over
view-2021.

Estrada, Sheryl. "Twitter to Pay Resource Group Leaders, Saying the Work
Shouldn't Be a 'Volunteer Activity.'" *HR Dive*, October 6, 2020. www.hrdive
.com/news/twitter-to-pay-resource-group-leaders-saying-the-work-should
nt-be-a-volu/586489/.

Farnham, Alan. "Female Crash Dummies Injured More: What Car Should
Women Buy?" ABC News, March 29, 2012. abcnews.go.com/Business/female
-crash-dummies-injured/story?id=16004267.

Feintzeig, Rachel. "The Boss Doesn't Want Your Résumé." *Wall Street Journal*,
January 5, 2016. www.wsj.com/articles/the-boss-doesnt-want-your-resume-145
2025908.

Fischer, Kristen. "These Companies Are Hiring—and They Don't Want Your
Resume." *Working Mother*, April 26, 2017. www.workingmother.com/these
-companies-are-hiring-and-they-dont-want-your-resume.

Friesen, Justin, Kerry Kawakami, Larissa Vingilis-Jaremko, Regis Caprara, David Sidhu, Amanda Williams, Kurt Hugenberg, Rosa Rodriguz-Bailon, Elena
Canadas, and Paula Niedenthal. "Perceiving Happiness in an Intergroup
Context: The Role of Race and Attention to the Eyes in Differentiating Between True and False Smiles." *Journal of Personality and Social Psychology*
116, no. 3 (2019): 275–395. https://doi.apa.org/doiLanding?doi=10.1037%2F
pspa0000139.

Fritz, Annette R. "The Implications of Developing and Implementing a Staff
Study in Minnesota Courts." 2011–2012 Phase III project, Institute for Court
Management Fellows Program, May 2012.

Gallup. "Transform Performance Management." Accessed March 22, 2021.
www.gallup.com/workplace/215927/maximize-performance-management
.aspx.

Garr, Stacia Sherman, and Candace Atamanik. "High-Impact Diversity and Inclusion: Maturity Model and Top Findings." Bersin by Deloitte. PowerPoint
presentation, May 2017.

Giles, Howard, and Tamara Rakić. "Language Attitudes: Social Determinants
and Consequences of Language Variation." In *The Oxford Handbook of Language and Social Psychology*, edited by Thomas M. Holtgraves, 11–26. Oxford:
Oxford University Press, 2014.

Goler, Lori, Janelle Gale, Brynn Harrington, and Adam Grant. "Why People
Really Quit Their Jobs." *Harvard Business Review*, January 11, 2018. https://
hbr.org/2018/01/why-people-really-quit-their-jobs.

Bibliography

Google Walkout for Real Change. "Standing with Dr. Timnit Gebru—#ISupportTimnit #BelieveBlackWomen." Medium, December 4, 2020. googlewalkout.medium.com/standing-with-dr-timnit-gebru-isupporttimnit-believeblackwomen-6dadc300d382.

Go2HR. "Employee Training Is Worth the Investment." Accessed December 14, 2020. www.go2hr.ca/training-development/employee-training-is-worth-the-investment.

Grant, Adam. *Think Again: The Power of Knowing What You Don't Know.* New York: Viking, 2021.

Harts, Minda, Sarah Lacy, and Eve Rodsky. "Women Are Drowning in Unpaid Labor at Home. Stop Making Them Do It at Work." *Fast Company*, August 19, 2020. www.fastcompany.com/90541130/women-are-drowning-in-unpaid-labor-at-home-stop-making-them-do-it-at-work.

Heifetz, Ronald A., and Marty Linsky. *Leadership on the Line: Staying Alive Through the Dangers of Change.* Boston: Harvard Business School Press, 2002.

Hekman, David R., Stefanie K. Johnson, Maw-Der Foo, and Wei Yang. "Does Diversity-Valuing Behavior Result in Diminished Performance Ratings for Non-White and Female Leaders?" *Academy of Management Journal* 60, no. 2 (March 3, 2016). journals.aom.org/doi/abs/10.5465/amj.2014.0538.

Heller, Dave. "Work Experience Poor Predictor of Future Job Performance." Phys.org, May 14, 2019. phys.org/news/2019-05-poor-predictor-future-job.html.

hooks, bell. "Sisterhood: Political Solidarity Between Women." *Feminist Review*, no. 23 (1986): 125–138. www.jstor.org/stable/1394725.

Hunt, Vivian, Sara Prince, Sundiatu Dixon-Fyle, and Lareina Yee. *Delivering Through Diversity.* New York: McKinsey & Company, 2018. www.mckinsey.com/~/media/mckinsey/business%20functions/organization/our%20insights/delivering%20through%20diversity/delivering-through-diversity_full-report.ashx#:~:text=Companies%20in%20the%20top%2Dquartile%20for%20gender%20diversity%20on%20their,likely%20to%20outperform%20on%20profitability.

Hutchison, Paul, Julie Christian, and Dominic Abrams. "The Social Psychology of Inclusion and Exclusion." In *Multidisciplinary Handbook of Social Exclusion Research*, edited by Dominic Abrams, Julie Christian, and David Gordon. Hoboken, NJ: Wiley, 2007.

Ibarra, Herminia, Nancy M. Carter, and Christine Silva. "Why Men Still Get More Promotions than Women." *Harvard Business Review*, September 2010. https://hbr.org/2010/09/why-men-still-get-more-promotions-than-women.

Bibliography

Jackson, Frances, and Emma Hansen, "Leadership Potential Versus Readiness." *Human Resources* (Summer 2016). www.sheffield.co.nz/Portals/0/Human%20 Resources%20Summer%20Issue%202016;%20Pages24-25;%20Leader ship%20Potential.pdf.

Jackson Lewis. "Court Rulings Stress National Importance of Diversity Goals but Set Limits on Methods." June 24, 2003. www.jacksonlewis.com/resources -publication/court-rulings-stress-national-importance-diversity-goals-set-lim its-methods.

Jarrett, Christian. "Who Are You Protecting When You Praise a Dud Perfor- mance?" *British Psychological Society Research Digest*, May 2, 2012. digest .bps.org.uk/2012/05/02/who-are-you-protecting-when-you-praise-a-dud-per formance/.

Johnson, Stefanie K., David R. Hekman, and Elsa T. Chan. "If There's Only One Woman in Your Candidate Pool, There's Statistically No Chance She'll Be Hired." *Harvard Business Review*, April 26, 2016. hbr.org/2016/04/if-theres -only-one-woman-in-your-candidate-pool-theres-statistically-no-chance -shell-be-hired.

Kang, Sonia K., Katherine A. DeCelles, András Tilcsik, and Sora Jun. "Whit- ened Résumés: Race and Self-Presentation in the Labor Market." *Admin- istrative Science Quarterly* 61, no. 3 (2016): 469–505. https://doi.org/10.1177 /0001839216639577.

Kellerman, Gabriella Rosen, and Andrew Reece. *The Value of Belonging at Work: Investing in Workplace Inclusion*. San Francisco: BetterUp, 2020. https://grow .betterup.com/resources/the-value-of-belonging-at-work-the-business-case -for-investing-in-workplace-inclusion-event.

Kirwan Institute for the Study of Race and Ethnicity. "Understanding Implicit Bias." Ohio State University, n.d. kirwaninstitute.osu.edu/research/under standing-implicit-bias/.

Ladders. *Eye-Tracking Study*. New York: Ladders, 2018. www.theladders.com /static/images/basicSite/pdfs/TheLadders-EyeTracking-StudyC2.pdf.

LaVito, Angelica. "Nike's Colin Kaepernick Ads Created $163.5 Million in Buzz Since It Began—and It's Not All Bad." CNBC, September 6, 2018. www .cnbc.com/2018/09/06/nikes-colin-kaepernick-ad-created-163point5-milli on-in-media-exposure.html.

Lean In. *The State of Black Women in Corporate America*. Palo Alto, CA: Lean In, 2020. https://leanin.org/research/state-of-black-women-in-corporate-america.

Lean In. "White Employees See Themselves as Allies—but Black Women and Latinas Disagree." June 19–25, 2020. leanin.org/research/allyship-at-work.

Bibliography

Lean In. *Women in the Workplace*. Palo Alto, CA, and New York: Lean In and McKinsey & Company, 2020. womenintheworkplace.com/.

Mann, Annamarie. "Why We Need Best Friends at Work." Gallup, January 15, 2018. www.gallup.com/workplace/236213/why-need-best-friends-work.aspx.

Maslow, A. H. "A Theory of Human Motivation." *Psychological Review* 50, no. 4 (1943): 370–396. https://doi.org/10.1037/h0054346.

McIntosh, Peggy. "White Privilege: Unpacking the Invisible Knapsack." *Peace and Freedom Magazine*, July–August 1989.

Mckesson, DeRay. "'I Learned Hope the Hard Way': On the Early Days of Black Lives Matter." *Guardian*, April 12, 2019. www.theguardian.com/world/2019/apr/12/black-lives-matter-deray-mckesson-ferguson-protests.

Merluzzi, Jennifer, and Adina Sterling. "Lasting Effects? Referrals and Career Mobility of Demographic Groups in Organizations." *ILR Review* 70, no. 1 (January 2017): 105–131. https://doi.org/10.1177/0019793916669507.

Merluzzi, Jennifer, and Adina Sterling. "Research: Black Employees Are More Likely to Be Promoted When They Were Referred by Another Employee." *Harvard Business Review*, February 28, 2017. hbr.org/2017/02/research-black-employees-are-more-likely-to-be-promoted-when-they-were-referred-by-another-employee.

Meyer, Robinson. "90% of Wikipedia's Editors Are Male—Here's What They're Doing About It." *Atlantic*, October 25, 2013. www.theatlantic.com/technology/archive/2013/10/90-of-wikipedias-editors-are-male-heres-what-theyre-doing-about-it/280882/.

Miller, Nicole. "The Evolution of Onboarding at Buffer: How We Welcome New Teammates." Buffer, April 10, 2020. buffer.com/resources/onboarding/.

Minkel, Alida. "HACR Latina Empow(h)er Initiative." Hispanic Association on Corporate Responsibility, March 3, 2020. www.blog.hacr.org/hri_blog/hacr-latina-empowher-initiative.

Modrin, Anelia. "How We Drive Inclusion and Diversity in Expedia Group." *Life at Expedia Group Blog*. Accessed January 26, 2021. blog.lifeatexpediagroup.com/experiences/how-we-drive-inclusion-and-diversity-in-expedia-group/.

Nahemow, Lucille, and M. Powell Lawton. "Similarity and Propinquity in Friendship Formation." *Journal of Personality and Social Psychology* 32, no. 2 (1975): 205–213. https://doi.org/10.1037/0022-3514.32.2.205.

Nellis, Stephen. "Apple Will Modify Executive Bonuses Based on Environmental Values in 2021." Reuters, January 5, 2021. www.reuters.com/article/us-apple-compensation/apple-will-modify-executive-bonuses-based-on-environmental-values-in-2021-idUSKBN29A2MK.

Bibliography

Nordwall, Stacey. "Connect with Coworkers, Make a Date with Donut." Culture Amp. Accessed August 16, 2020. www.cultureamp.com/blog/connect-with-co workers-make-a-date-with-donut/.

Pager, Devah, Bruce Western, and Naomi Sugie. "Sequencing Disadvantage: Barriers to Employment Facing Young Black and White Men with Criminal Records." *Annals of the American Academy of Political and Social Science* 623, no. 1 (2009): 195–213. www.ncbi.nlm.nih.gov/pmc/articles/PMC3583356/pdf /nihms-439026.pdf.

Pao, Ellen K. "Roadmap to Diversity and Inclusion." Medium, May 2, 2019. me dium.com/projectinclude/https-medium-com-projectinclude-targets-as-road map-to-diversity-and-inclusion-347e8e0b791b.

Passin, Gregg. "Using Compensation to Drive Action on Diversity, Equity and Inclusion." Mercer, n.d. www.mercer.us/our-thinking/career/using-compensa tion-to-drive-action-on-diversity-equity-and-inclusion.html.

Polk, Sam. "How Wall Street Bro Talk Keeps Women Down." *New York Times*, July 7, 2016. www.nytimes.com/2016/07/10/opinion/sunday/how-wall-street -bro-talk-keeps-women-down.html.

Pope, Devin G., Joseph Price, and Justin Wolfers. *Awareness Reduces Racial Bias*. Washington, DC: Brookings Institution, 2016. www.brookings.edu/wp -content/uploads/2016/06/awareness_reduces_racial_bias_wolfers.pdf.

Purdue University. "Staff Promotion Guidelines." N.d. www.purdue.edu/hr /mngcareer/compguidelines/stproinc.php.

Rigoni, Brandon, and Amy Adkins. "Millennial Job-Hoppers: What They Seek." Gallup, March 19, 2021. www.gallup.com/workplace/236471/millennial-job -hoppers-seek.aspx.

Robb, David. "Anita Hill Op-Ed: Hollywood Has Made Strides to Eliminate Sexual Harassment & Bias, but Can Still Do Better." *Deadline*, December 15, 2020. deadline.com/2020/12/anita-hill-op-ed-hollywood-sexual-harassment -bias-elimination-progress-report-1234656496/.

Rock, David, and Heidi Grant. "Why Diverse Teams Are Smarter." *Harvard Business Review*, November 4, 2016. hbr.org/2016/11/why-diverse-teams-are -smarter.

Romansky, Lauren, Mia Garrod, Katie Brown, and Kartik Deo. "How to Measure Inclusion in the Workplace." *Harvard Business Review*, May 27, 2021. https://hbr.org/2021/05/how-to-measure-inclusion-in-the-workplace.

Sandel, Michael J. *The Tyranny of Merit: What's Become of the Common Good?* New York: Farrar, Straus and Giroux, 2020.

Shields, Jon. "Report: 98% of Fortune 500 Companies Use Applicant Tracking Systems (ATS)." Jobscan, June 20, 2018. www.jobscan.co/blog/fortune-500-use-applicant-tracking-systems/.

Shunryu, Suzuki. *Zen Mind, Beginner's Mind.* Boulder, CO: Shambhala, 2020.

Smith, David G., Judith E. Rosenstein, Margaret C. Nikolov, and Darby A. Chaney. "The Power of Language: Gender, Status, and Agency in Performance Evaluations." *Sex Roles* 80 (2019): 159–171. https://doi.org/10.1007/s11199-018-0923-7.

Sorkin, Andrew Ross, Jason Karaian, Michael J. de la Merced, Lauren Hirsch, and Ephrat Livni. "Nasdaq Pushes for Diversity in the Boardroom." *New York Times,* December 1, 2020. www.nytimes.com/2020/12/01/business/dealbook/nasdaq-diversity-boards.html.

Sperance, Cameron, "Hilton's Diversity Strategy Underscores Recruiting Efforts in a Time of Deep Job Cuts." *Skift,* July 6, 2020. https://skift.com/2020/07/06/hiltons-diversity-strategy-underscores-recruiting-efforts-in-a-time-of-deep-job-cuts/.

Stieg, Cory. "How to Stay Committed to Your Goals: Tell Someone More Successful than You, Says New Study." CNBC, September 5, 2019. www.cnbc.com/2019/09/05/why-sharing-goals-with-someone-helps-you-achieve-them.html.

Sue, Derald Wing. *Microaggressions in Everyday Life: Race, Gender, and Sexual Orientation.* Hoboken, NJ: Wiley, 2010.

Teare, Gené. "Highlighting Notable Funding to Black Founders in 2020." *Crunchbase News,* February 12, 2021. https://news.crunchbase.com/news/highlighting-notable-funding-to-black-founders-in-2020/.

Thieda, Kate. "Brené Brown on Empathy vs. Sympathy." *Psychology Today,* August 12, 2014. www.psychologytoday.com/us/blog/partnering-in-mental-health/201408/bren-brown-empathy-vs-sympathy-0.

Thomas, Lauren. "Nike Sets Fresh Diversity Targets for 2025, and Ties Executive Compensation to Hitting Them." CNBC, March 11, 2021. www.cnbc.com/2021/03/11/nike-sets-diversity-goals-for-2025-ties-executive-comp-back-to-them.html.

Toossi, Mitra. "Labor Force Projections to 2024: The Labor Force Is Growing, but Slowly." *Monthly Labor Review,* December 2015. www.bls.gov/opub/mlr/2015/article/labor-force-projections-to-2024.htm.

Travis, Dnika J., and Jennifer Thorpe-Moscon. *Day-to-Day Experiences of Emotional Tax Among Women and Men of Color in the Workplace.* New York: Catalyst, 2018. www.catalyst.org/wp-content/uploads/2019/02/emotionaltax.pdf.

Travis, Dnika J., Jennifer Thorpe-Moscon, and Courtney McCluney. *Emotional Tax: How Black Women and Men Pay More at Work and How Leaders Can Take Action*. New York: Catalyst, 2016. www.catalyst.org/research/emotional-tax-how-black-women-and-men-pay-more-at-work-and-how-leaders-can-take-action/.

Trudel, Natalie. "Yes, You Can Eliminate the Annual Review, Improve Engagement and Still Get Workforce Metrics." *TLNT*, January 5, 2017. www.tlnt.com/yes-you-can-eliminate-the-annual-review-improve-engagement-and-still-get-workforce-metrics/.

Twaronite, Karyn. "Five Findings on the Importance of Belonging." EY, May 11, 2019. www.ey.com/en_us/diversity-inclusiveness/ey-belonging-barometer-workplace-study.

United Nations. "Norway Called 'Haven for Gender Equality,' as Women's Anti-discrimination Committee Examines Reports on Compliance with Convention." News release, January 20, 2003. www.un.org/press/en/2003/wom1377.doc.htm.

UN Women. "Women as Drivers of Economic Recovery and Resilience During COVID-19 and Beyond." July 14, 2020. www.unwomen.org/en/news/stories/2020/7/statement-joint-w20-women-during-covid-19-and-beyond.

Valve. *Handbook for New Employees*. Bellevue, WA: Valve, 2012. https://cdn.akamai.steamstatic.com/apps/valve/Valve_NewEmployeeHandbook.pdf.

Washington, Zuhairah, and Laura Morgan Roberts. "Women of Color Get Less Support at Work. Here's How Managers Can Change That." *Harvard Business Review*, March 4, 2019, https://hbr.org/2019/03/women-of-color-get-less-support-at-work-heres-how-managers-can-change-that.

Williams, Joan C., and Sky Mihaylo. "How the Best Bosses Interrupt Bias on Their Teams." *Harvard Business Review*, November–December 2019. hbr.org/2019/11/how-the-best-bosses-interrupt-bias-on-their-teams.

Willyerd, Karie. "Social Tools Can Improve Employee Onboarding." *Harvard Business Review*, December 21, 2012. hbr.org/2012/12/social-tools-can-improve-e.

World Economic Forum. *Unleashing the Power of Europe's Women Entrepreneurs: Six Ideas to Drive Big Change*. Geneva, Switzerland: World Economic Forum, 2020. www3.weforum.org/docs/WEF_Unleashing_the_power_of_Europes_women_entrepreneurs.pdf.

Zenger, Jack, and Joseph Folkman. "Your Employees Want the Negative Feedback You Hate to Give." *Harvard Business Review*, January 15, 2014. https://hbr.org/2014/01/your-employees-want-the-negative-feedback-you-hate-to-give.

Jeffrey Mossier

Daisy Auger-Domínguez has revolutionized people policy and practice at some of the world's leading companies, including Google, Disney, and Viacom. She is currently the chief people officer at Vice Media Group. Auger-Domínguez is on a mission to make workplaces more equitable and inclusive and has been featured in *Harvard Business Review, Forbes, Hispanic Executive,* and more. She frequently speaks on leadership, workplace culture, equity, and inclusion. Auger-Domínguez lives in Brooklyn, New York, with her husband, Christopher, and their daughter, Emma.